transitions

Queer Theories

Donald E. Hall

First published 2003 by
PALGRAVE MACMILLAN
Houndmills, Basingstoke, Hampshire RG21 6XS and
175 Fifth Avenue, New York, N.Y. 10010
Companies and representatives throughout the world

PALGRAVE MACMILLAN is the global academic imprint of the Palgrave
Macmillan division of St. Martin's Press, LLC and of Palgrave Macmillan Ltd.
Macmillan® is a registered trademark in the United States, United Kingdom
and other countries. Palgrave is a registered trademark in the European
Union and other countries.

ISBN 0–333–77539–2 hardback
ISBN 0–333–77540–6 paperback

This book is printed on paper suitable for recycling and made from fully
managed and sustained forest sources.

A catalogue record for this book is available from the British Library.

Library of Congress Cataloging-in-Publication Data
Hall, Donald E. (Donald Eugene), 1960–
    Queer theories / Donald E. Hall
        p. cm. – (Transitions)
    Includes bibliographical references and index.
    ISBN 0-333-77539-2 (cloth) – ISBN 0-333-77540-6 (paper)
    1. Gay and lesbian studies. 2. Homosexuality in literature.
    I. Title. II. Transitions (Palgrave Macmillan (Firm))

HQ75.15 .H35 2002
305.9'066407–dc21   2002026771

10 9 8 7 6 5 4 3 2 1
12 11 10 09 08 07 06 05 04 03

Printed in China

Queer Theories

transitions

General Editor: Julian Wolfreys

Published titles
BATAILLE Fred Botting and Scott Wilson
NEW HISTORICISM AND CULTURAL MATERIALISM John Brannigan
POSTMODERN NARRATIVE THEORY Mark Currie
FORMALIST CRITICISM AND READER-RESPONSE THEORY Todd F. Davis
  and Kenneth Womack
QUEER THEORIES Donald E. Hall
MARXIST LITERARY AND CULTURAL THEORY Moyra Haslett
ALTHUSSER Warren Montag
JACQUES LACAN Jean-Michel Rabaté
LITERARY FEMINISMS Ruth Robbins
DECONSTRUCTION•DERRIDA Julian Wolfreys

ORWELL TO THE PRESENT: LITERATURE IN ENGLAND, 1945–2000 John
  Brannigan
CHAUCER TO SHAKESPEARE, 1337–1580 SunHee Kim Gertz
BURKE TO BYRON, BARBAULD TO BAILLIE, 1790–1830 Jane Stabler
MILTON TO POPE, 1650–1720 Kay Gilliland Stevenson
SIDNEY TO MILTON, 1580–1660 Marion Wynne-Davies

Forthcoming titles
TERRY EAGLETON David Alderson
JULIA KRISTEVA AND LITERARY THEORY Megan Becker-Leckrone
NATIONAL IDENTITY John Brannigan
HÉLÈNE CIXOUS: WRITING AND SEXUAL DIFFERENCE Abigail Bray
HOMI BHABHA Eleanor Byrne
GENDER Claire Colebrook
IDEOLOGY James Decker
POSTMODERNISM•POSTMODERNITY Martin McQuillan
ROLAND BARTHES Martin McQuillan
RACE Brian G. Niro
MODERNITY David Punter
PSYCHOANALYSIS AND LITERATURE Nicholas Rand
SUBJECTIVITY Ruth Robbins
POSTCOLONIAL THEORY Malini Johan Schueller
TRANSGRESSION Julian Wolfreys

IMAGE TO APOCALYPSE, 1910–1945 Jane Goldman
POPE TO BURNEY, 1714–1779 Moyra Haslett
PATER TO FORSTER, 1873–1924 Ruth Robbins
DICKENS TO HARDY, 1837–1884 Julian Wolfreys

For Bill

Contents

General Editor's Preface

> Transitions: *transition* n. of action. 1. A passing or passage from one condition, action or (rarely) place, to another. 2. Passage in thought, speech, or writing, from one subject to another. 3. **a**. The passing from one note to another **b**. The passing from one key to another, modulation. 4. The passage from an earlier to a later stage of development or formation ... change from an earlier style to a later; a style of intermediate or mixed character ... the historical passage of language from one well-defined stage to another.

The aim of *Transitions* is to explore passages and movements in critical thought, and in the development of literary and cultural interpretation. This series also seeks to examine the possibilities for reading, analysis and other critical engagements which the very idea of transition makes possible. The writers in this series unfold the movements and modulations of critical thinking over the last generation, from the first emergences of what is now recognised as literary theory. They examine as well how the transitional nature of theoretical and critical thinking is still very much in operation, guaranteed by the hybridity and heterogeneity of the field of literary studies. The authors in the series share the common understanding that, now more than ever, critical thought is both in a state of transition and can best be defined by developing for the student reader an understanding of this protean quality.

This series desires, then, to enable the reader to transform her/his own reading and writing transactions by comprehending past developments. Each book in the series offers a guide to the poetics and politics of interpretative paradigms, schools and bodies of thought, while transforming these, if not into tools or methodologies, then into conduits for directing and channelling thought. As well as transforming the critical past by interpreting it from the perspective of the present day, each study enacts transitional readings of a number of well-known literary texts, all of which are themselves conceivable as having been transitional texts at the moments of their first appearance. The readings offered in these books seek, through close critical reading and theoretical engagement, to demonstrate certain possibilities in critical thinking to the student reader.

It is hoped that the student will find this series liberating because rigid methodologies are not being put into place. As all the dictionary definitions of the idea of transition above suggest, what is important is the action, the passage: of thought, of analysis, of critical response. Rather than seeking to help you locate yourself in relation to any particular school or discipline, this series aims to put you into action, as readers and writers, travellers between positions, where the movement between poles comes to be seen as of more importance than the locations themselves.

Julian Wolfreys

Introduction:
What "Queer Theories"
Can do for You

The body of abstract theory and applied readings that came to be known as "queer theory" during the 1990s (and that will be pluralized here – more on that in a moment) is dauntingly complex and diverse. In some ways, the task ahead of us – me as writer attempting to provide a complete overview of the topic, and you as a reader working to acquire comprehensive knowledge – is impossible. Perhaps the best that we can both do is simply to relax and lower our expectations. And, in fact, the theories that we will be discussing here demand a recognition of partiality, of tendentiousness, of epistemological limitations. For readers expecting or insisting upon a guide to mastering "queer theory," this book will inevitably disappoint. For those who are willing to allow – or perhaps even to embrace – diversity, partiality, and the impossibility of comprehensiveness, this book may provide useful information and even a few pleasures.

To allow you to sort out your expectations and decide whether or not this book is right for you, I first want this introduction to expose, shamelessly, how this book does and does not perform. I will then spend a few pages providing some preliminary, working definitions of "queer," so at least we all know, more or less, what we will be talking about in coming chapters. Indeed, if there is one thing for which "queer theory" generally has little respect, it is hidden agendas with their unspoken, uninterrogated norms and assumptions. While "confession" and other forms of self-revelation and self-exposure often depend upon facile notions of comprehensive self-knowledge and spurious, seductive forms of "forgiveness," recognizing such complications does not mean that we must sit in sullen silence or resign ourselves to the impossibility of useful action, productive communication, and laudable, defensible forms of social change. As

I

we shall see, language – as it structures thoughts, social images, and both purposeful and unintentional articulation – provides the base matter of our identities, and the parameters and limitations of our ability to know and act, but also the *only* material we have with which to work to improve our lives and those of others.

So herewith – in a fashion so un-queer that perhaps it *is* queer – are some of the core principles, assumptions and beliefs underlying *Queer Theories* to help you decide if it is to your taste and worth your very valuable time and effort:

1 This book will discuss sexuality, which is often considered a highly "private" matter, but which is complexly related to social life

While later chapters will work to distinguish between "queer" investigations of sexuality and other medical, legal, philosophical, and literary/cultural critical discussions of sexuality, it is important first to establish that sexuality (in its many and highly varied manifestations, as both acted upon and un-acted upon forms of erotic desire) is thoroughly related to social existence, even if it is often carried on in relative privacy – in the bedroom or the inside of one's own head. As we will explore in Chapters 1 and 2, social attitudes, as well as laws, scientific categories, and medical diagnoses, serve to legitimate – sometimes overtly, sometimes subtly – certain forms of sexual expression and to castigate (often severely) others. In exploring the differing valuations and norms concerning "proper" and "improper" forms of sexual desire and activity, we find that sexuality is thoroughly interconnected with (if never wholly determined by) religion, economics, prevailing scientific paradigms, the social sciences, aesthetics, and other flows of cultural expression and social valuation. In studying sexuality, we are offered a highly productive starting point for inquiring into human social organization and systems of belief. This is not at all to suggest that sexuality offers the single *most* important avenue for social and cultural understanding. As companion books in the "Transitions" series demonstrate quite well, other theories and methodologies offer their own unique opportunities and compelling insights. But this volume demands that readers recognize and accept the significant utility of the study of sexuality, however much a singular focus on class, gender, race, or ethnicity might offer its own important avenues for critical investigation. And, as we shall see, all of these (and more) are potentially interrelated.

2 Yet at the same time this book suggests that sexual "identity," though a useful and powerful construct, is also an artificial and limited one

The concept of a socially significant, politically charged, specifically "sexual identity" is a relatively recent one, dating more or less from the late nineteenth century (though certainly with some important antecedents), as my next chapter will explore. But even though self-identification through sexuality has carried tremendous weight and power in the past 100–150 years, it is vital to recognize also its highly limited nature. While some theorists of sexuality believe that sexual "identity" is innate or even biologically determined, this volume will consistently question that assertion and suggest strongly that at the very least the ways sexuality is expressed and valued have changed dramatically over time, and that sexual "identity" is only one of many identities that we all hold simultaneously. I may self-identify as "queer," but I am also many other things. In discussing "sexual identity" we must recognize its always partial connection to the myriad of roles we assume as social beings, even as we value the insights it does offer.

Furthermore, this book will suggest that it is important (both for intellectual and social activist purposes) that we question aggressively the means by which society actually determines an individual's sexual "identity." Does it depend upon interpersonal activity involving genital contact? The narrowness of that definition would deny an identity to anyone who has yet to act upon her or his desires, as well as others for whom genital contact is not the primary means for erotic gratification. Is it perhaps simply desire, then, that determines identity? But desire is hardly simple, and certainly we must ask what forms of desire would determine an "identity"? As we will explore in later chapters, the identifiers "heterosexual" and "homosexual" are hardly sufficient to account for the manifestations of erotic interest that most people feel as they explore sexuality over time, through erotica, and in fantasy. So, is one's sexual "identity" perhaps determined by what one calls oneself? Certainly this would come closest to what many people believe is our inherent right to sexually self-define as we wish, but would conveniently ignore the complications posed by individuals who nervously deny the full range of their sexual desires, who even work futilely to "change" desires that are powerful or deeply ingrained, and who may or may not over time come to accept desires that society or family deems criminal or illegitimate.

This volume will weigh in on such controversies, but it cannot and will not pretend to resolve them definitively. In fact, easy, static answers are wholly incompatible with the body of work we have come to call "queer theory."

3 As the above commentary indicates, the "queer" study of sexuality is related to several other bodies of theory and applied analysis that call into question received notions and facile binary definitions

We cannot discuss "queer" theory without discussing post-structuralism, post-modernism, and the insights of philosophers whose theories do not address sexuality directly. In upcoming chapters, we will examine the insights not only of Michel Foucault, Eve Sedgwick, and Judith Butler, whose work has resonated throughout "queer theory" and is clearly engaged with studies in sexuality, but also theorists such as Friedrich Nietzsche, Jean-Paul Sartre, and Jacques Derrida, whose insights will help us understand the development of the "queer" analysis of sexuality, as well as the "queer" manipulation of identity or identities. Thus we will move often between text and context and in a couple of ways: the text of a work of literature and the context of its social creation and reception, of course, but also the text of "queer" forms of theorization and their context of philosophical and literary critical thought. In doing so, we will be venturing into some of the most exciting and difficult concepts and theories enlivening intellectual discussions and applied critical activity today.

4 But as abstract – even abstruse – as such theory is at times, it is still understandable by, and useful and accessible to, a broad audience of careful readers and eager thinkers, however daunting its language may appear at first glance

This book's primary audience is students at the advanced undergraduate through the graduate levels. While the theories underlying "queer" analysis are complex, they are not outside of the range of understanding of such a readership. Indeed, underlying all of the books in the "Transitions" series is the belief that contemporary theory and critical methodologies can be made available to under-graduate and graduate students, however turgid the language of their primary theorists may be. A book such as this one cannot be compre-hensive (no book can be), but certainly it can provide an accessible introduction to its topic and direct readers to other and more advanced works in the field.

But there is an additional notion underlying the present book that I wish to foreground here. I will suggest that many of the insights of contemporary "queer" analysis help us understand the lived realities and day-to-day activities of diverse individuals today, whatever their sexual identity may be. In its emphasis upon the disruptive, the constructed, the tactical, and performative, queer analysis reveals some of the ways in which many late-modern individuals experience the fractured and contingent nature of human existence in the twenty-first century. Thus this book, and especially its conclusion, will make provocative links between the insights of contemporary "queer" theorists and the everyday lives of some of its readers. Indeed, that emphasis on coalition building, on making links among diverse groups, is one of the most important impulses underlying "queer" forms of theorization.

5 This book suggests that over a decade after the genesis of the
   term, what is often called "queer theory" must be rendered
   plural now, given its many forms and insights, hence the
   "Queer Theories" of its title

If, as we will explore later, the concept "queer" emphasizes the disruptive, the fractured, the tactical and contingent, then certainly any implication that queer theorization is itself a simple monolith would be hypocritical. Simply put, there is no "queer theory" in the singular, only many different voices and sometimes overlapping, sometimes divergent perspectives that can be loosely called "queer theories." This book will emphasize and work through that pluralization, teasing out possibilities for what may and may not be forms of queer theory, while offering few strict rules or rigid exclusions.

6 Our discussion of queer theories demands an inside/outside perspective, in which we recognize our own discursive constraints and the limitations of our perspectives, but, at the same time, work energetically with the language and concepts available to us

Queer theories generally recognize the partiality and tendentiousness of knowledge and perspectives; such limitations will be emphasized throughout this book. Yet this inability to claim or access comprehensive or transcendent knowledge does not have to breed cynicism or hopelessness. It is possible to reflect broadly on our constraints and limitations, to admit as well that we cannot know all of them, and still to recognize the necessity of political action, applied critical analysis, and forthright intellectual activity. As Diana Fuss notes in her introduction to *Inside/Out*, a foundational "queer theory" text from 1991, "Change may well happen by working on the insides of our inherited sexual vocabularies and turning them inside out, giving them a new face" (7). One of the most persistent myths concerning "queer" and other forms of post-structuralist thought and postmodern perspectives is that they are defeatist. As we will explore in upcoming chapters, queer thinking has led to highly effective political organizing, dynamic cultural critical production, and powerful translations of the "theoretical" into the "applied" and "practical."

Indeed, one of the most important aspects of the "meta"-consciousness that I will emphasize derives from the aforementioned recognition of the partiality of perspective. Throughout this book I will suggest that queer theories in their diversity and at times dissonance demand that we retain as a point of reference an open-ended communication model. Certainly, no queer theorist self-incorporating her or his own theory's emphasis on partiality can ever claim to offer final and definitive insights or complete interpretations. Queer theorization demands a broad acknowledgement of the need for continued discussion, for diversity in perspective and articulation, and for challenging and disruptive speech, even that which challenges and disrupts queer claims themselves. I will argue that the rubric "queer" must embrace and encourage a variety of styles, forms, perspectives, and insights, none of which can accurately claim the status of the "natural," "definitive," or "real."

7 Queer theories demand a questioning of the conventional, which should include the conventions followed by the present book, even as we recognize that conventions allow for effective communication and other useful forms of social interaction

Self-styled "queers," even when aggressively questioning the norms of society, rarely go so far in their questioning that they simply ignore red lights at intersections or their landlords' demands for rent payments. They might question the concept of "red lights" or "rent payments" in theory, but still broadly look out for their own and others' security and interests by following the "norms" of society in many of their day-to-day practices.

This book will operate similarly. Throughout we will be exploring a body of theory that exposes conventions and social norms as artificial and based in a broad dynamic of power relations that often oppress sexually nonconforming individuals. And in doing so, I wish to question as well the conventions of presenting such theoretical material, avoiding claims of mastery and absolute authority that are inconsistent with the theories being discussed. Furthermore, I will reflect in meta-theoretical fashion on the possibilities and heretofore unrealized potentials of the exciting body of work that this book takes as its focus. In doing so, I will occasionally "queer" the flow of my discussion with asides, personal intrusions, theoretical provocations, and sometimes unanswerable complications. These "Queries," as I will term them, are positioned between chapters to provide a break in the dryness of the book's presentation and to offer a useful gloss on the material just discussed. Yet accessibility to students and a demystification of abstract theoretical concepts will always take precedence here over playfulness and a queering of the norms of scholarly presentation. Throughout this book, I will suggest that a simultaneous tactical deployment of *and* critical engagement with the "rules" of conventional behavior represents queer activity at some of its most sophisticated and provocative.

8 Queer theories must themselves be queered often and energetically

The diverse theories and perspectives that this book will investigate are still developing, changing, and struggling with their own issues of normal practice and common purpose. Thus I will argue that the field itself needs constant critical scrutiny and challenge, from within and without. In fact, its own blindspots, lapses, inconsistencies, and nervous avoidances must be foregrounded if it is to avoid becoming yet another manifestation of the normalizing forces that it claims to critique and to work to undermine. While all bodies of theory need rules and conventions, those also always demand vigilant attention as potential constraints and oppressive limitations. And, I will suggest, what is most important to investigate is what practitioners within the field generally avoid discussing.

The above underlying premises and beliefs give the reader, I hope, some useful information about what this book will do and how it will do it. I would also like to mention here some of its most significant predecessors. Perhaps one of the most enduring "norms" of scholarly and textbook production is for the author to claim that her or his work is *more* comprehensive, *more* useful and complete than others in the field. I am not going to do that. I can only claim that the present book is usefully different.

The best-known and most widely used book on the general topic of the present investigation is Annamarie Jagose's 1996 overview, *Queer Theory: An Introduction*. I have used her valuable book several times in my own classes, and I have great respect for it. It is readable, well researched, and nicely succinct. Yet at the same time I believe it is also quite limited (otherwise I would not have agreed to write the present volume). Unlike my own, Jagose's interests are not in applying the theory that she discusses. She does not take readers from the intriguing concepts that she explains to actual textual readings and interpretations. Furthermore, while she usefully avoids discussing "queer theory" as a static entity, she certainly does not attempt on her own to stretch its boundaries or question its norms. I will venture into somewhat more dangerous territory in later chapters.

Another very useful overview covering some of the same information provided here is Joseph Bristow's *Sexuality*, which was published in Routledge's "New Critical Idiom" series in 1997. Because he too avoids textual applications, Bristow can devote more time to exploring the work of some key theorists. His discussion of Freud and Lacan, in particular, is much more detailed than what you will find in my second and third chapters. I have recommended Bristow often to graduate students needing a solid grounding in sexuality-related theories, especially of those two thinkers. But it is telling that Bristow's index lists only ten pages devoted to "queer theory" specifically, and in foregrounding the perspectives of other critics, he, like Jagose, only rarely offers his own critique of the theories that he discusses so authoritatively.

One book that does take some overt risks, and for which I have considerable respect for that very reason, is Alan Sinfield's *Gay and After* from 1998. Sinfield, as I will mention in later chapters, is one of the present day's most interesting and provocative queer theorists and interpreters of literary texts. *Gay and After* is an enjoyable and profitable "read" for anyone interested in queer theory. Yet as a collection of diverse essays, it is not particularly useful for students wishing to learn about the history, context, and diverse practitioners of queer theory. Furthermore, it gives scant attention to the specific ways in which lesbian experience and theoretical articulations have contributed importantly to – and sometimes necessarily and admirably fracture – the field. Ambitiously exploring and pushing the boundaries of "queer theory," *Gay and After* gives much less attention than Jagose's book or the present one to the back-story of its own theoretical and critical articulations.

Yet all three of these books are valuable and engaging, and in queer fashion, I want to recommend them highly to the present book's readers. If you are intrigued by the material I present here, they might be your next reading experience. Perhaps the queerest thing that we can do as masterful scholars and authoritative critics is to commend and recommend our competitors. Jagose's very brief book is more succinct than my own, Bristow's covers some key theorists more fully, and Sinfield's is more aggressively theoretical. All have their unique merits that you should not ignore.

But this book also has its merits and I want to talk a bit now about its basic organization. Part I opens with "A Brief, Slanted History of 'Homosexual' Activity" (Chapter 1) which examines the development of sexual "identity" as a concept and the many ways in which theories of sexuality have affected the interpretation of lives and texts before "queer" came into critical currency in the early 1990s. I then move on to a discussion of "Who and What is 'Queer'?" (Chapter 2) in which I examine the specifics of "queer" as a critical concept that has antecedents in existential philosophy and post-structuralist thought. In "Queering Class, Race, Gender, and Sexual Orientation" (Chapter

3) I then address the limitations of "queer theory" as it was mani-fested through much of the 1990s, exploring what remained unstated, unexamined, and even nervously avoided by the field.

Part II of the book offers readings of several texts, drawing on and exemplifying the concepts previously explored, but designed primar-ily to spur your continued exploration. "The Yellow Wall-Paper," *Dr. Jekyll and Mr. Hyde, Orlando, Giovanni's Room,* and *The Color Purple* provide intriguing textual material for queer readings. In Part III, I conclude by musing on the future of "queer theory," where it might go and what might doom it to irrelevance. Throughout these and earlier sections, I regularly pose questions and offer asides – the "Queries" that I mention above – that work to push readers to think about their own assumptions and practices even when I have no easy answers or facile reassurances to offer to replace comforting norms or safe conventions. Throughout, I insist upon a necessary *methodologi-cal* queerness that involves diverse reading strategies and multiple interpretative stances. While every act of interpretation or critical argumentation must be internally consistent and well supported, or risk being rejected by readers, all acts are finally limited and partial. Throughout I emphasize numerous queer possibilities rather than insist upon a single queer formula.

And this opening up of diverse potentials is intended, quite frankly, to make this body of theories – these many queer possibilities – avail-able and attractive to you. Indeed, underlying all contemporary criti-cal analysis inflected with identity politics and a perception of identity-based oppression (and imbued, of course, with the desire to challenge or redress that oppression) is a certain, often unspoken, identity-*altering* agenda. Whether admitting it openly or not, feminist theory and analysis in all of its diverse forms works very hard to turn you into a feminist or feminist-allied man. Likewise, Marxist and materialist theory in its diverse manifestations today wants to convert you to its particular and important cause: the challenging of an exploitative class structure and the capitalist system that perpetuates it. Certainly these are the understandable subtexts of Ruth Robbins's *Literary Feminisms* and Moyra Haslett's *Marxist Literary and Cultural Theories,* both fine additions to the "Transitions" series in which this volume also appears. Rarely are you asked for your exclusive alle-giance – you may even be urged to attach yourself in multiple ways to a set of complex, interrelated projects and revisionary practices (as we see with John Brannigan's *New Historicism and Cultural Materialism,* also in the "Transitions" series) – but underlying most broad theoretical musings and discrete acts of analysis today is an attempt to change the world by first changing you, the reader of the "theory" text.

The fact that such an agenda is normally covert can itself be interpreted variously. Such a lack of openness could be understood as a Machiavellian tactic: lure readers into an argument or reading, and then work slowly and steadily to transform their beliefs without alerting or alarming them. Covert agendas might also be attributable to the unfortunate formal legacy of more traditional literary criticism that can replicate oppressive beliefs while refusing to admit that criticism always conveys social and political beliefs. Simply following the convention of *not* speaking overtly about one's intentions vis-à-vis the reader helps legitimize the articulation, for a veneer of disinterested communication with the reader is maintained, even when the interests of the readings offered are quite overt.

It is always safer to participate in the normal, formal practices of theory writing and criticism, no matter how radical one's agenda. All roads lead to Rome, one might say. The norm is overdetermined or it wouldn't be so powerful. It is almost always unspoken or it wouldn't be so intractable.

But to reiterate an important point here: queer theories have no love for the normally covert or hidden. This book represents an overt act of proselytizing. *I am going to try to queer you.* At least a little, anyway.

This does not mean that I am going to ask you to experiment with homosex (or heterosex) or urge you to question your gender identity (though certainly I think experimentation and questioning are generally very good things and if you need or have been waiting for a permission-giving device, then by all means let me serve that purpose too). Nor would I ever point out certain aspects of your experiences or identity performance and call you "a" queer. No, that would not be appropriate at all.

Indeed, as Eve Sedgwick so accurately points out, "there are important senses in which 'queer' can signify only *when attached to the first person. . . .* [W]hat it takes – all it takes – to make the description 'queer' a true one is the impulsion *to* use it in the first person" (*Tendencies* 9). But certainly "impulsions" come from somewhere and queer theories do not shy away from working to activate impulsions through difficult, uncomfortable, discomforting questions.

So . . . are you "queer," have you been "queered," are you *a* queer?

Don't answer now. I haven't even told you yet what I mean by "queer." At least let me offer a few tentative definitions while I let these questions work on you. And don't misunderstand me, I'm not at all interested in having you tell me anything about your past or present. I'm really asking if you want to join our little queer club, a volunteer organization devoted to working very hard to queer our *future . . .* together.

Queer – the adjective

"Queer" can be a lot of things, but it cannot be unwilling to affiliate with others who are uncomfortable with or oppressed by a sometimes violent, sometimes dreary and debilitating dominant culture. In Sedgwick's words, "Queer is a continuing moment, movement, motive – recurrent, eddying, *troublant.* The word 'queer' itself means *across* – it comes from the Indo-European root -*twerkw,* which also yields the German *quer* (traverse), Latin *torquere* (to twist), English *athwart.* . . . Keenly, it is relational and strange" (*Tendencies* xii). Sedgwick's pointing out that connection to "across" and "athwart" is worth discussing briefly. In later chapters we will discuss the Victorian drive to categorize and classify, to fix individuals and their many social characteristics into schemas of scientific and pseudo-scientific understanding. As part of – and in response to – an unmooring of traditional, static notions of class, gender, and racial identities, there was a general social drive for new forms of secure, fixed identity – a desire to chart, delineate, understand (and thereby render less threatening) potentially fluid and morphic social existence through selectively focusing on certain aspects of behavior, personality, physiology, or a belief system, and pinning a defining identity label on the individual thereby. "What are you?" – a question that took on a new urgency in the modern era because the possible answers were myriad – drove an intertwined scientific, economic, and political emphasis on providing one-dimensional answers. And certainly a spurious one-dimensionality can represent a relatively safe and comfortable space for many people. But not for all, and the fact that reductive answers about identity are so very inadequate still today drives the response of some who resist, who two-, three-, and multidimensionalize, who seek to complicate thoroughly the possible answers to that interrogatory "What are you?"

Thus it is broadly useful to begin to think of the adjective "queer" in this way: it is to abrade the classifications, to sit athwart conventional categories or traverse several. It is to be at once a girl and an athlete, simultaneously a rural Southerner and an electronic music fan, at the same time an African-American adolescent living in the inner city and an intellectual. Queer – the adjective – means that there is no *easy* answer to the question above, no single word, no simple slot into which complex personalities, behaviors, desires, abilities, and ambitions can be placed. In this way, we are all queer, if we will simply admit it. We are all athwart if we expose and repudiate some of the comforting lies told about us and that we tell ourselves.

Queer – the noun

Yet fear of "discomfort" hardly captures the power of classification systems to hold us in/to one-dimensional identifications. One of the underlying thrusts of the drive to categorize and fix securely is to delineate "healthy" normality from abject abnormality in clear and powerful ways. Indeed, systems of identification always convey social values as they chart people. While objectivity is often claimed – indeed, the credibility of the drive to classify depends upon claims of objectivity – the impulse is invariably to distinguish the proper from the improper, to assign values to identities and activities.

To be a woman is to be a lesser version of a man. To be "of color" is to be a lesser version of being "white." To be an effeminate man is to be a lesser version of a masculine man. To be a homosexual is to be a lesser version of a heterosexual.

One version of being "a queer" is simply to occupy the lower half of that last hierarchized binary. As sexual activity became a particularly urgent means by which individuals were classified during the nineteenth century (we'll talk about sexual "science" in Chapters 2 and 3), slurs and pejoratives were marshaled to "put people in their place" and make sure that they understood the degraded nature of that place. While scientific discourse often (though sometimes barely) masked the disapprobation associated with a particular identity, popular language exposed it and rendered it unmistakable. Thus, however "scientifically" Victorian racial classification systems seemed to chart the so-called "natural" abilities of the races, popular slurs made sure that individuals within the system never forgot the value assigned to them. And however obscurely and pseudo-scientifically the medical establishment discussed the newly potent designation of "homosexual" in the late nineteenth century, popular discourse found ways of translating the hierarchized nature of the hetero/homo binary into clear and unequivocal language. A "queer" was something that you clearly did not want to be. If possible, change or be changed. And if it is impossible to change, then certainly be silent and celibate.

Queer – the verb

For the broad social fear is always that the abnormal and degraded will not stay in their assigned place, that "secure" social systems and identities will become unmoored, and that lived complexities will undermine facile designations of who we are and who we should be. Sexuality and desire in particular have a dangerous and infectious quality because they are so unlike the (supposed) "concretes" that underlie other social identities, such as genitalia (for gender identity), skin color (for racial identity), and financial assets (for class identity). The fear is always that the "queer" noun will take on a transitive verb form, will spread its queerness, convert others, awaken discontent, and undermine the system.

And this is an understandable and credible, though hardly necessary or laudable, fear. Since sexuality and desire are so very amorphous, so hard to know or pin down, so potentially changeable in small and sometimes dramatic ways over time, "queering" does pose a particular threat to systems of classification that assert their timelessness and fixity. It may not destroy such systems but it certainly presses upon them, torturing their lines of demarcation, pressuring their easy designations. Furthermore, if the oppressed find coalitions across various forms of oppression – gender, race, sexuality, social class – they will greatly outnumber their oppressors. And, certainly, if they take the worst slur that society can hurl against them – "queer" or "nigger" – and undermine its power through different usages, a tool of those oppressors is potentially, palpably weakened.

And this is why I want to "queer" you. Throughout this book, I want to enlist your help in putting pressure on simplistic notions of identity and in disturbing the value systems that underlie designations of normal and abnormal identity, sexual identity in particular. And we can do some of that work through queer interventions in the form of cultural, textual, and specifically literary analysis.

Queer – the theories

And now we come to the crux of the present volume, appearing as part of the "Transitions" series. Theories that attempt to homogenize, normalize, categorize, and hierarchize are pervasive across the fields of the social sciences and humanities. Essentialist theories, that locate or seek a trans-historical, enduring or core essence to human identity have even been used in the service of progressive causes – feminist and gay/lesbian. While I will discuss the lure, utility, and finally limitations of such essentializing moves in upcoming chapters, here it is important to note that such moves separate and categorize in much the same way that theories degrading women and homosexuals long did. "Queer" theories – in this book's usage of the term – work to challenge and undercut any attempt to render "identity" singular, fixed, or normal.

As a rubric in wide use among academics, "queer" dates from the early 1990s, with one of the most succinct and still useful delineations of its utility coming from Michael Warner in his introduction to the collection *Fear of a Queer Planet: Queer Politics and Social Theory* from 1993: "[Queer] represents, among other things, an aggressive impulse of generalization; it rejects a minoritizing logic of toleration or simple political interest-representation in favor of a more thorough resistance to regimes of the normal. . . . For both academics and activists, "queer" gets a critical edge by defining itself against the normal rather than the heterosexual, and normal includes normal business in the academy" (xxvi).

Warner's use of the term "regimes of the normal" points to the ways that notions of normality – of proper place and role – represent a mode of government, a form of management of peoples, their activities, and expressions of selfhood. This is not to posit a simple dynamic of intent – with a willful group of oppressors (government officials, high-ranking scientists, and nefarious corporate executives) banding together to oppress all who deviate from their idea of the norm – feminists, gays and lesbians, ethnic minorities, activists of all persuasions. That perception of intent and conscious conspiracy – though it may accurately describe an occasion or particular situation – fails to capture the complex ways that "regimes of the normal" endure over time. In positing any "us/them" dynamic, theories of oppression fail to account for how "we" often oppress ourselves. We – however "oppressed" we are – are always part of those "regimes of the normal" in ways that exceed our own consciousness. Queer theories always recognize our own acculturation into notions of normality in ways that demand ongoing critical attention to the actions and belief systems comprising our "selves."

And this is the challenge of aggressively generalizing with the term "queer." As Warner notes, "queer" may display a certain "brilliance as a naming strategy" but it also "suggests the difficulty in defining the population whose interests are at stake in queer politics" (xxvi). I will discuss at greater length "who and what is 'queer'" in Chapter 2, but certainly with such a term that rejects notions of the normal, it is a continuing challenge to resist a clear demarcation of "legitimate" queerness. While "queer" as a specific term of political activism arose as part of the fight for AIDS funding and against the rank homophobia of the Reagan/Bush regime in the 1980s and early 1990s, and has long, as a term of opprobrium, been directed explicitly against the sexually nonconforming, "queer" does not demand a litmus test of a certain type of (homo)sexual activity. In attempting to queer you, I am not asking you to "mess around" with someone of the same sex . . . simply to "mess up" notions of normality.

Thus among the many forms of disruptive desire, iconoclastic impulses, uncomfortable questionings of normality, and investigations of the gaily (in Nietzsche's sense) *ab*-normal that we will discuss in the coming pages, I hope that you will see something concerning your "self" or one of your many selves. I am a middle-class, white man, atheist, professor, occasional rave-goer, writer, returned Peace Corps volunteer, intellectual, and among many other things, a happy queer. As I will reiterate often, at the very least, and perhaps at the very best, queer theories multiply and complicate our identity bases to the point that we are less likely to look at others and desire to "put" them in their "place." None of us has a single, fixed place, as scary as that freedom (from fixity) may be. Indeed, attempts to name and enforce the "normal" are largely born of fear – though certainly abetted by economic and other needs – and this book will succeed if it reduces *your* fear of the queer.

The only thing to be afraid of is the messiness and complexity that is life itself. Though, granted, that can be very scary indeed.

A Query

She asked it very matter-of-factly, "Are you a *queer*?" This was in chemistry class (while Mr. Shelby was across the hall flirting with Mrs. Arnold, the "expert" guidance counselor who tried to talk me *out* of going to college . . . so much for experts). I was 15 and Joan suddenly commanded the attention of the entire room as she turned the identity spotlight directly on me. Of course I knew all too well that I desired other boys (especially a dark, lanky one who mercifully was not in the room at that moment), had recently "come out" to a couple of close friends, and even had a small stash of gay rights material hidden in my bedroom closet (waiting to be found a year later by my parents). But this was rural Alabama in 1975 and I had a well-honed survivor's instinct. "No," I said dryly, and went back to doodling on my notebook cover. "Well, are you *gay*?" was her immediate follow-up (and I'll never know if she was making a subtle distinction or trying to trick me through sham political sensitivity). "*No*," keeping to my story and my doodling. "Do you even know what gay *means*?" she persisted. Did I ever. "Yes," continuing my doodling. Silence. Bored, she and the class turned their attention elsewhere. "Well, I was *just* curious," was her parting remark.

I felt awful. Not particularly threatened or physically unsafe. Unlike many others, my school was not a very violent place (all of the would-be oppressors were drunk, stoned, or dead after overdosing on angel dust), though certainly it was no place to celebrate difference. No, I felt awful because of the lie. I knew what I "was" (confusion only came much later), was even comfortable with what I "was," but also knew better than *ever* to turn around in the hallway when someone yelled, "Hey, queer!" To be sure, I always wanted to turn around and say something smart and sarcastic. After all, I was not-so-secretly proud of being abnormal – bookish, ambitious, self-aware – in that bunch of losers (which, more than anything specifically sexual, may have been what they were calling me on). "Hey, queer!" No response. No confession. And (just as I hoped) never any persistence or counter-response on their part. Only an occasional "Hey, queer!" to see if maybe this time I would choose to identify or if I had finally figured something out about myself, something that they already suspected and perhaps suspected ("Do you even know what gay *means*?") that I was simply too naïve to know about myself.

Ha. Queer youths are usually very far removed from "naïve." Not cynical exactly, but knowing and tactically self-protective certainly. It would take me three more years before I felt I could own up in very public fashion to being "gay" and another 15 before I would give into the "impulsion to use [queer] in the first person."

But the "impulsion" was certainly there, the defiant abnormality was already part of my performance and personality. I became *a* queer – the noun – when I first used the term to self-identify in the early 1990s, but I certainly was queer – the adjective – long before then. And the utility of reconciling adjectives with nouns and then energizing them into verbs – of transforming descriptors into identities into actions – is something I want to talk about with you throughout the pages of this book.

Part I

The Social Construction of Queer Theories

I A Brief, Slanted History of "Homosexual" Activity

Is a "queer" history even possible? Without a doubt, queers of various sorts have existed throughout history: individuals who have challenged openly or simply lived abrasively toward notions of the sexual and social norm. And as the coming pages will explore, it is clear that there has always been some form of sexual activity between men and between women, though how that activity manifested itself and the ways in which it was socially castigated or tolerated have varied greatly.

Yet the concept of "a" queer history is nevertheless a problematic one. One of the most useful insights of late twentieth-century critical theory and reconceptualizations of historiography is that "history" is always an artificial construct, one that depends upon numerous acts of interpretation, exclusion, and information shaping that reflect inevitably and indelibly the beliefs and biases of the historian or critic. The construction of any simple historical "timeline" is particularly problematic from such a theoretical perspective. Even a single life does not "develop" in neatly linear fashion; there are contradictions, reversals, recurrences, and anomalous actions that make biography writing an act always of creative writing. And when you take the complexity of a single life and exponentially increase it by the complexity of all lives, the notion that human history is reducible to a nice, clean line of causes, effects, progressions, and developments is really a bit ridiculous (however popular and comforting those wall charts showing the advance of world "civilization" may be).

But even more to the point here, linearity becomes particularly artificial for our purposes because queers have lived often in ignorance of each other and of queer-relevant historical information from the near, as well as distant, past. Sexuality itself has frequently been ignored as

part of historical record keeping, and sexual nonconformity, in particular, has often (though not always) gone unrecorded. Indeed, it was
commonly feared that simply discussing sexual nonconformity would
give people ideas about forms of sexual expression and gratification
that would never have occurred to them otherwise. And certainly
there is something to that fear. It is not that we have to have a name
for our desires before they urge themselves upon us; desire may be
there already for any number of reasons (though also hearing about
different sexual pleasures and possibilities may, itself, generate new
and different forms of desire). But certainly naming something and
giving it a history (either within an individual life or over a great span
of years) does make it available as a way of organizing one's identity
and of seeing and proactively creating affiliations.

Indeed, history writing – as reductive, biased, and creative as it may
inevitably be – is a singularly important political act. I would caution
that it needs questioning – queering – aggressively so it is never naturalized or concretized, but it is vital as a component of identity-
creation and communal validation. There would be no popular and
effective lesbian and gay rights movement today without a process of
historical data-recovery, which opens up the possibility of affirming
contemporary lives by looking backwards over time to find that we
are not alone in our experiences of oppression and struggles for
acceptance. History *motivates* by offering examples of what can
happen if one fails to organize and fight back, by stoking one's anger
over the many horrors perpetrated by generations of oppressors, and
by creating a "telos" (an end-point or goal): the present moment
where action simply must be taken or a future moment of "liberation"
that one must fight to realize.

Thus to help me achieve some of the goals I articulated in my introduction, I will engage in this chapter in a bit of slanted and selective
history writing. And as we move toward the interpretation of an
admittedly select set of literary texts in the next section of this book,
the history that will be most useful for us is that of Great Britain and
the United States, though certainly the following chapter and others
will venture onto the Continent at times. But in so selecting, I do not
want to forget that Anglo-American history as it will be discussed here
is not only an act of creative writing for what it includes within its own
"story," but also for the vast numbers of peoples and stories across the
globe and through time that it must ignore. Thus at the end of this
chapter I will "query" world cultures briefly and suggest some other

sources of information for students who understandably and commendably wish to turn to the wealth and complexity of sexualities and sociosexual normalities outside of our limited scope in this book. There are many, many histories still to be written, used, and learned from. As lesbian historian Leila Rupp has suggested, "History, for most historians [today], is not the one 'true story.' Rather it is a story as best we can tell it, given the evidence, our own assumptions and values, and the perspective we take from our own place in a particular society, at a specific point in time" (*A Desired Past* 13–14).

So let me begin to set some of the parameters for our own slanted little story with a question or two. When and why did something so small and (potentially) insignificant as a man touching another man's penis or a woman caressing another woman's genitalia become a source of profound horror and a seeming threat to the very foundations of human moral, religious, and political structures? Why have such expressions of desire and acts of tenderness motivated torture, murder, and vehement, frothing diatribes by politicians, clergy, and medical personnel? Why does an act of love (or simply piqued sexual interest) between two individuals of the same biological sex still today generate genocidal hatred? Even more concretely put, why, when I hold the hand of my boyfriend at a restaurant, do some people want to kill me?

To answer these questions we do have to move backwards through time, to look at changing ideas, references, and resonances, some of which are still used today to justify harshly different valuations of what we now term hetero- and homosexuality. And in moving across millennia, we immediately face the problem of terminology, for there is no term or phrase that accurately subsumes both my holding hands with my boyfriend in Los Angeles in the twenty-first century *and* anal intercourse between an adult man and an adolescent boy in ancient Greece. I could call that latter activity "gay," as some have, but that is simply a backwards projection, a limited and imprecise usage that obscures far too many complexities for a book such as this one. "Gay" represents a modern stance concerning a well-formulated, highly politicized sexual identity. Some have argued that it is most appropriate to see "gay" as a late twentieth-century identity label; others have traced its usage back to the last decades of the nineteenth century. But certainly "I am gay" is only possible as a statement in a world in which sexuality is perceived as having an identity-determining capacity, and even then only gains weight and meaning in a context in

which "I am straight" (or something to that effect) is the generally
approved social norm. That is not how people thought of themselves
(or their "selves") for most of human history, as difficult as it may be
for some of us to understand that fact, since we are looking backwards
through the lens of our own language and reference systems.

This point is worth taking a moment to explore since it is central to
the rest of the book. Perhaps the easiest way to conceptualize such a
dramatic epistemological shift for the student new to this discussion
is to think of some physical or preferential characteristic today that
does not carry any particular weight. Let us say a preference for hot
cereal over cold cereal for breakfast. That is not a distinction that we
generally think about or to which we attribute any social value. Of
course, if I am eating cold cereal one morning in a restaurant and I see
someone else eating hot oatmeal, I suppose I might think to myself,
"ick, how can she eat that?" but probably it would not even register
with me. And I am quite sure that I would never place her in a category of "hot-cereal-eater" that would color my perception of her
through the rest of the day and forever afterwards. If we work together
in the same office and I happen to see her in the hallway, images of
her eating oatmeal would not suddenly spring to mind, nauseating
me, and making me wish her dead or incarcerated. That is simply not
how we in the twenty-first century classify individuals. Perhaps in the
future we may rearrange our worldviews in such a way that we will
divide up the world into categories of people arranged by breakfast
preferences. At that point, if the hot-cereal-eaters are in the majority
or have particular political sway, cold-cereal-eating might be
outlawed and cold-cereal-eaters violently oppressed. "Coldies," existing covertly, might then form secret support networks; a few may risk
arrest by campaigning publicly for a decriminalization of cold-cereal-
eating, etc. Those individuals might not be able to look back on our
day and imagine that it was possible that we did not see the profound
identity difference between hot-cereal-eaters and cold-cereal-eaters.
They would be looking at us through the lens of their own identity
constructs.

Obviously the above analogy is a simplistic and problematic one.
Sexuality and desire were never as wholly inconsequential as breakfast food preferences are today. But it is important to recognize that
we cannot extrapolate from our own worldviews and think of them as
"natural" or "normal" across vast expanses of time. Nor can we even
use them accurately across cultures today. If I walk hand-in-hand

with another man on the streets of Los Angeles, I am correctly interpreted as someone who has sexual contact with other men. If two men walk hand-in-hand down a road in rural Congo or India, it would be wholly erroneous to assume that they are sexually active with each other. I will return to such complexities throughout this book. But here is vital to remember that facile impositions of one individual's or group's conception of the "normal" or "natural" is precisely what the queer theories that we will explore later engage, critique, and ultimately reject as oppressive and grossly reductive.

In looking backwards over centuries, all we can do is attempt to tease out the identity constructs that were available and circulating in a culture and at a particular time. "Gay" as a term signaling an assertion of self-aware and self-respecting sexual identity is one best left for referencing the twentieth century and today. And it is most accurately used for men alone. "Lesbian" as an identifying term distinct from "gay" identity is also centrally important here, even though lesbians and gay men have often interacted politically and socially and in ways also worth noting. "Homosexual" and "heterosexual" too are recent identifiers, dating from late nineteenth-century medical terminology. They are not at all accurate as terms for labeling identities from previous centuries, though they are useful for describing specific activities between members of the same sex or different sexes. In other words, two men from the medieval era, who had anal intercourse, could be said to have engaged in "homosexual" activity (as a descriptor of sexual contact between members of the same sex), even if it would be wholly erroneous to describe them as self-aware "homosexuals" of the nineteenth- or twentieth-century variety. In the coming pages I will use "homosexual" only in that manner, to describe acts not individuals. And even then I acknowledge fully that it is an anachronistic and problematic usage (which is why I put "homosexual" in quotation marks in this chapter's title). It is simply a convenient one that I will complicate as necessary.

So with these complications out of the way, let us return to the question posed earlier: when and why did one woman touching another's flesh or one man fondling another's body become invested with the power to elicit hyperbolic, even hysterical, social reactions? It was not always so. As historian David M. Halperin and philosopher Michel Foucault have explored, sexual paradigms during the Classical Greek era were far different. While we know much more about how men organized their sexual lives during that and most other eras than

we do about how women interacted sexually, we do know that homosexual activity, within certain boundaries, was not regarded as a
threat to society. Indeed, in some narrowly defined manifestations, it
was idealized and celebrated. Greek mythology makes many references to same-sex erotic desire, especially between adult men and
what we would now term "adolescent" boys. And other philosophical
and literary writings, as well as artistic representations, from the era
suggest that such contact was countenanced by (perhaps was even
common among) the privileged Greek citizenry. While this may seem
shocking to us, and we may wish to project backwards our contemporary notions of "child abuse" to condemn it, such an anachronistic
imposition tells us much more about the power of our categories than
anything particularly useful about the Greeks. That sexual contact
between patrician men and boys was "naturalized" at the time
prompts us to see our own systems of organizing social/sexual relations as similarly time-bound. The "natural" has little trans-historical
grounding.

Indeed, as Halperin explores in *One Hundred Years of
Homosexuality*, adult male sexuality during the Classical era had
much more to do with power status and social positioning than it did
with any expression of identity-determining desire for the same or
other sex. Sexual contact between two adult men or two adult women,
while it no doubt occurred, was not itself an activity that provided a
basis for self-assertions of identity, as far as we know. Social standing
– what we might loosely call social "class" – was the means by which
individuals conceived of themselves and their place in the world.
Pederastic activity was one means by which privileged men manifested their dominance over others. Of course, how *dominance* specifically piqued sexual desire and what that may or may not tell us about
sexual relationships during other eras or today is a topic still demanding considerable scrutiny, research, and theorizing.

And beyond those intergenerational manifestations, same-sex
desire was referenced in several important ways during the Greek era
that resonated through later time periods and that deserve special
note here. During the sixth century BC, the poet Sappho wrote nine
books of emotionally charged and erotic verses, many concerning
young women (though only a few of them survive today as anything
other than tiny fragments). Both the term "Sapphic" and, of course,
"Lesbian" (which derives from the name of her home island, Lesbos)
have come down to us through the ages as terms for women who

desire other women. And Sappho's iconic status is no twentieth-century projection backwards; she and her homoerotic verses were very well known during her own day, and her poetry was highly celebrated by Plato and others.

And Plato is another major source of Classical articulation on same-sex desire that has implications still. His dialogues contain various references to pederastic desire as mentioned above, but also in his *Symposium*, he foregrounds a major statement by Aristophanes that has relevance to our discussion of identity construction even in the twenty-first century. In his statement, Aristophanes theorizes that the world was once made up of conjoined beings, some of mixed sex, others of two men or two women. When Zeus divided these conjoined beings into separate individuals, sexuality was determined by the search for one's missing half, either of the same or different sex. This broad understanding of sexuality as metaphysically determined (even divinely ordained) is something that we will see queer theories question aggressively, as useful as it may be for the purposes of arguing that a particular identity is "natural." While the search for a "soul mate" may be celebrated widely even today in popular discourse, queer theories will treat with skepticism the transcendental bases of such terminology.

But even if (we might say) some things thus stay the same, others certainly change dramatically. The Greek era's relative tolerance for select forms of homosexual activity (and expressions of homoerotic desire in literature) gave way to very harsh proscriptions against all sexual activity outside of heterosexual marriage during the Christian era. While John Boswell in *Christianity, Social Tolerance, and Homosexuality* (an immensely popular work from 1980, which I will mention again at the end of this chapter) suggests that the early church sometimes countenanced same-sex relations, Carolyn Dinshaw and other recent medievalists have carefully pointed out the many horrors perpetrated against "sodomites" during the entire era. Dinshaw summarizes, responds to, and substantially revises Boswell's readings as she explores the severe penalties for all erotic contact between members of the same sex. From church records, we know that sexual activity certainly occurred in the same-sex communities of convents and monasteries, but also that biblical injunctions against such contact (contained primarily in Leviticus and the story of divine wrath against Sodom and Gomorrah) fueled a persecution of homosexually active individuals there and across society. Sodomites were punished with castration, incarceration, and by the thirteenth century (if not earlier) public execution. Fueling this escalating persecution was the distinct fear that homosexual activity within religious communities would threaten the involved individuals' primary allegiance to the church hierarchy. Across society, one might also see the increased persecution of sodomites as a result of the ascendancy of a network of Christian theocratic states that was determined to repudiate pagan/Greek activities, enforce a gender order that kept women in a state of sexual and social servitude to men (and men channeling their sexual energies into creating new church members), and divide individuals into clear-cut domestic units that rendered political and social control much easier to achieve and maintain. Indeed, the persecution of such individuals was thus overdetermined, demonstrating for us how a "norm" is often multiply reinforced. Thus it is important to recognize that a medieval man engaging in anal intercourse with another man was committing a "crime against nature" that was really a crime against the church and the state. The category of "nature" is always influenced by – and in some instances wholly determined by – such political interests.

Yet, as noted, these and other "crimes" certainly still occurred among men and also among women. Historian Judith Brown has carefully searched the historical archive for medieval church articulations on and persecutions of women who had sexual contact with other women, and has offered some important insights. She first explores the context for St. Augustine's fifth-century warnings to his sister against homosexual carnality and carefully accounts for new prohibitions against nuns sleeping together devised by councils of Paris and Rouen in the early thirteenth century. Yet after probing these few references, she stresses that given the clear "knowledge that Europeans had about the possibility of lesbian sexuality, their [relative] neglect of the subject in law, theology, and literature suggests an almost active willingness to *dis*believe" ("Lesbian Sexuality" 69). She concludes that "Even more than male sodomy, sodomy between females was 'the sin which cannot be named'" and such "[s]ilence bred confusion and confusion bred fear. On these foundations Western society built an impenetrable barrier that has lasted for nearly two centuries" (75).

Indeed, "naming" something – even in prohibitive fashion – does carry with it the possibility of identification "with" as well as "against," as we will explore more fully in our next chapter. Explicit proscriptions against male sodomy served to heighten the possibility that some individuals who enjoyed, for whatever reason, sexual activity with another man would seek out ways of organizing, arranging, and structuring their time, energy, and movements in order to gratify secretively their desires. Oppression often breeds very creative forms of resistance. Sodomy between men was made a crime punishable by death in English civil law starting in the sixteenth century. Early seventeenth-century laws in the American colonies were similarly harsh. Yet we know that around the same time in England houses of male prostitution began to appear in London and that men developed networks of subcultural connection through which they could meet other men who also desired sex. As Alan Bray and other historians have explored, "molly-houses" were meeting places for men who wished to arrange sexual encounters with other men. Most of these individuals were probably married and as always it would be erroneous to call them "gay" or "homosexual" since those terms were unavailable to them. But unlike previous eras, a social and cultural space started to open up whereby a secretive identity, one clearly centering on homosexual contact, began to develop – and in ways that we can broadly see as a precursor to a modern notion of homosexual identity. Thus even though it would be reductive to chart the linear "rise" of a homosexual identity, it is vital to recognize how traditions and cultural/subcultural systems do develop over time. Identity constructs are belief systems that spread by word of mouth, by movements of people, and through the printed word and other media (the stage, the web today, etc.), all over time. Without seeing the patterns of social organization that resulted from increased persecution of homosexual activity during the medieval era and the creative arrangements that we know existed in the Renaissance, it would be hard to appreciate how the specific parameters of homosexuality today developed.

And certainly the narrowness of notions of "proper" sexual activity led to resistance of some very interesting sorts. The "libertine" identity of the seventeenth and eighteenth centuries, as explored by Randolph Trumbach and other scholars, was a radical sexual identity theorized by upper-class men who wished to challenge the power of the church and state to control their right to use their own genitalia as they wished. Its limitation to a certain class and gender tells us much about how narrow some "liberation" or liberationist movements can often be – representing only the interests of a few privileged individuals – but it also reveals to us something about what was happening during the seventeenth and eighteenth centuries regarding a prolifer-ating discourse of individual rights (over and above the rights of the church, king, or civil government). This is a watershed era during which notions of "natural" social roles and unquestionable obedience to the aristocracy and church hierarchy began to give way to a sense of changeable and challengeable social relationships. Such increased social flexibility and fluidity were abetted by challenges to biblical beliefs posed by science and the new mobility in social class fueled by urbanization, industrialization, and a growing mercantile economy. The "libertine" identity portrayed in the writings of the Marquis de Sade and others, in which sexual gratification of practically any sort – with members of the same or other sex, in whatever combination or grouping desired – is an important manifestation of a counter-discourse that reflected a new mind-set of challenge to what had been deemed normal and natural. In this way, libertinage serves as some-thing of a precursor to queer theories today, though with its own rich historical context and complex internal rules, which George Haggerty has explored in *Men in Love: Masculinity and Sexuality in the Eighteenth Century*. And certainly de Sade's incarceration and the continued persecution and execution of sexual nonconformists make very clear just how threatening sexual "individualism" was, even when other manifestations and celebrations of individual rights proliferated. The right to the "pursuit of happiness," as proclaimed in the U.S. Declaration of Independence, did not include the right to pursue sexual contact with another man or woman, however happy that might make one.

As we draw closer to our own day, the forms and functionings of sexuality become ever more recognizable. In Michel Foucault's well-known assessment from *The History of Sexuality: An Introduction*, "[t]he nineteenth-century homosexual became a personage, a past, a case history, and a childhood, in addition to being a type of life, a life form, and a morphology, with an indiscreet anatomy and possibly a mysterious physiology" (43). While he is clearly over-simplifying when he asserts that "1870" stands as the precise date of the "birth" of the "medical category of homosexuality" (43), Foucault makes an important larger point that we continue to live today with certain powerful Victorian classifications and identity categorizations. And while I will discuss Foucault at much greater length in my next chapter, he does provide us here with a useful marker of historical shifts in the conceptualization of same-sex desire.

As the breakdown of "natural," "fixed" social identities continued through the nineteenth century – with the continuing erosion of birthright in the determination of class identity, the challenge posed by the women's movement to "natural" spheres in gender identity, and the undermining of religious authority through scientific research and evolutionary theory – the disquieting potential for the loss of all fixed social references and stable definitions abetted the rise of the so-called "social sciences": sociology, psychology, and anthropology, among them. Claiming scientific objectivity, practitioners in these fields set about charting human behavior and social organization in ways that served to define and maintain forms of social "order" that often protected the interests of select privileged groups. Nineteenth-century theorists of race, such as W. B. Stevenson and Joseph Arthur Gobineau, devised elaborate charts that classified individuals by skin tone and physiology into "higher" and "lower" forms of life and social development. As I have discussed in *Fixing Patriarchy*, theorists of gender, responding to the women's movement of the era, attempted to reinforce skewed notions of men's and women's roles by marshaling quasi-scientific "evidence" to "prove" women's inferior capacities outside of the domestic sphere. And as Foucault has explored, the medical and scientific community set out to chart sexual normality and abnormality, working to define and justify proper expressions of sexual desire, and diagnose, account for, and perhaps "cure" improper expressions of same-sex desires and other "perversions," ones that threatened the interests of a still expanding, reproduction-dependent economy organized and regulated through monogamous, patriarchally controlled domestic units.

Indeed, nineteenth-century sexologists began to construct elaborate theories detailing "normal" and "abnormal" sexualities, their manifestations, genesis, and social consequences. As Jonathan Ned Katz points out in *The Invention of Heterosexuality*:

> In August, 1869, a German medical journal published an article by Dr. K.F.O. Westphal that first named an emotion he called "Die contrare Sexualempfindung" ("contrary sexual feeling"). That emotion was "contrary" to the proper, procreative "sexual feeling" of men and women. Westphal's contrary sexual feeling was the first, and became one of the best known, contenders in the late-nineteenth-century name-that-perversion contest. (54)

Other sexologists of the era began to work diligently to further refine
sexual categories. Richard von Krafft-Ebing's encyclopedic
Psychopathia Sexualis from 1886 thoroughly pathologizes homosexuality, seeing it and a wide array of other "perversions" not only as
manifestations of individual illness but clear indicators of a degener-
ating society. What an individual did with her or his own genitals and
other body parts was thus ever more highly politicized and overloaded with meaning. Anxieties over social dissolution, circulating
because of a wide array of economic, religious, and political uncer-
tainties, fixated (not solely, but certainly powerfully) on the figure of
the sexual nonconformist. Having always been carried on in private,
sexuality was "a" secret (perhaps "the" secret) that once fully revealed
and properly controlled would secure us all. Not surprisingly, Krafft-
Ebing seems especially disturbed by the possibility that an individual
might move from sexual conformity to nonconformity by "choice,"
which he calls "cultivated pederasty" and terms "one of the saddest
pages in the history of human delinquency" (601). As we will explore
later, temporal changes in sexuality or sexual self-identification
and eager explorations across identity boundaries are particularly
disquieting for the fixers and categorizers of identity.

Yet, as always, those expressions of explicit condemnation continued to breed resistance. Another early sexologist, Karl Ulrichs, devised
an elaborate schema in his writings from the 1860s and 1870s to
explain homosexuality as "natural," partially through references back
to Plato, just as we have explored here. Ultimately, Ulrichs based his
defense of homosexuality on the premise that same-sex desiring individuals had the soul of the other sex's body trapped within them.
Ulrichs thereby meant to validate homosexuality as metaphysically
determined, yet as Joseph Bristow has noted, "this idea would have a
lasting and damaging influence on twentieth-century prejudices
against homosexuals. For it set the trend for imagining that lesbians
and gay men were 'inverts'" (*Sexuality* 21–2). "Inverted" individuals
were (supposedly) recognizable because they always demonstrated
the gender characteristics of the sex of the soul within them: gay men
were theorized as always effeminate and lesbians as always masculine. This conflation and confusion of gender and sexuality gained
further implicit support in Havelock Ellis's treatise *Sexual Inversion*
from 1897, which decried social prejudices against homosexuals but
still used a model of easily recognizable "normal" and "abnormal"
behavior that attempted only to replace vicious homophobia with

something like pity for the invert. Such pathos resonated through literary characterizations even well into the twentieth century, with Radclyffe Hall's characterizations of miserable "inverted" women in *The Well of Loneliness* (1928) standing as the starkest example.

How did these changing theories and scientific paradigms affect the activities and daily lives of men and women during the nineteenth century who actually engaged in homosexual activity? Here as always it is difficult to know precisely. Most people going about their day-to-day activities do not leave written records of their thoughts and actions; the few documents that are readily available include arrest and court records, autobiographies, and personal letters. We do know from the very frank autobiographical accounts of the Victorian writer John Addington Symonds that same-sex erotic activity was rampant in boys' boarding schools at mid-century. Furthermore, we have many legal documents to chart an increasing persecution of "homosexuals" toward the end of the century, as that term began to circulate and as fears of social disintegration and changeable social identity became ever more fixated on the scapegoat of the sexual degenerate. The best-documented case was the 1890s trials of Oscar Wilde, the popular and eccentric Victorian playwright. Wilde unwisely and unsuccessfully challenged in court the labeling of him as a "somdomite" (a misspelling of sodomite) by the father of his lover, Alfred Douglas. In that libel case and the subsequent prosecution of him for "crimes against nature," the Victorian press publicized in wildly inflammatory ways Wilde's eccentric dress, effeminate manner, and haughty demeanor, all held up as important signifiers of his unnatural sexuality and the threat he posed to "normal," middle-class values. But even though Wilde's case was certainly a tragic one – he died in 1900 after having served two years in prison at hard labor – the figure of Wilde the aesthete, dandy, and campy witticist, also became a powerful one as a new public icon for homosexual men in Britain and America. As the first person widely and publicly identified as "a" homosexual, Wilde influenced generations of men who came to model themselves after (or sometimes define themselves against) him.

But the dramatic figure of Wilde obscures the many ways that same-sex desiring men lived their lives in hidden and anonymous fashion during the nineteenth century, as in centuries before and decades afterwards. As Jeffrey Weeks, Angus McClaren, and William Cohen have explored through court documents from the era, we know that male prostitution existed, that men were occasionally arrested for dressing as women, and that others were prosecuted for soliciting and engaging in "indecent" acts in parks and elsewhere. And, of course, untold numbers of men carried on active sexual lives with other men in ways that were never noticed or known. Victorian pornography details sexual activity between men and women, men and men, and women and women, in pairs and groups, that can hardly be deemed sociologically reliable, but certainly tells us something about the possibilities that existed within the imagination (and perhaps lived experiences) of some Victorians. As I have explored in my overview of erotica from the period, "Graphic Sexuality and the Erasure of a Polymorphous Perversity," sexually explicit writings from the century demonstrate some clear shifts in points of reference and internal delineations of acceptable and unacceptable same-sex activity over the course of the century. These, too, however, are clearly most relevant to the lives – in or outside of print texts – of literate-class men.

We know much less about working-class sex lives and, as always, relatively little about women's sex lives of the period. Historian Leila Rupp tells of her close personal relationship with her "maiden" Aunt Leila (born just after the end of the "Victorian era") but admits that even she does not know if her now-deceased aunt was "a lesbian." Even though Aunt Leila lived all of her adult life with another woman, and even shared a bed with her "friend," Rupp writes,

> I don't know anything about Aunt Leila's desire, sexual behavior, or self-conception. But of course we don't know about such things for most people in the past. And that's the problem. The difficulty of locating sources that document same-sex love and sexuality is legendary. Reflecting the modern Western association of women with love and men with sex, the evidence in the case of women, as the story of Aunt Leila so aptly illustrates, tends to reveal [only] emotional attachments to other women. . . . It's not that women never had sex . . . just that our evidence is skewed.   (*A Desired Past* 5)

Thus historian Lillian Faderman, in *Surpassing the Love of Men*, has traced the "romantic" friendships of women across many centuries in Britain and America, but acknowledges that it is impossible to know when and in what form sexual contact occurred between women who cohabited or publicly expressed their ardent feelings for each other. She, Rupp, and others remind us that it would be foolish to surmise that sexual activity between women was rare or nonexistent simply because it was not written about or was rarely mentioned in the annals of legal activity. Patriarchal belief systems, serving the interests of men and male-dominated institutions such as the church, expressly denied women the capacity or right to feel sexual desires except as channeled into the structure of marriage and reproduction. Of course, prostitution, adultery, and other forms of castigated and punished sexual expression were discussed in legal and other venues as a mechanism whereby "good" women (chaste and cheerful wives, devoted mothers, etc.) were differentiated from fallen or "bad" women (whores, etc.): the former were pure, loyal to men, and, in theory, always sexually naïve.

That women's sexuality was little discussed except in such exemplary cases had complex implications. The fact that women's independently acted-upon sexuality was thought improbable, except among greedy and unnatural prostitutes and morally bankrupt adulteresses, meant that laws often wholly ignored lesbianism, even when sexual contact between men was outlawed and severely punished. As we have seen, homosexual activity between men was a crime punishable by death for many centuries in Britain. Homosexual activity between women was never explicitly criminalized. And, as Rupp suggests above, the common patriarchal association between women and emotion and the greater scope allowed for women's emotional expression meant that women could openly express affection toward each other in public without anyone interpreting it as an indicator of sexual activity. Though we would never want to ignore the many ways that women were harshly oppressed by sexist ideologies, it is clear that such obtuse beliefs provided a very useful cover for women who did live sexually nonconformist lives. Only with the rise of the women's rights movement – and its dramatic successes in the twentieth century – did popular perceptions widen to recognize and explicitly castigate sexual activity between women.

And this does bring us to the remarkable and well-documented activity of the twentieth century. The rise of political rights movements – which worked to redress social injustices of race, class, and gender – began in the eighteenth century and proliferated during the nineteenth century. As we discussed above, this was not because oppression itself necessarily increased during that time period (though sometimes it did) but more directly because individuals newly thought of themselves as having inherent rights that the state and privileged groups too often intruded upon or denied them. And thus we can say that "identity" became ever more "political" as individuals banded together in organizations – small and large, highly public, and sometimes very secretive – to explore their commonalities, discuss their common experiences of injustice, and strategize to change oppressive laws, policies, and social perceptions. Twentieth-century "lesbian and gay" rights movements were greatly indebted to women's rights movements and African-American rights movements from previous generations. The somewhat later manifestation of sexual rights movements when compared to most others is attributable to several factors. One, sexuality is less directly tied to specific physical characteristics and clear outer markers of identity, as I mentioned in my introduction, thus social designation and self-perception occurred at a later date. With the social category of "homosexual" arising only in the nineteenth century, the overt politicization of that identity base lagged behind the politicization of well-defined categories such as "woman" or "Black." Furthermore, sexuality itself was often held to be unmentionable and the breaking of silence on "unnatural" sexual activity involved an especially deep shame and embarrassment that had to be overcome. While the self-identifying statement "I am a woman" or "I am working class" certainly carried with it an extraordinary range of cultural valuations and expectations, it did not carry with it the embarrassment or the likelihood of immediate public scorn and violent reaction that the revelation "I am a homosexual" did.

And certainly we cannot discuss the general social stigma (and sense of shame) associated with homosexuality that lingered through much of the twentieth century without mentioning its most influential early theoretician, Sigmund Freud, whose systemization of the field of psychology in the decades around the turn of the century gave the discipline a new legitimacy and social power. His complicated legacy endures to this day. While Freud's statements on homosexuality are inconsistent over the course of his career, in most of his writings he does portray it as a state of misdirected erotic energies resulting from childhood traumas and unfinished developmental processes. Lesbian historian Margaret Cruikshank has noted that Freud

> speculated that homosexuality involved a narcissistic search for a love that symbolizes the self, a castration fear for men and penis envy

for women. He did not regard it as a sickness, however, or as a condition that could be changed, and thus he opposed criminal punish-
ments for homosexuality. Freud believed that the natural sexual
feelings of children are both homosexual and heterosexual and that
social conditioning usefully represses both bisexuality and homosexuality. Thus a homosexual person is arrested in his or her development. Followers of Freud, especially in the United States, interpreted
this to mean that homosexuals are perpetually adolescents, imma-
ture, blocked in some way, incapable of leading normal lives.
Abandoning Freud's tolerant views, his disciples advocated treatment
for homosexuality.   (*The Gay and Lesbian Liberation Movement* 7)

Yet I would reiterate that Freud was certainly no paragon of tolerance.
In his *Three Essays on the Theory of Sexuality* (1905) he fans fear and
bigotry in warning that "The education of boys by male persons . . .
seems to encourage homosexuality" (96) and clearly links homosexuality with mental illness in numerous claims such as "The unconscious mental life of all neurotics (without exception) shows inverted
impulses, fixation of their libido upon persons of their own sex" (32).
As Peter Gay notes in *The Tender Passion*, "For Freud, heterosexual
genital love-making was . . . an achievement, the culmination of a
long, never painless, and never quite complete evolution. [This]
perception of sexual unfolding retained the normative hierarchy that
had gone barely challenged through most of the Christian centuries"
(251–2). Freud's heterocentric, normative system of value and reference heavily influenced generations of psychoanalysts and therapists,
whose all-too-frequent condescension toward homosexuals reinforced a sense of self-hatred and shame. And Freud's theories and
values were widely known even beyond the medical community. As
Lillian Faderman notes in *Surpassing the Love of Men*, "It would not
have been necessary to read Freud's essays on 'The Sexual
Aberrations' or 'The Psychogenesis of a Case of Homosexuality in a
Woman' in order to know that love between women was now an indi-
cation of childhood trauma and arrested development. Writers of
popular literature, who may or may not have gone back to the original
sources themselves, regurgitated the information for mass delecta-
tion" (315).

Yet in spite of this pathologizing of homosexuality, individuals
began to risk popular scorn and embarrassment, as well as imprison-
ment, in increasing numbers during the twentieth century to assert
that homosexuality was not a criminal, degenerate, or mentally disor-

dered state. At the same time Freud and other sexologists were devising elaborate theories proving the centrality of heterosexuality to a healthy society, Edward Carpenter in *The Intermediate Sex* (1908) and other works was arguing that the increasing incidence of "uranism" (or homosexuality) was the harbinger of a new day of sexual freedom for all. And while an open political rights movement on lesbian and gay issues only developed toward the end of the twentieth century, private movements and scattered public actions date from the last decades of the nineteenth century and proliferated thereafter. In Germany, Magnus Hirschfeld founded the Institute for Sexology in 1919 that was specifically devoted to furthering rights for women and homosexuals; while his Institute was destroyed by the Nazis in 1933 (and the Third Reich went on to incarcerate and murder many thousands of homosexuals), Hirschfeld's work was internationally known and planted the seeds of other activist organizations in Europe and America. George Chauncy's *Gay New York*, Lillian Faderman's *To Believe in Women*, and Leila Rupp's *A Desired Past* all document the many and inventive ways that lesbians and gay men created supportive communities in the United States, especially after the turn of the twentieth century. What these historians reveal is just how creative and brave oppressed individuals can be as they create their own codes of behavior in order to recognize each other without risking public discovery, and also begin to form neighborhoods and social groups that allow them a space for self-expression and validation. Chauncy's remarkable book shows that in certain areas of New York City during the period of the 1890s to the 1930s men lived relatively open lives as self-proclaimed "fairies" and "queers," in ways recognized by the general public and even commented upon by the press, though they always thereby risked arrest, harassment, and other forms of persecution.

What Chauncy, Faderman, and Rupp urge us to recognize today is that as much as we like to consider ourselves in the twenty-first century as uniquely self-aware and political, earlier generations were certainly capable of dramatic political statements and were hardly the self-hating and silent individuals that we may too often consider them to be. In simply existing "queerly," people were living in ways that had a political impact, sometimes large, sometimes small and more diffusive. Of course, if we define the "political" more narrowly as well-organized efforts to challenge laws, policies, and perceptions, then lesbian and gay political movements only developed in Britain and

America during the middle and later decades of the twentieth century. The first political "action groups" date from the 1950s, with the creation of the Mattachine Society and the Daughters of Bilitis on the west coast of the United States. The former began as a small movement of men, led by Harry Hay in Los Angeles, with ideological ties to the anti-Korean War movement and Communist Party (though it became considerably less radical later in the decade), and the latter as a small group of women, led by Del Martin and Phyllis Lyon in San Francisco, seeking to create an alternative to the covert bar scene of the day. Both groups generated publications, *One* and *The Ladder* (respectively), that began to circulate and that helped inaugurate a national gay and lesbian rights consciousness. Recent queer, as well as gay and lesbian, rights movements owe much to the path-breaking work of such groups.

Equally foundational to a deepening twentieth-century consciousness and politicization of sexuality (and with implications that still bear consideration) were the Kinsey Reports on sexuality first published in the 1940s and 1950s. While Kinsey's methodology was problematic and his statistics generally unreliable, the "facts" and "figures" of the first Kinsey Report on male sexuality still linger in our system of reference today. As Chauncy notes,

> [M]ost recent commentary on the Kinsey Report has focused on (and criticized) its supposed estimate that 10 percent of the population were homosexuals, [but] Kinsey himself never made such an estimate and argued explicitly that such estimates could not be based on his findings. His research is much more helpful if used, as Kinsey intended, to examine the extent of occasional homosexual behavior among men who may or may not have identified themselves as "homosexual." Only 4 percent of the men he interviewed reported having been exclusively homosexual in their behavior throughout their lives, but 37 percent acknowledged having engaged in at least one postadolescent homosexual encounter to the point of orgasm, and fully a quarter of them acknowledged having had "more than incidental homosexual experience or reactions" for at least three years between the ages of sixteen and fifty-five. (*Gay New York* 70)

Somewhat lower but similar patterns of experience were charted among women surveyed for the report on women's sexuality published in 1953. As John D'Emilio has explored in *Sexual Politics, Sexual Communities*, these reports had wide-ranging significance both inside and outside of the lesbian and gay community. The star-tlingly high numbers of homosexual activity (though not "identity") that Kinsey reported served at times "not to ameliorate hostility toward gay men and lesbians, but to magnify the proportions of the danger they allegedly posed" (37). But D'Emilio also points out that

> [a]mong homosexuals and lesbians themselves, Kinsey had a more clearly beneficial impact. Scientific evidence appeared to confirm what many gay people in the 1940s were experiencing – the sense of belonging to a group. Moreover, by revealing that millions of Americans exhibited a strong erotic interest in their own sex, the reports implicitly encouraged those still struggling in isolation against their sexual preference to accept their homosexual inclina-tions and search for sexual comrades.   (37)

And Chauncy makes an important additional point worth mentioning here, for as understandable as these usages of Kinsey were for the purposes of self-validation, the implications of Kinsey's research – that sexuality can change dramatically over time and in response to context, and that sexual activity does not necessarily have to lead to self-identification – have yet to be fully acknowledged and grappled with by most sexual rights movements even today. As we will explore in the next chapter, it is easy but finally reductive to read onto complex human behavior and emotions the artificial binary "hetero-sexual/homosexual" and categorize often diverse activities and multi-faceted identities as belonging to one "side" alone. Indeed, self-validation along those lines by lesbians and gay men has often led to a facile diagnosis of "not accepting" one's "true" homosexual self if one has occasional or passing erotic contact with members of both sexes. Even one homosexual encounter can be taken by some as proof of "really" being lesbian or gay, and of living in an unhealthy state of denial if one fails to self-identify as such.

Yet certainly a general discourse of validation was working to heighten the political awareness, commitment, and activity of groups of lesbians and gay men after the mid-century. And if there is a water-shed moment demonstrating this – one that is now commonly hailed by lesbian and gay rights groups – it is the "Stonewall Riots" begin-ning on June 28, 1969. In the middle of a routine raid by vice cops on a gay bar in New York, several hundred incensed patrons, tired of harassment, resisted by throwing bottles, rocks, and other objects at police. Skirmishes between the law and groups of angry lesbian, gay, and transgendered individuals continued for several days. While obviously it is reductive to call this the "birth" of the gay civil rights movement, since individuals and groups had been doing important work for many years, the Stonewall Riots are certainly important as a marker and as a common point of reference (one that continues to be celebrated today in the form of annual "gay and lesbian" pride festivals and marches throughout the month of June). The late 1960s saw an increasing radicalization of social movements working for the civil rights of women and minorities, and Stonewall was an important manifestation of a newly broadened concern with oppression and a new willingness to take to the streets to demand an end to discrimination. Dennis Altman, in *Homosexual: Oppression and Liberation* from 1971, offers some superb insights into and historical details concerning these early days of the specifically "gay liberation" movement in New York. Guy Hocquenghem provides important information on French activities and organizations of the same era in *Homosexual Desire* (1972). Jeffrey Weeks is equally incisive in his analysis of British social history in *Coming Out* (1977). I recommend these books highly for readers pursuing research on that era.

And this willingness to challenge oppression also manifested itself *within* civil rights movements and organizations, as well as in the larger public sphere. The relationship between the women's movement and the lesbian rights movement was strained in the third quarter of the twentieth century. Liberal feminists, wishing to achieve parity with men in business, education, and the political arena, often sought to distance themselves from lesbians seeking civil rights. The epithet "dyke" hurled against all feminists served to fracture women's rights organizations, with the most infamous example of divisiveness being Betty Friedan's characterization of a "lavender menace" seeking to take over the National Organization for Women (NOW) during the late 1960s. This led to overt resistance by lesbians within the organization, who used that term in 1970 to begin a successful campaign of consciousness-raising among all organization members, resulting in an explicit commitment by NOW in 1971 to work for lesbian rights.

Similar strides were made during the 1970s and 1980s to bring to the foreground of consciousness the double-oppression (sometimes triple- or quadruple-oppression, when one considers gender and social class) of lesbians and gay men of color. Audre Lorde was an eloquent spokesperson, in prose and poetry, for the necessary inclusion of sexuality in discussions of civil rights for African-Americans and women. Similarly, Essex Hemphill and Joseph Beam in *Brother to Brother* and other works worked to challenge the heterosexism and chauvinism inherent in masculinist discourse within some sectors of the African-American male community. In *The Greatest Taboo: Homosexuality in Black Communities*, edited by Delroy Constantine-Simms, we find investigations both of the richness of African-American gay and lesbian life, and of the long and continuing struggles to challenge the homophobia of national movements such as the Nation of Islam. Multiple identities involving race, class, gender, and sexuality have also been theorized and superbly complicated by Cherrie Moraga and Gloria Anzaldúa in *This Bridge Called My Back* and other works. I will return to some of these theories, investigations, and fine complications in later chapters.

As all of this implies, a perception of anything like a homogeneous lesbian and gay rights movement would hardly be an accurate one. Lesbians and gays, white and of color, have sometimes worked together and sometimes in highly divergent ways. While we will explore the "queer" movement of the late 1980s and early 1990s in some detail in the next chapter, it is important here to recognize that coalitions among individuals whose only commonality is an experience of oppression based on sexual activity are always fragile ones, especially when gender, race, and class diversity is obscured temporarily by a political agenda that concentrates on sexual identity alone. The entrenched sexism of some gay men, the culturally encoded racism of some white lesbians and gays, the powerful classism of middle-class individuals of both sexes, and the many ways that religious and political beliefs beyond specific sexual identity issues fracture any sense of simple social identity mean that current gay and lesbian politics are certainly fractious and friction-filled.

And this divisiveness has sometimes arisen over a particular polarity that bears some final words of clarification in this chapter, that of "essentialism" and "constructionism." Essentialism implies a belief in a core "essence" to identity, one that endures through time. An essentialist stance might involve references to biological differences or some continuity in self-awareness that derives from a specific sexual or gender identity. For instance, a theorist or critic with essentialist leanings might emphasize that same-sex desiring individuals have always existed and that however much their context may have changed, they were, without a doubt, aware of their sexual desires and they must have thought of themselves as belonging to a distinct group of similar individuals. As the reference to "essence" implies, some essentialists draw on metaphysics: popular works that explore or extol the "gay soul," the "gay spirit," etc. imply a Platonic realm beyond this world in which timeless entities or essences exist (with sexualities, obviously). Those leaps of faith are ones that I will not pursue here. But perhaps the most clear-cut essentialist claims in gay studies recently are far removed from such metaphysics, are being generated by scientists, including Simon LeVay, who seek a firm biological basis for homosexuality. While LeVay's research, in particular, has been heavily criticized for its questionable methodology, he and others continue their search for gay genes, gay brains, and other biological and physiological characteristics that distinguish (and presumably have distinguished for many centuries) homosexuals from heterosexuals.

Working from a different set of premises and methodologies, "constructionists" look not to biology or the metaphysical realm but to language and belief systems as determinants of identity. While we will explore this strand of thinking more fully in the next chapter (since queer theories are, in fact, constructionist theories) here it is worth emphasizing that constructionists look always to historical context to see what categories and concepts were available at the time in question and how those may or may not have involved forms of self-awareness and identification on the basis of sexual desire or activity. A very strict constructionist would even reject the use of the adjective "homosexual" to describe activities from centuries long past, as I have used it above.

Obviously the explanations above are simplifications. Few literary or cultural critics are so simplistic as to reference an enduring "gay soul" or "gay brain," or to ignore wholly changing historical contexts. But certainly in the early years of lesbian and gay studies, essentializing moves were made that had an important political purpose: to locate gays and lesbians throughout time with whom current readers and activists could identify and feel kinship. This was a necessary process of recovery. Same-sex desire, homoeroticism, and lesbian- and gay-relevant themes and implications have long been ignored by historians, literary critics, textbook writers, and anthologists. As an often viciously oppressed minority, lesbians and gays in the twentieth and twenty-first centuries have desperately needed ways of affirming themselves in the face of condescension and scorn by psychologists, clergy, and law-makers. To locate and celebrate "lesbians" and "gays" throughout history is a powerful way of countering the derision and dismissal of a larger homophobic culture. It may be anachronistic and simplistic from the standpoint of historically nuanced research to call Shakespeare "gay" or Sappho a "lesbian," but from the standpoint of identity-affirmation, it is fully understandable why a movement would want to make such claims and why readers and activists would find them so important and integral to their senses of self-worth. Theorist Diana Fuss makes an important point in *Essentially Speaking* when she suggests that essentialism has been self-consciously "deployed" (20) at times to meet communal and contextually under-standable needs.

Indeed, and as Fuss explores at length, nowhere have the conflicts between essentialism and constructionism been played out more clearly than in the field of feminist criticism and theory. While I can only suggest that readers interested in exploring the many varieties and complexities of feminist theory consult Ruth Robbins's superb *Literary Feminisms*, a companion to the present volume, it is worth noting here that profound disagreements have arisen over whether or not women have certain "essential" characteristics that differentiate them from men: nurturance, emotional responsiveness, etc. Robbins usefully traces a series of conflicts, convergences, and divergences in feminist thought that includes many of the same moves that we are examining here: recovery of voices from the past, an exploration of ways of identifying across time periods, and differing visions for what a less gender-oppressive world would be. As mentioned above, lesbian feminism has itself been a complicating force within the field of feminism and a driving force behind the creation of gay and lesbian studies as a legitimate field of inquiry, though the fields are not coex-tensive. Gayle Rubin has pointed out famously in "Thinking Sex: Notes for a Radical Theory of the Politics of Sexuality" that sexuality studies and gender studies are quite different avenues of inquiry, while certainly overlapping and influencing each other at times. Yet without the discussion of identity politics that spurred and continues to invigorate feminist studies, the fields of lesbian/gay/queer studies would be impoverished, if not impossible.

While I do not want to set up a hard and fast, reductive distinction here (for the terms are used interchangeably at times), a move toward an increasingly thorough constructionism does signal a difference between what we might term "gay and lesbian" and "queer" studies.

Yet to point this out is still to recognize that some of the most powerful, identity-solidifying and validating voices have come from lesbian
feminists and gay men writing before "queer" forms of theorization.
Jane Rule's *Lesbian Images* from 1975 opens with a galvanizing
discussion of social attitudes toward "lesbians and homosexual men"
from ancient times to the present. Judy Grahn's *Another Mother
Tongue: Gay Words, Gay Worlds* (1984) examines "gay" imagery from
around the world in very affirmative ways, while often reading other
cultures through the lens of Anglo-American constructs. And even in
the early years of lesbian literary and cultural criticism, historicizing
moves often complicated more essentialist models. Adrienne Rich's
"Compulsory Heterosexuality and Lesbian Existence" (1980) and
Bonnie Zimmerman's "What Has Never Been: An Overview of Lesbian
Feminist Criticism" (1981) helped inaugurate the study of oppression
based on sexuality. The former offers a still compelling paradigm of
entrenched heterocentrism that allows for the critique of language
and political structures; the latter urges powerfully that "we [not]
forget to apply rigorous historical and cross-cultural tools to our
scholarship" (215). In this way both helped provide important
groundwork for the rigorously historical critical work of the 1990s and
beyond. As Linda Garber notes in *Identity Poetics*, all of the writers
above (and many others) "took a firmly rooted, multiply located stand
based on an identity forged through multiple differences – expressing
an identity poetics" that laid the groundwork for the queer theories of
later years, and in ways that a simple binary of essentialism/construc-
tionism fails to capture (97).

Similarly foundational, if not "queer" in the precise sense that we
will use the term in our next chapter, was the path-breaking, identity-
affirming work of gay critics John Boswell and Robert K. Martin during
the 1980s. Boswell's *Christianity, Social Tolerance, and Homosexuality*, though using the term "gay" in an anachronistic fashion
(and, as mentioned above, offering readings that have been heavily
criticized for their historical selectivity) was instrumental in legitimiz-
ing "gay" scholarship and continues to sell well because of its gay-
affirmative stance. Similarly, Martin in *The Homosexual Tradition in
American Poetry* (1979) provided an important corrective to traditional literary history's erasure of the many homoerotic themes and
images in American literature, even as "homosexual" is again
deployed very loosely. While essentializing at times in ways that now
seem methodologically suspect, such articulations are historically

contextualizable and understandable in that they served to carve out
a space for the discussion of same-sex desire in spite of social opprobrium and traditional disciplinary dismissal.

Thus we might even say that identity must be affirmed powerfully
before it can be "deconstructed" rigorously and responsibly. And even
as it is deconstructed, the need for continuing affirmation does not
disappear or necessarily diminish. As we explore queer theories in our
next chapter, I will return often to that need to continue to legitimate
a sense of collective, powerful, and empowering identity even as intellectual inquiry calls into question the very notion of "sexual" identity.
It is not an "either/or" situation. As always, such binaries are intellectually sloppy and reductive. In a recent attack on the entire field of
"queer theory," gay anthropologist Max Kirsch (in *Queer Theory and
Social Change*) quotes approvingly two lesbian critics who charge,

> we cannot afford to allow privileged patriarchal discourse (of which
> Post-structuralism is but a new variant) to erase the collective iden-
> tity lesbians have only recently begun to establish. . . . For what has in
> fact resulted from the incorporation of a deconstructive discourse, in
> academic "feminist," discourse at least, is that the word *lesbian* has
> been placed in quotation marks, whether used or mentioned, and the
> existence of real lesbians has been denied, once again.   (7)

Kirsh notes that "identity, however short-lived, [is] essential" (7). But,
I would argue, that does not mean that it cannot be critiqued rigorously as an essential "construct." Putting time-bound concepts and
identifiers in quotation marks does not deny anyone's existence today
or yesterday. Indeed, intellectual complication (in the service of
greater freedom of expression and activity for sexual nonconformists)
should never be equated simplistically with a wholesale denial of
nonconformist sexual expression by religious fundamentalists and
other homophobes. Historicizing and "deconstructing" are ways of
differently imagining our future as well as understanding our past.
Identity is always a fiction, in the sense that it must suppress
complexity and isolate a defining characteristic (or a limited set of
characteristics) from a wide range of possibilities, but to say this is in
no way to deny the fact that I may be killed or imprisoned because of
it. We can grapple intelligently with *both* aspects of "identity": its
reality and its fictionality. Even revisionary, newly empowering
notions of "identity" inevitably suppress certain complications and

supposedly "peripheral" activities. Of course, when it is *my* complication or peripheral activity that is suppressed, that may feel to me like as much an act of violence or oppression as that which may have spurred identity creation and affirmation in the first place.

A Query

So what has been left out of the above "slanted" history? Most of the world and most of human diversity, of course. It is impossible to discuss the vast majority of sexual systems and human relationships that have existed across time and the globe; indeed, most of them we simply know nothing about. And even the ones about which we do know something, we so often and inevitably interpret through the lens of our own systems of reference, bringing with us value judgments and "moral" premises that may seem wholly appropriate – "natural" – to us, but hardly so to those being described.

Let me mention a fairly well-known case in point: the Sambia of New Guinea. In *Guardians of the Flute* (1981) and, most recently, *Sambia Sexual Culture* (1999) anthropologist Gilbert Herdt has detailed the intricate sexual systems of the Sambian men whose activities over a lifetime entail by social mandate both homosexual and heterosexual contact: "Sambia sexual lifeways required that men engage in same-sex relations before marriage, with exclusive relations with their wife afterward, creating multiple desired person-objects. Thus, Sambia sexuality and cultural reality are based upon a capacity to experience multiple sexual desires and social relations" (*Sambia* 20). But beyond the multiplicity of their desires, it is the specifics of the Sambia's same-sex rituals and behaviors that have startled many:

> Sambia practice secret homoerotic fellatio, which is taught and insti-
> tuted in first-stage initiation [into adulthood]. Boys learn to ingest
> semen from older youths through oral sexual contacts. First- and
> second-stage initiates may only serve as fellators; they are forbidden
> to reverse erotic roles with older partners. Third-stage pubescent
> bachelors and older youths thus act as fellateds, inseminating prepu-
> bescent boys. All males pass through both erotic stages, being first
> fellators and then fellated; there are no exceptions. . . . Boys must
> drink semen to grow big and strong. (*Sambia* 60–1)

Many people have since written about the Sambia's unique rites of passage, with one of the clearest and most useful commentaries being provided by Rupp:

> In the highlands of New Guinea, Sambia boys can grow into adulthood only if they swallow the semen of older men, so male initiation rites involve fellatio. Participating in such an act in either role is expected, is not deviant, and means nothing about one's "sexuality." And is the act itself even "sexual"? Is it significant that young boys become men by putting mouth to penis rather than by eating semen with a bowl and spoon? (*A Desired Past* 8)

Indeed, how do we interpret such a "foreign" system of reference and set of norms? Traditionally, missionaries, for example, might automatically reference their own cultural values and condemn such behavior as lewd, disgusting, or unnatural. But Rupp's questions linger, challenging us to leave our responses more open-ended and unsure of themselves. Such skepticism about our own ability to pass judgment definitively does not make all critical reactions impossible or all investigations across cultures futile, but it does prod us to problematize our "gut-level" responses with reflection and to use those other systems of reference to question our own, rather than simply and always the reverse. As Carol Vance so aptly remarks regarding the Sambia ("Social Construction Theory"), we must remind ourselves continuously that "New Guinea is not Amsterdam or Greenwich Village" (22), and that there are no "natural" definitions and points of reference that pertain to all of those locales.

And if this leads to enormous semantic problems for individuals exploring diverse cultures vicariously or in written critiques, then for those Anglo-Americans actually working in Asian, African, and Central and South American countries, the challenges are truly extraordinary. Thus Jeremy Seabrook, a British HIV educator working in India, writes in *Love in a Different Climate* about his struggles to talk with men about their homosexual activities, when they do not see their practices as in any way "identity"-determining. Seabrook uses the term "men who have sex with men" or MSM to refer to such men, many of whom are happily married but who occasionally hire male prostitutes or have casual, anonymous sex with another man. Yet Seabrook also discovers that in urban areas where Western television and films are beginning to restructure people's perceptions, new cate-

gories such as "gay" and "bisexual" are quickly replacing more traditional patterns of behavior and systems of reference.

Thus Peter Drucker's collection of essays entitled *Different
Rainbows* charts the rise of specifically lesbian and gay rights movements in countries where the concepts "lesbian" and "gay" are relatively new imports. In his nuanced and intellectually provocative
introduction, Drucker teases out the many implications of what such
identity constructs newly allow and what they potentially destroy in
traditional cultures, while at the same time he recognizes the important work of new, self-aware queer groups in developing nations, who
are demanding civil rights and respect and whose struggles against
brutality and oppression deserve our attention. Among his contributors are individuals writing about the varied contexts of Latin
America, South Africa, Kenya, and China.

For students interested in the diversity of world sexualities and
sexual norms, the books above provide excellent starting-points.
Additionally, *Same-Sex Love in India*, edited by Ruth Vanita and
Saleem Kidwai, provides a dramatic array of historical and contemporary documents portraying erotic love between women and between
men on the Indian subcontinent. Stephen O. Murray and Will
Roscoe's *Boy-Wives and Female Husbands* also provides an eye-
opening collection of missionary and explorer accounts, primary
documents, and recent writings on African same-sex erotic activity.
Murray's *Homosexualities* similarly samples writings on same-sex
activity through time and from across the globe as he looks for
patterns of self-awareness and identification even when "gay" and
"lesbian" are wholly foreign concepts. Finally, John C. Hawley's
Postcolonial, Queer collects important writings exposing neocolonial-
ism in some manifestations of queer theory and advancing postcolonial perspectives concerning world sexualities and same-sex contact.
While such works are (unfortunately, but inevitably) peripheral to the
present study because of its focus on British and American literature
and applications of critical theory, they are provocative and
commendable. Read them when you have the time.

2   Who and What is "Queer"?

As I suggested at the beginning of my last chapter, the imposition of a neat "timeline" onto the complexity of lesbian- and gay-relevant "histories" through the millennia and across the globe would be reductive indeed. And as we turn now to the last two decades of the twentieth century, we see an unprecedented jumble of both oppressive and progressive activities across Anglo-American society, and a sometimes muted, sometimes deafening cacophony of voices within the community formed by gays, lesbians, and other sexual nonconformists. To a certain extent, the 1980s provide stunning evidence of the ability of an oppressed and internally divided group to come together to work on certain, discretely defined political agenda items, while the next decade (discussed here and in Chapter 3) shows just how difficult – really, impossible – it is to sustain political cohesion when a moment of piqued crisis settles into long-term worry and when short-term, clear-cut goals give way to far differing visions of a less oppressive future or alternative system of sociosexual valuation. In this chapter and the next, I will explore those sometimes smoothed-over fissures and enduring fractures, before moving on to our literary textual applications of "queer theories" in Chapters 4–6.

While internal divisiveness and diversity of outlook have always characterized lesbian and gay groups and movements, that heterogeneity was temporarily mitigated by the severity of the HIV/AIDS crisis. The summer of 1981 saw the first manifestation of unexplainable sickness and death among gay men in Los Angeles (and soon thereafter other major metropolitan areas of the United States). First termed GRID – Gay Related Immunodeficiency – the mysterious illness sent waves of fear through the urban gay community, as growing numbers of previously healthy men became ill and died gruesome deaths from strange, rarely seen forms of cancer and bacteriological infections. Re-termed AIDS – Acquired Immune Deficiency Syndrome – in 1982 and by mid-decade linked to a previously unknown retrovirus (HIV), the mounting crisis galvanized the gay and lesbian community and became a source of hysteria for much of the general population, yet it went wholly unmentioned by U.S. President Ronald Reagan and only cursorily addressed by other politicians and Reagan's political appointees.

Mounting death tolls and shocking political indifference was a combustible mixture. The simmering anger at laws continuing to criminalize homosexual activity, at media stereotyping, socially accepted slurs and scapegoating, at politicians – particularly Reagan – who seemed willing to turn a blind eye toward the impending death of an entire generation of gay men, sparked an intense reaction. Political organizing and action as usual seemed ineffective, if not wholly inappropriate, given the increasing number of deaths. Women and men of various races, sexualities, and belief systems put aside other agendas, identity allegiances, and disagreements to form coalitions to raise money and awareness, and secure greater public funding for and government action on AIDS research and prevention. The Gay Men's Health Crisis in New York, the many organizations around the U.S. sponsoring AIDS walks and AIDS rides, and the Names (AIDS Quilt) Project are striking examples. This is not to say that profound differences of opinion and priority did not continue to exist and manifest themselves (particularly on nonmonogamous and otherwise nonconformist sexual practices), but certainly the mid-1980s saw the establishment of linkages on discrete issues that often over-rode disagreements.

In particular, two organizations warrant attention here. While always involving small numbers of individuals, ACT UP (the AIDS Coalition to Unleash Power) and Queer Nation were formed to demand public recognition of the severity of the AIDS crisis and challenge directly homophobic governmental policies and social attitudes. In its highly theatrical public demonstrations and "in your face" direct-action events played to the cameras of the national media, ACT UP was literally an instance of an oppressed minority, sickened by prejudice, loudly and explicitly refusing "to take it anymore." And, in particular, the fact that the membership ranks of both ACT UP and Queer Nation were heavily weighted toward young, urban, college-age and college-going students is important to note, for this population provided a link between a radical activist consciousness and the radical theorizations that would come to be known as "queer theory." I speak from first-hand experience here. As Ph.D. students in an English department in the Washington, DC, area in the late 1980s, my friends and I marched with ACT UP, and some of my fellow, theory-savvy grad students were intimately involved in weekly strategy meetings of the organization and such well-orchestrated ACT UP events as the "takeover" of the FDA building in 1988. Lauren Berlant and Elizabeth Freeman offer the following recounting, drawn also from some of their own personal experiences, as well as those of friends:

> Founded at an ACT UP New York meeting in April of 1990, Queer Nation aimed to extend the kinds of democratic counterpolitics deployed on behalf of AIDS activism for the transformation of public sexual discourse in general. . . . Queer Nation [took] from ACT UP [a] complex understanding of political space as fundamental to its insistence on making all public spheres truly safe for all of the persons who occupy them, not just in psychic loyalty but in everyday and embodied experience. To be safe in the national sense means not just safe from bashing, not just safe from discrimination, but safe *for* demonstration, in the mode of patriotic ritual, which always involves a deployment of affect, knowledge, spectacle, and, crucially, a kind of banality, ordinariness, popularity.   ("Queer Nationality" 150–1)

Queer Nation's public demonstrations included kiss-ins, leaflet and manifesto distributions, and other "in your face" displays of same-sex affection (especially in such "ordinary" spaces as shopping malls, straight bars, etc.) to make their well-known overall point: "We're here, we're queer, get used to it!"

We can see in the examples of ACT UP and Queer Nation, as well as other 1980s and 1990s movements, how clear and vicious oppression breeds creative and energetic forms of resistance, as the undeniable homophobia of the American government in the face of the AIDS crisis led to a heightened political urgency and particular intensity of response. I would not want to argue for a simple formula or physics of political activity – there is no algorithm of give-and-take among oppressors and the oppressed – but clearly moments/periods of heightened group consciousness and cohesive reaction do occur when external forces help push communities together. "Queer," a term commonly used to deride and vilify same-sex desiring people, was reclaimed by Queer Nation and others as a umbrella term to celebrate, rather than castigate, difference from the "norm" at a time when the oppressiveness and implicit violence of that norm was clear and undeniable. Just as other oppressed groups and individuals have "turned the tables," so to speak, on oppressors by occupying and rewriting the meaning of slurs (such as "bitch" or "nigger" in music culture and certain intracommunal usages), political action groups responding angrily to governmentally sanctioned homophobia took back a term that drew immediate attention to itself as a (now positive) marker of difference, and that more broadly drew attention to the way language has long been used to categorize and devalue human lives and lifestyles.

And the brief chronology above – which will lead us in a moment to the "birth" of "queer theory" in the academy – reveals an important but oft-neglected point. "Theory" generally lags behind popular changes and trends. In other words, "queer theory" as it burst onto the scene of English and cultural studies departments in the 1990s was only describing, analyzing, and giving a certain intellectual nuance and depth to an already existing phenomenon. "Queer theory" as practiced in universities certainly did not reclaim the word "queer." It only continued a reclamation and usage that had already started in Queer Nation and other venues (and even those recent reclamations drew on a very long history of self-empowering usages of the term "queer," as George Chauncy has explored in *Gay New York*). Just as postmodern theorists and existential philosophers did not originate the social conditions that they analyze, so too have queer theoreticians worked only to make sense of an already deeply entrenched set of questionings and abrasions of normality. It is important always to remember such basic temporalities, since too often the academy becomes the scapegoat of finger-pointing politicians and social conservatives, and can also self-congratulate a little too broadly for innovations and experimentations for which it cannot claim creative ownership.

With that bit of historical context-setting behind us, what I will now do is give first a brief accounting of the core articulations of queer theory's academic manifestation from the early 1990s and then move backwards to trace some of the intellectual history behind its concepts and provocations, before returning to explore a variety of recent theorists and theories. Just as queer theories as they are multiply manifested today cannot be appreciated without the specifically gay- and lesbian-relevant history of the last chapter, so too is it necessary for us to trace the roots of queer theories to questions posed by several generations of philosophers and radical thinkers.

The first high-profile use of the term "queer theory" was in a special issue of the feminist journal *differences* from the summer of 1991 (one that collected essays drawn from an academic conference held in 1990). Edited by Teresa de Lauretis and entitled "Queer Theory: Lesbian and Gay Sexualities," the issue contained essays on a diverse array of cultural representations and manifestations of same-sex desire. Tellingly (for she later changed her mind about its value), de Lauretis in her introduction makes only a quick case for the umbrella term "queer theory." She writes, "The term 'queer,' juxtaposed to the 'lesbian and gay' of the subtitle, is intended to mark a certain critical distance from the latter, by now established and often convenient formula" (iv). As she traces some of the different usages of terms such as "homosexual," "gay," and "lesbian," de Lauretis returns briefly to the utility of the catch-all phrase: "the term 'Queer Theory' was arrived at in the effort to avoid all of these fine distinctions in our discursive protocols, not to adhere to any one of these terms, not to assume their ideological liabilities, but instead both to transgress and transcend them – or at the very least problematize them" (v). A more sustained case for the term "queer theory" is made in the first essay of the issue, written by performance theorist Sue-Ellen Case: "Queer theory, unlike lesbian theory or gay male theory, is not gender specific. In fact, like the term 'homosexual,' queer foregrounds same-sex desire without designating which sex is desiring" (2). Queer theory, she argues, "works not at the site of gender, but at the site of ontology, to shift the ground of being itself," and she suggests, "queer revels constitute a kind of activism that attacks the dominant notion of the natural. The queer is the taboo-breaker, the monstrous, the uncanny" (3).

Case's shift from a discussion of "gender" to a broader interest in "ontology" – the very question of "being" – is important to note. As I mentioned in my introduction, this marking out of a much larger terrain for "queer" investigations was given further support in Michael Warner's impressive 1993 collection *Fear of a Queer Planet: Queer Politics and Social Theory*. In his introduction, Warner writes,

> "queer" represents, among other things, an aggressive impulse of generalization; it rejects a minoritizing logic of toleration or simple political interest representation in favor of a more thorough resis-

tance to regimes of the normal. . . . For both academics and activists, "queer" gets a critical edge by defining itself against the normal rather than the heterosexual, and normal includes normal business in the academy.   (xxvi)

If we conjoin Case's and Warner's statements, we see how "normal being" (as well as possibilities for "abnormal being") becomes the common terrain of investigation in queer theorization and critique. But as abstruse as this may sound, there is from "queer theory's" outset a clear interest in the day-to-day, in the mundane activities that constitute "normal being": "Queers do a kind of practical social reflection just in finding ways of being queer. (Alternately many people invest the better part of their lives to avoid such self-understanding and the social reflection it would imply)" (*Fear of a Queer Planet* xiii). Indeed, the practicalities and performances of *everyday social being* provide a very different field of interest for "queer theories" than is suggested by the nonsynonymous umbrella term "lesbian and gay studies."

If we take Warner at his word and see "queer" as "pointing out a wide field of normalization," at the same time it "suggests the difficulty in defining the population whose interests are at stake in queer politics," then it is useful to indulge in his "aggressive impulse of generalization" (xxvi) and call some individuals and their theories queer-relevant or "proto-queer" even if their own personal sexualities may or may not have passed some (inevitably arbitrary and dubious) litmus test of "normality" or "abnormality." Indeed, by aggressively "queering" intellectual history in this way, we, in fact, continue the queer project of suggesting broad alliances, as we find telling traces of the "abnormal" even among "normal" (canonical, heterosexual) philosophers and theorists (of course, the credibility of the very concept "normality" is thereby rendered highly questionable). Warner, in effect, does precisely that in pointing to Hannah Arendt (1906–75) and her subtle investigations of how "conformism" operates as a key characteristic of modern society, before asking,

> Can we not hear in the resonances of queer protest an objection to the normalization of behavior in this broad sense, and thus to the cultural phenomenon of societalization. If queers, incessantly told to alter their "behavior," can be understood as protesting not just the normal behavior of the social but the *idea* of normal behavior, they

will bring skepticism to the methodologies founded on that idea.
(xxvii)

In this significantly broadened sense, even Hannah Arendt was hardly the first "queer" theorist. Queer-relevant philosophical questionings of normal behavior go back at least a century earlier (and even that imprecise dating ignores the less intellectualized but certainly "lived" investigations of normality conducted by the libertines and sexual nonconformists of earlier centuries that I mentioned in my last chapter).

So, then, would it be appropriate to call the nineteenth-century British philosopher John Stuart Mill a "queer theorist"? Not exactly, but certainly the vigorous intellectual investigations of how society defines the "natural" that are expressed memorably in Mill's essay "Nature" (written in the 1850s, published in 1874) certainly should be appreciated as queer-theory-relevant. When Mill writes that the arbitrary terms "nature" and "natural" are generally used simply to preempt and obscure objections to that which an individual "is already inclined to approve" (323) and that "[c]onformity to nature, has no connection whatever with right and wrong" (340), Mill is helping lay the intellectual groundwork for later investigations of the "normal," including those performed by queer theory. Similarly, in works such as "On Liberty" (1859), where he probes the tyranny of the majority and the necessity for safeguarding individualism and minority groups' objections to the social norm, Mill certainly speaks for appreciating a lived nonconformity and skepticism that is also queer-relevant. Indeed, the question for Mill, as for queer theorists today, is how presuppositions behind commonly used terms often remain wholly uninvestigated and, more specifically, how categories of language convey values while denying their socially constructed nature. And in Mill's case this thorough skepticism concerning social conventions was reflected in his perception of gender roles and even his own sexual life; not only was he a vocal feminist, but, as Phyllis Rose writes in *Parallel Lives: Five Victorian Marriages*, Mill and his (at first married lover and then) wife, Harriet Taylor, "were daring people. They endorsed Robert Owen's radical definition of chastity as sexual intercourse with affection, prostitution as sexual intercourse without it. They did not, in thinking about sexual conduct, 'consider the ordinances of society binding on a subject so entirely personal'" (111). Of course, that Mill never addressed in any way same-sex eroticism demonstrates some of the narrow boundaries even on relatively "radical" thought in the nineteenth century (and today), but while such limits among otherwise nonconformist thinkers are important to acknowledge (for they constitute some of the most difficult barriers to surmount), they should not hinder us from using Mill queerly, perhaps even against his own wishes, as a precursor to theorists who do attack directly the heterocentric parameters of notions of the sociosexual norm.

The same queer usage is possible with the philosopher who took up most intensely the late nineteenth-century challenge to received notions of normality, Friedrich Nietzsche. Of course, Nietzsche, like Mill, might even be broadly called "queer" since he lived at variance with some of the narrow sociosexual norms of his day – he visited prostitutes, he had an intense passionate devotion to another man (Richard Wagner), and he perhaps went mad and died from a venereal infection (syphilis) – though certainly he also explicitly condemned gender nonconformity among men and was no promoter of social and sexual rights for women. But beyond any realized or unrealized "lived" queerness, it is Nietzsche's skepticism toward – even hatred of – the notion of broad "norms" and other constraints on human thought and experimentation that make him important for us to consider here. As Robert Solomon and Kathleen Higgins have suggested in *What Nietzsche Really Said,* "One of Nietzsche's most prominent innovations, providing a bridge to the twentieth century, is his insistence that there is no absolute knowledge that transcends all possible perspectives: knowledge is always constrained by one's perspective . . . and that perspective depends on our physiological constitution, our skills of inquiring and interpreting, our culture, and our language" (35–6).

Indeed, Nietzsche's influence on twentieth-century philosophy in general was immense. From Nietzsche's *The Genealogy of Morals* (1887) and other works, Michel Foucault (whom I discuss below) borrowed the notion of "genealogy." Dave Robinson (in *Nietzsche and Postmodernism*) provides a succinct overview of this important concept:

> Nietzsche's "genealogical" histories are so called because they examine the historical *origins* of certain concepts that are thought to lack a history. His sociological and psychological investigations reveal that those concepts often thought to be universal, eternal or divinely

ordered are in fact contingent human constructs with specific histories, and so are in no way "natural" or "given." Genealogical history is descriptive and interpretative, but also evaluative. In Nietzsche's genealogy, for example, Christian moral beliefs in humility and obedience have a long track record, but they are still a social phenomenon with a specific and rather dubious history, and are now no longer valuable or worth preserving. Michel Foucault's subsequent genealogical investigations into madness, medicine, sexuality, punishment and the self are clearly influenced by those of Nietzsche. (69–70)

In *The Gay Science* (1882, with no sexual reference intended in the translation of the German "froehliche" as "gay"), Nietzsche famously proclaimed "God is dead" and then set out to explore exuberantly, gaily, the implications of this state of freedom:

> we philosophers and "free spirits" feel, when we hear the news that "the old god is dead," as if a new dawn shone on us; our heart overflows with gratitude, amazement, premonitions, expectation. At long last the horizon appears free to us again, even if it should not be bright; at long last our ships may venture out again, venture out to face any danger; all the daring of the lover of knowledge is permitted again; the sea, *our* sea, lies open again; perhaps there has never yet been such an "open sea." (280)

In his calls there and elsewhere to live bravely, creatively, and intensely, Nietzsche prefigures the iconoclasm and attempts to put abstract theory into lived practices that are central to late-twentieth-century queer (and many other identity-political) theories. That Nietzsche seems to swerve at times into solipsism and arrogant dismissal of the pain and difficulties of the lowly "herd" (as he termed social conformists) serves to remind queer theorists even today of the need to preserve an appreciation of the powerful limitations socialized within individuals who may not be able to break easily from "herd" behaviors, ones that might be seen more generously as mundane manifestations of deep-seated, desperate, and understandable (if not at all laudable) desires for general social approval and sanctioned, relatively secure meaning.

Of course Nietzsche is often classified with the group of twentieth-century philosophers called "existentialists," whose work further explored that "amazing" state of freedom accorded by the "death" of faith in transcendental, divine meaning. Indeed, while philosophers such as Jean-Paul Sartre and Albert Camus are, again, not exactly "queer" in their investigations of specifically sociosexual normality, their intellectual probings of the "existential" condition, wherein human existence predates any human "essence" (with the latter – often imagined as a "soul" beholden to divine law – therefore necessarily a human invention), certainly bears on later investigations of constructions of natural or normal sexual conduct. In works such as "Existentialism is a Humanism" and elsewhere, Sartre adds his voice to Nietzsche's in calling for a creative and exuberant embracing of the state of freedom accorded humans by way of their full recognition and honest acceptance of the lack of sacred mandates or other transcendental sources of meaning or value. This is why Sartre finds much to praise in his friend Jean Genet's transgressive explorations of homosexual passion (in works such as *Our Lady of the Flowers* and *Querelle*, as well as his daily life), even though Sartre's groundbreaking study *Saint Genet: Actor and Martyr* is often (in Guy Hocquenghem's words) a "faithful reflection of [the dominant sexual] discourse" (*Homosexual Desire*   124). Thus Sartre's own perspectives and limits become startlingly clear when he writes that the forces/choices accounting for Genet's homosexuality have "made him a woman" (79) and that "amorous passivity . . . inclines him to homosexuality" (81). Certainly Sartre and the existentialists were social constructionists in that they argued for human agency in all designations of right and wrong, higher and lower, and proper and improper. That Sartre's own less than radical gender politics may have failed to reflect fully the iconoclasm of his philosophical assertions serves as an important reminder to us about how rigorous *we* must be in allowing theory to disturb even our most cherished preconceptions.

André Gide, an existentialist who was certainly "queer" in sexuality as well as philosophical bent, deserves mention here too. In books such as *The Immoralist* (1902) and *Corydon* (1924), Gide explores a specifically sexual state of "freedom," even if, at times, his preconceptions about acceptable "homosexual" acts seem rather limited. As Leo Bersani notes, "Gide thought of 'inverts' – grown men who like to be anally penetrated – as morally or intellectually deformed, and it is one of the least attractive aspects of Gide's presumed defense of homosexuality in *Corydon* that the argument excludes what most of us would identify as homosexual desire" (*Homos* 121). But certainly Gide pushed existential iconoclasm into the terrain of the sexual in ways that Sartre and Camus never did. He queerly de-links sexuality from a necessary basis in domestic or even affectional relationships. Bersani argues that Gide, in *The Immoralist,* constructs

> a model for intimacies devoid of intimacy. [He] proposes that we move irresponsibly among other bodies, somewhat indifferent to them, demanding nothing more than that they be as available to contact as we are, and that, no longer owned by others, they also renounce self-ownership and agree to that loss of boundaries which will allow them to be, with use, shifting points of rest in a universal and mobile communication of being. If homosexuality in this form is difficult to know, this is because it no longer defines a self.   (128)

While Bersani criticizes Gide and *The Immoralist* for the timidity with which, finally, both treat sexuality in all of its possible manifestations among adult men, it is certainly important for us to see that Gide disrupted notions of selfhood in such a way that philosophical challenges to notions of "normal" sexual behavior and identity – of "normal" sexual selfhood – are given legitimacy and are seen as well within the boundaries of what existential philosophers theorize *about.* Gide insists that sexuality has no special, separate legitimacy or protected state that renders it off-limits for iconoclastic investigation.

To cover all of the many theorists and philosophers of the twentieth century whose work is related to, and (arguably) partially responsible for, the queer investigations of sexuality of the last decade of the century is impossible here. But certainly those individuals broadly termed "post-structuralists" were especially influential. If "structuralism" can be understood as the search for clear and certain relationships between the structure of language and our perception of reality – a scientific pursuit really – then post-structuralism is skeptical of any possible delineation of cause and effect or discovery of stable, knowable structures underlying perception. Both trace their insights back to the field of linguistics, the study of language. And for this and other reasons, it is important to mention the psychoanalytic work of Jacques Lacan, for he too argued for the central role of language in the creation of human relationships and senses of selfhood. Revising significantly the work of Freud, Lacan argued that an individual's "self" is formed through the internalization of larger social constructs and hierarchies of value in the process of acquiring language. The child thus becomes acculturated through her or his encounter with the "Symbolic" – which comprises language, images, and other means by which society communicates and replicates. That social values are decidedly phallocentric (male power centered) and heterocentric is clearly revealed through Lacan's theories, though at the same time, such entrenched values are potentially challengeable given their socially constructed status. While this is only a cursory reference to Lacan's complex theories, Joseph Bristow in *Sexuality* gives a lengthier explanation of Lacan's perspectives on desire and identity formation for those students interested in the work of this challenging but rewarding psychoanalytic theorist.

Another important contributor to the body of post-structuralist thought that helped spur the generation of "queer" forms of theory was Jacques Derrida. As Julian Wolfreys has explored in *Deconstruction•Derrida*, Derrida revised structuralist insights into the binary construction of meaning – male/female, light/dark, proper/improper – to reveal how those binaries are always weighted toward the first term, which is held at greater social value, but which also always needs the second term to substantiate that value. The binary heterosexual/homosexual, while structuring our conceptions of human identity, obviously does not accord equal value to both identities. But as degraded or debased as that second term in the binary may be, it marks the always fragile boundaries of the first term. How can anyone think of him or herself as "heterosexual" without the clear contrast provided by the images, traits, and markers provided by social conceptions of the "homosexual"? What we might broadly term the "deconstruction" of this binary would therefore hinge on the investigation not only of their socially constructed nature, but also of the tenuousness of the means by which the supposedly secure and sanctified first term maintains its privilege. Derrida thus provided to queer theorists the singularly important recognition of sexual systems as anxious, confused, and self-inflated in a way that masks a thorough instability, even though this recognition does not deny that such systems are highly entrenched and difficult to overcome or even simply to revise.

And this mind-set and milieu of interrogation, skepticism, and deconstructive passion was both evidenced in and stoked by the theorizations during the 1970s and 1980s of the "French feminists": Julia Kristeva, Luce Irigaray, and Hélène Cixous. As I mentioned in my first chapter, Ruth Robbins does a superb job at exploring the theories of these central twentieth-century thinkers in her *Literary Feminisms.* In particular, Irigaray and Cixous are important to mention here. Irigaray challenges in both theory and in print presentation the "normal" practices of phallocentric culture. In *Speculum of the Other Woman, This Sex Which is Not One,* and other works she strives to reimagine "desire" in ways that operate outside of heterosexual/heterocentric norms, though at times she seems to imagine women's desires as coming from their unique genital/sexual configuration in ways that have been heavily criticized for essentialist implications. Much more interested in undercutting any such biological foundationalism was (and is) Hélène Cixous, who in "Sorties" challenges the stability of social meanings privileging maleness and masculine authority, asking "What would happen to logocentrism, to the great philosophical systems, to the order of the world in general if the rock upon which they founded this church should crumble?" (65). And part of what she works to confront is the homophobia of both philosophy and broader society, saying:

> There have always been those uncertain, poetic persons who have not let themselves be reduced to dummies programmed by pitiless repression of the homosexual element. Men or women: beings who are complex, mobile, open. Accepting the other sex as a component makes them much richer, more various, stronger, and – to the extent that they are mobile – very fragile. It is only in this condition that we invent. Thinkers, artists, those who create new values, "philosophers" in the mad Nietzschean manner, inventors and wreckers of concepts and forms, those who change life cannot help but be stirred by anomalies – complementary or contradictory. That doesn't mean that you have to be homosexual to create. But it does mean that there is no *invention* possible, whether it be philosophical or poetic, without there being in the inventing subject an abundance of the other, of variety. . . .   (83–4)

Cixous's most intriguing challenge is a call for a "reconsideration of *bisexuality*," by which she means "the location within oneself of the presence of both sexes, evident and insistent in different ways according to the individual, the nonexclusion of difference or of a sex, and starting with this 'permission' one gives oneself, the multiplication of the effects of desire's inscription on every part of the body and the other body" (84–5). While I will return to this challenge in my next chapter, it is important to note here that Cixous evokes the possibility of mutable sexual relationships and selfhood without prescribing what form desire might take from a deconstruction of the hetero/homosexual binary.

To see queer theory as thus wholly enmeshed in discussions of identity, multiple identities, and the possibilities of *changing* identity is vital. As I mentioned in my previous chapter, Linda Garber has pointed out the indispensable work of lesbian feminist theorists such as Judy Grahn, Adrienne Rich, and Audre Lorde, who understood identity always as plural and contingent, as they "questioned the institution of heterosexuality and self-consciously worked to create lesbian identity and community" (*Identity Poetics* 11). In particular, Garber notes Lorde's "perpetually shifting location, simultaneously occupying seemingly contradictory spaces" as exemplified in the poem "School Note": "for the embattled / there is no place / that cannot be / home / nor is" (quoted by Garber 98). Dennis Altman, in 1971, also offered some sophisticated analysis of identity issues in *Homosexual: Oppression and Liberation*. While he works from a "liberation" model that posits a form of freedom from social constraints and sexual "repression" that some later theorists dismiss as too rudimentary, his is an explicitly constructionist argument in which he suggests importantly that "the very concept of homosexuality is a social one, and one cannot understand the homosexual experience without recognizing the extent to which we have developed a certain identity and behavior derived from social norms" (2). At about the same time in France, Hocquenghem was proclaiming that "[c]apitalist society manufactures homosexuals just as it produces proletarians, constantly defining its own limits: homosexuality is a manufactured product of the normal world" (*Homosexual Desire* 50). François Lyotard's declaration in *The Postmodern Condition* (1984) of the end of "master narratives" of truth and identity during the latter half of the twentieth century is also relevant to the genesis of "queer theory," as is Michel de Certeau's investigations in *The Practice of Everyday Life* (1984) of the numerous ways that individuals deploy power in their day-to-day activities and the choices that they make as they tactically engage larger social structures and impositions of value and meaning. Lyotard and de Certeau provide evidence of a burgeoning interest in the last quarter of the twentieth century in what one might call the micro-physics of power and the ways in which individuals can negotiate their own forms of self-expression that may abrade larger designations of normality and propriety.

But certainly no theorist of identity has been more central to "queer" theorizations than Michel Foucault, whose insights and investigations changed the way that academics and activists both thought about and responded to the power of sociosexual norms. When Altman in 1971 states, "What is needed in fact is a theory of sexuality and of the place sexuality occupies within human life" (58), he was answered, we might say, by the French publication in 1976 (and English translation in 1978) of the first volume of Foucault's *History of Sexuality*. And while I will examine here in necessarily brief fashion a few basic concepts underlying Foucauldian analysis, I will return often to Foucault in later chapters as I continue to explore the many possible varieties and utilities of queer analysis.

The first Foucauldian concept that is central to queer theorization is that linking "discourse" and "identity." In various early works, Foucault foregrounds a constructionist notion of identity that explores how mental illness (in *Madness and Civilization*) and criminality (in *Discipline and Punish*) are historically contingent and changing concepts, used to cordon off groups of people in such a way that evolving economic and political interests are protected and advanced. "Discourse" is Foucault's base matter for critical investigation. Discourse comprises language, images, unspoken beliefs and prejudices, laws and scientific concepts, and all other means by which human values are communicated, "naturalized," and reproduced. In ways that broadly correspond to Lacan's notion of the "Symbolic," Foucault suggests that individual personhood (subjectivity) is created through an internalization of discursive categories and the interests and biases that they reflect. This is not to suggest that oppression, for example, is a simple unilateral or unilinear action, for one of Foucault's most important insights (in *Discipline and Punish*) is that our internalization of social categories and expectations of "proper" behavior make the intervention of authorities or repressive agencies (such as the police) relatively rare. We operate as disciplining agents on each other and ourselves through our expectations of "normal" behavior and our sometimes subtle, sometimes overt, communications of disapproval. A broad mechanism of social discipline is achieved in the modern era through the conformist impulses and self-conceptions of well-socialized individuals. Although Foucault does not reference Nietzsche specifically in this instance, it is not difficult to see traces of the earlier philosopher's categorization of the passive "herd" in some of Foucault's theories. But unlike

Nietzsche, Foucault is not interested in broadly disparaging conformists as much as he is in understanding the mechanisms by which conformity – even among philosophers and other intellectuals – is maintained.

Foucault's insights into the means by which new types of sexual "normality" became socially entrenched during the nineteenth century are particularly relevant to our discussion here. In his groundbreaking study, *The History of Sexuality: An Introduction*, Foucault examined the rise of "sexual science" during the Victorian era and its seemingly powerful prescriptions of normal and abnormal behavior. But Foucault significantly revises earlier overviews of the era in several ways. First, he demonstrates just how vocal the supposedly "prudish" Victorians were about sexuality. Rather than nervously avoiding the subject, nineteenth-century researchers, scientists, politicians, writers, etc. spoke about sexuality at historically unprecedented lengths and volume. The "discourse" on and involving sexuality – from child-rearing manuals to psychological theories of deviance – was incessant. Thus a model of "repression" (such as Altman uses to imagine and idealize a state of "liberation") is wholly inadequate to describe a situation of insistent discussion of and new modes of identification through "sexuality" in the past 100–150 years. Indeed, Foucault explores at length how certain sexual categories, especially "homosexual" and "heterosexual," were ones that not only were oppressive towards nonconformists but also became new and *empowering* ways by which individuals identified themselves.

This is why Foucault became a central figure not only for queer academics but also queer activists in the late twentieth century. In his notion of the "tactical polyvalence of discourse" Foucault opened up the conceptualization of power from a simple model of oppressor and oppressed to a multidimensional investigation of oppression, reaction, metamorphosis, and group empowerment over time that has complicated and enriched our understanding. Thus however useful it might be to point out the homophobia of the turn-of-the-century psychoanalytic community, let us say, it is also important to acknowledge how such vectors of oppression became a rallying point for groups of individuals, who became self-aware and politicized through and in response to oppression. This is not to make an excuse for or otherwise dismiss discrimination or brutality, but it is to open up for philosophical and historical consideration the ways notions of "normality" and "abnormality" create identity groups that find political voices and tactics through, and over and above, the characteristics that are ascribed to them.

Foucault's theories are much more complex and multifaceted than is indicated in the few strands that I isolate above, but certainly in his reconceptualizations of discourse, sexuality, and power, we find the core of most queer theories of the 1990s and today. Whether they reference most explicitly theories of psychology, performance, class, or genre, queer theorists generally work from a constructionist model that is highly indebted to Foucault. Only those commentators who wholly reject the possibility for political agency in the deployment of post-structuralist theory (which includes Foucault's work) regularly dismiss or deride his work. I will query one such objection in the interval following this chapter. But David Halperin makes an important point in his 1995 study *Saint Foucault: Towards a Gay Hagiography*, when he locates in Foucault the intellectual impulse behind the assumption of "queer" as a theoretical, activist, and identificatory position, for following Foucault,

> (Homo)sexual identity can now be constituted not substantively but oppositionally, not by *what* it is but by *where* it is and *how* it operates. Those who knowingly occupy such a marginal location, who assume a de-essentialized identity that is purely positional in character, are properly speaking not gay but *queer*.
>
> Unlike gay identity, which, though deliberately proclaimed in an act of affirmation, is nonetheless rooted in the positive fact of homosexual object-choice, queer identity need not be grounded in any positive truth or in any stable reality. As the very word implies, "queer" does not name some natural kind or refer to some determinate object; it acquires its meaning from its oppositional relation to the norm. Queer is by definition *whatever* is at odds with the normal, the legitimate, the dominant. *There is nothing in particular to which it necessarily refers*. It is an identity without an essence. (61–2)

While I take slight issue with Halperin's assertion that queerness is necessarily determined by an "oppositional" positioning, rather than, in my opinion, an "abrasive" one ("opposition" to me is limited in its binary construction and configuration of resistance), I do agree that Foucault's insights have generated "the possibility of a *queer politics* defined not by the struggle to liberate a common, repressed preexisting nature but by an ongoing process of self-constitution and self-transformation – a queer politics anchored in the perilous and shifting sands of non-identity, positionality, discursive reversibility, and collective self-invention" (*Saint Foucault* 122). It is not at all an exaggeration to say that without Nietzsche there would have been no Foucault as we knew him, and also without Foucault there would be no Donald E. Hall as I am constituted today. To Foucault I am indebted partially but importantly for my own queer "self."

And certainly I am not the only one. Queer theories and theoreticians today abound and most are explicitly indebted to Foucault. Indeed, the first whom I wish to mention here was also one of the first to reference Foucault's *History of Sexuality: An Introduction* in overt and intellectually invigorating ways. Gayle Rubin, in "Thinking Sex: Notes for a Radical Theory of the Politics of Sexuality," memorably differentiates radical sex studies from feminism (however deeply indebted the former is to the latter), arguing that

> it is essential to separate gender and sexuality analytically to reflect more accurately their separate social existences. This goes against the grain of much contemporary feminist thought, which treats sexuality as a derivation of gender. For instance, lesbian feminist ideology has mostly analyzed the oppression of lesbians in terms of the oppression of women. However, lesbians are also oppressed as queers and perverts, by the operation of sexual, not gender, stratification. Although it pains many lesbians to think about it, the fact is that lesbians have shared many of the sociological features and suffered from many of the same social penalties as have gay men, sado-masochists, transvestites, and prostitutes. (33)

Taking a strict constructionist approach, Rubin reminds us: "The realm of sexuality also has its own internal politics, inequities, and modes of oppression. As with other aspects of human behavior, the concrete institutional forms of sexuality at any given time and place are products of human activity" (4). And Rubin here usefully, if implicitly, broadens the discussion of modes of oppression to the *internal* politics of queer communities as well as their external relationships to more obvious oppressors and institutions.

Indeed, that drive to investigate the "internal" as well as "external" aspects of sexual life and identification is central to the work of Eve Sedgwick, one of the most important figures in queer studies of the 1990s. Her profound influence on the field actually dates from the mid-1980s, with the publication of her groundbreaking book *Between*

Men: English Literature and Male Homosocial Desire. In it, Sedgwick explores how male psychosocial relations have through the centuries worked not only to control women but also increasingly to excise unacceptable manifestations of specifically "homosexual" desire from "homosocial" male bondings and other relationships. In doing so, Sedgwick offers still important, historically nuanced readings of erotic triangles and shifting forms of anxiety in works by Shakespeare, Tennyson, and Dickens, among others.

But Sedgwick's most important contribution to the burgeoning field of queer studies was her 1990 book *Epistemology of the Closet.* To frame theoretically her close readings of Melville, Wilde, James, and Proust, Sedgwick offers first an "Axiomatic" introduction that makes a compelling case for the study of sexuality, specifically, in literature and culture. In her first chapter, she then explores the shifting and uncertain grounds of our "knowledge" of homosexuality. In distinguishing between "minoritizing" and "universalizing" paradigms in the discussion of same-sex desire, she reveals the thoroughly confused nature of debates over whether "homosexuality" is distinct to a small group of individuals or a characteristic fundamental to everyone's sexuality or sexual development. Rather than arguing one side or the other, she sets out as her particular interest an exploration of how

> the persistence of the deadlock itself has been the single most power-ful feature of the important twentieth-century understandings of sexuality whether hetero or homo, and a determining feature too of all the social relations routed, in this sexualized century, through understandings of sexuality. This deadlock has by now been too deeply constitutive of our very resources for asking questions about sexuality for us to have any realistic hope of adjudicating it in the future. What we can do is to understand better the structuring, the mechanisms, and the immense consequences of the incoherent dispensation under which we now live. (*Epistemology* 91)

While her (one might say) pessimism in this passage over "adjudicating" differing understandings of sexuality may be seen as somewhat energy-deflating for some theorists, certainly the intellectual excitement of her close readings and provocative "axioms" helped energize queer studies for a decade and more. She also helped thereby to solidify the new field's specific interest in thinking *about* categories rather than arguing for the singular legitimacy of one particular mode of categorization.

Given that "queer" was not a term available to her as a literary and cultural critic in 1990, her articulations on the word and its implications were much anticipated and certainly important and provocative when delivered in *Tendencies* in 1993. In her preface and first chapter, "Queer and Now," Sedgwick traces changing meanings of the word "queer" (as I quote in my own introduction) and then offers an inclusive, widely embracing understanding of its contemporary possibilities that I find very useful (and will therefore cite at length):

> one of the things "queer" can refer to: the open mesh of possibilities, gaps, overlaps, dissonances and resonances, lapses and excesses of meaning when the constituent elements of anyone's gender, of anyone's sexuality are made (or *can't be* made) to signify monolithically. The experimental linguistic, epistemological, representational, political adventures attaching to the very many of us who may at times be moved to describe ourselves as (among many other possibilities) pushy femmes, radical faeries, fantasists, drags, clones, leatherfolk, ladies in tuxedoes, feminist women or feminist men, masturbators, bulldaggers, divas, Snap! queens, butch bottoms, storytellers, transsexuals, aunties, wannabes, lesbian-identified men or lesbians who sleep with men, or . . . people able to relish, learn from, or identify with such. . . .
>
> . . . "[G]ay" and "lesbian" still present themselves (however delusively) as objective, empirical categories governed by empirical rules of evidence (however contested). "Queer" seems to hinge much more radically and explicitly on a person's undertaking particular, performative acts of experimental self-perception and filiation. A hypothesis worth making explicit: that there are important senses in which "queer" can signify only *when attached to the first person*. One possible corollary: that what it takes – all it takes – to make the description "queer" a true one is the impulse *to* use it in the first person.   (8–9)

This expansive definition of "queer" and broad, if implicit, invitation to "join" the queer movement (so to speak) underlies also the present book. Sedgwick's teasing out of the possibilities for "experimental" identificatory moves and changes in "self-perception" make *Tendencies* perhaps her most activist/activating work. In it Sedgwick at once "reads" and participates in the intellectual excitement of the birth of "queer" theory and "queer" as an abrasive, alternative, self-chosen identity category. Her specific reference to the "performative" above and throughout *Tendencies* makes explicit her intellectual debt to the work of Judith Butler, whom I discuss below. In all three of the books just mentioned, Sedgwick as no other theorist of her day both captures and interprets a moment in time.

But as much as Sedgwick provides us with a definitional touchstone of an expansive notion of "queerness," she certainly was not the only important theorist working at the time of "queer theory's" explosion onto the academic scene. In *Essentially Speaking* from 1989, and as discussed earlier, Diana Fuss rejects a simple binary of construction-ism/essentialism, arguing instead for a continuing critical conscious-ness vis-à-vis the necessary, strategic deployment of identity categories. She addresses forthrightly the fear, still widely circulating today, that "once we have deconstructed identity, we will have nothing (nothing, that is, which is stable and secure) upon which to base a politics" (104). Fuss quotes theorist Elaine Marks in retorting "'there must be a sense of identity, even though it would be fictitious'. . . . Fictions of identity, importantly, are no less powerful for being fictions" (104). Fuss builds on this recognition of multiple identity needs and contingent groundings in her introduction to *Inside/Out: Lesbian Theories, Gay Theories* in 1991. She rejects the idea of simple "epistemological breaks" with the past, calling instead for a project of creative abrasion:

> Perhaps what we, as gay and lesbian readers of culture, cannot escape at *this* moment in our histories is an "analysis interminable," a responsibility to exert sustained pressure from/on the margins to reshape and to reorient the field of sexual difference to include sexual differences. . . . Sexual identity may be less a function of knowledge than performance, or, in Foucauldian terms, less a matter of final discovery than perpetual reinvention. (6–7)

The impulse of her work and that of the contributors to *Inside/Out* is thus to "shift away from the interrogative mode and toward the perfor-mative mode – toward the imaginative enactment of sexual redefini-tions, reborderizations, and rearticulations" (7). This disruptive potential – of never fully leaving behind the past, its categories and vocabularies, but still working toward a *differing* (not wholly different) future – is what first drove and still sustains queer theorizations and activisms. And perhaps the most important point that can be gleaned from the above is that it is *not* necessary to imagine a utopia or prescribed (and therefore necessarily *proscribing*) configuration of "liberation" or sexual freeplay/freedom in order to retain an energetic involvement with identity political work, critique, and change.

How to disrupt it, *how* to change it (with "it" being identity – sexual, gender, or . . . fill in the blank for oneself) are among the questions asked by Judith Butler, whose investigations of the "performance" of identity have been widely referenced in queer theorizations of the past decade and more. "Drag" and other disruptive performances of gender and sexual identity are important exempla for Butler. In a key essay from 1991, entitled "Imitation and Gender Insubordination," she argues that

> Drag constitutes the mundane way in which genders are appropriated, theatricalized, worn, and done; it implies that all gendering is a kind of impersonation and approximation. If this is true, it seems, there is no original or primary gender that drag imitates, but *gender is a kind of imitation for which there is no original*; in fact, it is a kind of imitation that produces the very notion of the original as an *effect* and consequence of the imitation itself. In other words, the naturalistic effects of heterosexualized genders are produced through imitative strategies; what they imitate is a phantasmatic ideal of heterosexual identity, one that is produced by the imitation of its effect. In this sense, the "reality" of heterosexual identities is performatively constituted through an imitation that sets itself up as the origin and the ground of all imitations. In other words, heterosexuality is always in the process of imitating and approximating its own phantasmatic idealization of itself – *and failing*. Precisely because it is bound to fail, and yet endeavors to succeed, the project of heterosexual identity is propelled into an endless repetition of itself. Indeed, in its efforts to naturalize itself as the original, heterosexuality must be understood as a compulsive and compulsory repetition that can only produce the *effect* of its own originality; in other words, compulsory heterosexual identities, those ontologically consolidated phantasms of "man" and "woman," are theatrically produced effects that posture as grounds, origins, the normative measure of the real.   (21)

Butler uses this assertion of the thoroughly artificial, performative, necessarily repetitive nature of heterosexualized genders, indeed heterosexual identity itself, as the basis for locating a noteworthy frailty:

if heterosexuality is compelled to *repeat itself* in order to establish the
illusion of its own uniformity and identity, then this is an identity
permanently at risk, for what if it fails to repeat, or if the very exercise
of repetition is redeployed for a very different performative purpose?
If there is, as it were, always a compulsion to repeat, repetition never
fully accomplishes identity. That there is a need for a repetition at all
is a sign that identity is not self-identical. It requires to be instituted
again and again, which is to say that it runs the risk of becoming *de-*
instituted at every interval.   (24)

Elsewhere in the same essay, she writes that the "parodic replication
and resignification of heterosexual constructs within non-heterosex-
ual frames bring into relief the utterly constructed status of the so-
called original" (23), and that if "every performance repeats itself to
institute the effect of identity, then every repetition requires an interval between the acts, as it were, in which risk and excess threaten to
disrupt the identity being constituted" (28). This, at the very least,
seems to imply that the structure of heterosexual genders and even
heterosexuality itself is quite fragile. Thus in the last section of her
enormously influential book *Gender Trouble* (1990), tellingly entitled
"From Parody to Politics," Butler issues a call to action: "The critical
task is . . . to locate strategies of subversive repetition enabled by
those constructions, to affirm the local possibilities of intervention
through participating in precisely those practices of repetition that
constitute identity and, therefore, present the immanent possibility of
contesting them" (188).

Before summarizing some of her later qualifications and refine-
ments, it is important here to take a moment and reflect on why
Butler's reflections and injunctions from 1990–1 were so energizing
for queer theorists and activists alike (though certainly presented here
in very abbreviated fashion). While social constructionist theory
always implied a diachronic mutability to definitions and social roles,
few social constructionist theoreticians offered any precise avenue for
effecting change; especially lacking was a tactic specific to the field of
sexual nonconformity. Class critics had Marx and his many interlocu-
tors; feminists had diverse theoreticians and a long history of political
response. But Butler came along at a time when intellectuals and
theory-hungry activists, feeling oppressed by narrow and anachronistic notions of sexual identity, needed a sophisticated rallying call and
action plan. While Butler soon became very uncomfortable with the

amount of adulation she received (with academic fans – and a fanzine – focusing on her private life rather than her ideas), she certainly deserved (and still deserves) praise for offering a useful, if often over-simplified, strategy: parody the "norm" and work to change thereby a structure of normal roles and relations. This proactive stance came at the same time that "Queer Nation" was staging its own theatrical assaults on shopping malls and straight bars and as ACT UP continued its angry demonstrations against the continuing homophobia of the first Bush regime. Butler at least implied that by continuing and deepening such highly visible (and even highly enjoyable) differing "performances," the power of middle-class, neo-Puritanical notions of normality might begin to weaken and their structures/institutions become far less stable and secure.

And even though Butler's statements in 1990–1 might ascribe too much disruptive power to the "queer" performer and underemphasize the enduring power of the "norm," there is certainly much to be said for the energy of her work, energy that comes from a sense that things *can* change and that an individual or group *can* have an effect through concrete interventions and disruptive actions. Butler later cautioned against jumping too quickly to assume that we might, let us say, change our "genders" as quickly and effortlessly as theatrical roles, and she certainly offered some important qualifications concerning the thoroughly entrenched nature of "normal" and normalized gender and sexual roles and relations. She explained the possibility of misunderstanding her point in *Gender Trouble* to an interviewer in 1992:

> The bad reading goes something like this: I can get up in the morning, look in my closet, and decide which gender I want to be today. I can take out a piece of clothing and change my gender, stylize it, and then that evening I can change it again and be something radically other, so that what you get is something like the commodification of gender, and the understanding of taking on a gender as a kind of consumerism.   (Quoted in Glover and Kaplan xxvii)

In David Glover and Cora Kaplan's commentary on the above quotation, they point out that the "flaw in this picture"

> lies in its failure to take into account the contradictory mode in which we inhabit our sense of gender, not as an identity that we freely embrace, but one that we also struggle against, that sustains us at the

same time it constrains us. Like the everyday use of language from which it partly derives, gender underpins our capacity to make decisions and act upon them, while constantly slipping out of our control and ensnaring us in complex webs of meaning that no single individual can ever hope to master.　(xxvii)

And certainly Butler never actually implied that such a degree of agency or "mastery" was ever possible in the parodic intervention into normal notions of gender and sexuality. In her 1999 preface to the tenth-anniversary edition of *Gender Trouble*, she warns, for instance, against taking her "example" of drag as "*the* paradigm of subversive action or, indeed, as a model for political agency" (xxii, my emphasis). She makes an important point that I will return to in a moment, that "subversive performances always run the risk of becoming deadening clichés through their repetition and, most importantly, through their repetition within commodity culture where 'subversion' carries market value" (xxi). "Rather," she writes, "the aim of the text was to open up the field of possibility without dictating which kinds of possibilities ought to be realized. One might wonder what use 'opening up possibilities' finally is, but no one who has understood what it is to live in the social world as what is 'impossible,' illegible, unrealizable, unreal, and illegitimate is likely to pose that question" (viii). In those instances wherein

> the *reality* of gender is . . . put into crisis: it becomes unclear how to distinguish the real from the unreal. And this is the occasion in which we come to understand that what we take to be "real," what we invoke as the naturalized knowledge of gender is, in fact, a changeable and revisable reality. Call it subversive or call it something else. Although this insight does not in itself constitute a political revolution, no political revolution is possible without a radical shift in one's notion of the possible and the real.　(xxiii)

Thus while it would be a mistake to overestimate the political importance of such disruptions and "shifts," so too would it be foolish to underestimate their necessity. In *Fixing Patriarchy* (1996) I take issue with Butler's rather astonishing optimism in her concluding words to *Gender Trouble*, when she writes,

> If identities were no longer fixed . . . a new configuration of politics would surely emerge from the ruins of the old. Cultural configura-

tions of sex and gender might then proliferate or, rather, their present proliferation might then become articulatable within the discourses that establish intelligible cultural life, confounding the very binarism of sex, and exposing its fundamental unnaturalness.   (189–90)

As I said then and still believe now: don't hold your breath, for there is nothing "sure" about the matter. But certainly I cannot deny that the abrasion, troubling, unfixing, or disruption of gender and sexual identity is necessary, if never sufficient, for a "new configuration of politics" of a queer sort. And though Butler obviously did not know when she wrote *Gender Trouble* that it would become widely "cited as one of the founding texts of queer theory" (vii), it is clear why "the book was taken up by Queer Nation, [even as] some of its reflections on the theatricality of queer self-presentation resonated with the tactics of Act Up" (xvii), for Butler's theorization of performativity does *motivate* by implying an undetermined, undeterminable, but still *better* future that does not depend upon the essentialism that underpins and necessarily limits most gay/lesbian political activism and intra-communal activation, as traced in my last chapter.

And this indeterminacy but sense still of indeterminate optimism was what characterized and characterizes still queer theorizations at their most engaging. In an important 1995 column entitled "What Does Queer Theory Teach Us about *X*?" Lauren Berlant and Michael Warner signal and in some ways celebrate this indeterminacy:

> We have been invited to pin the queer theory tail on the donkey. But here we cannot but stay and make a pause, and stand half amazed at this poor donkey's present condition. Queer theory has already incited a vast labor of metacommentary, a virtual industry: special issues, sections of journals, omnibus reviews, anthologies, and dictionary entries. Yet the term itself is less than five years old. Why do people feel the need to introduce, anatomize, and theorize something that can barely be said yet to exist?   (343)

As they go on to suggest, "Queer is hot" yet any reduction of the many varieties of "queer commentary" "to a single discourse, let alone a propositional program" is premature, if not impossible (343). They write,

> Queer commentary has involved a certain amount of experimenting, of prancing and squatting on the academic stage. This is partly to

remind people that there *is* an academic stage and that its protocols and proprieties have maintained an invisible heteronormativity, one that infiltrates our profession, our knowledge, and this editorial. This does not mean we embrace, or disavow, the indecorous per se. Indecorum can be a way of bringing some dignity to the abject. But it is also a way of changing the public for academic work, of keeping the door ajar. (348)

By the time they wrote their column, "queer" as a term of political consciousness and agency had certainly moved beyond the narrow realm of the academy and even the slightly larger realm of political activism. It was circulating widely in television, popular reportage, music, and film. This carried both potentials and, of course, problems. Berlant and Warner point out that

> There are even components of the national mass media, such as *Details* and MTV, that have cultivated a language of queerness in their highly capitalized forums. . . .
> Given such conditions, the rhetoric of queering identity in mass youth culture can seem like a luxury. There are those who dismiss the rhetoric as consumerist and then trivialize all queer issues as matters of "lifestyle." But even if that perception were true, is lifestyle really unconnected to violence and world transformation? Politics so often turns on competing standards of seriousness that any narrow understanding of violence, need, and interest should be resisted. (346)

Yet even with the undeniable weight of their last assertion, the "consumerist" appropriation of queer "prancing and squatting" certainly had its legitimate critics. Butler's caution above concerning the "market value" of "subversion" echoed the concern of others. It is telling that one of the first academics to use "queer theory" as a term and rubric quickly abandoned it. In a concluding essay to "More Gender Trouble: Feminism Meets Queer Theory" (a 1994 special issue of *differences*), Teresa de Lauretis explains her use of "lesbian" in the title of a recent book: "As for 'queer theory,' my insistent specification *lesbian* may well be taken as a taking of distance from what, since I proposed it as a working hypothesis for lesbian and gay studies in this very journal . . . , has quickly become a conceptually vacuous creature of the publishing industry" (297).

While my next chapter will go into some detail concerning possible objections to and avoidances inherent to date in the "queer theory" paradigm, it is certainly worth noting that consumer culture quickly seized upon it (even if de Lauretis's dismissal of it as "conceptually vacuous" seems both broad and undertheorized). A catchy and provocative term such as "queer" – especially embracing as it does all sorts of sexy transgressions and possible innovations – was practically tailor-made for the marketplace. By the mid- to late-1990s pop cultural references to "queerness" abounded. In an episode of *The Simpsons*, the townspeople of Springfield engage in a march protesting government inaction against a rogue bear that has been wandering into town; they reference Queer Nation in chanting "We're here, we're queer, we don't want anymore bears!" In another episode Homer whines to a gay character that homosexuals had no right to take the word "queer" for themselves, because "That's *our* word to call you!" "Queer" as a positive marker of sexy but unspecified difference was used in popular song lyrics, and by the end of the decade, a soap-opera-like television show entitled *Queer as Folk* openly explored queer lives, loves, and sexual adventures for a wide viewership in Britain and America. In the academy, queer conferences abounded, special issues of journals devoted to the topic proliferated, and publishers marketed numerous books and anthologies that used "queer" in their titles.

But at the same time as all of this "prancing and squatting on the academic stage" and elsewhere was going on, there were some very painful reminders that American society, in particular, had not simply moved beyond "old politics" and identity categories into a new era of sexual and gender free-play. The horrific murder of Matthew Shepard in 1998, the hysterical debates over "gay marriage" during the same time period, and the intense and ongoing fundamentalist and right-wing political challenges to even modest legal protections against discrimination on the basis of sexual "orientation" all point out the profound disjunction at times between "theoretical" (and even pop cultural) experimentations and the homophobic violence of everyday life. Indeed, the gulf between postmodern perspectives on the contingency of identity and more essentialist usages of "lesbian" and "gay" identity as a rallying tool and communal comfort zone sparked intense debates within the lesbian and gay community as well as between homophobes and those challenging homophobia. As Berlant and Warner point out, "the organs of the national gay press – in particular, the *Advocate, Out, Deneuve, Ten Percent* – have been either oblivious or hostile to queer theory" (347). Queer *theory* in particular was seen as abstruse and elitist by an American lesbian and gay reading (and nonreading) public that could be just as anti-intellectual as the larger American culture of which it was and is an oppressed subset.

But while broad dismissals of all academic work and specialized language are easy to see as predictable manifestations of entrenched anti-intellectualism, there are certainly thoughtful objections that have been raised to "queer" and other recent theories' forms of self-presentation. In an interview I conducted with feminist theorist Sandra Gilbert, I was taken with an important point that she made when asked about the current state of the field of feminist literary criticism:

> I'm afraid that what *was* feminist criticism and what is now more likely to be gender studies (and that's fine with me) have become just another sector of the academic technocracy, that they have lost their political urgency and become "established" in a really clichéd ivory-tower way. Some of the leading gender theorists speak in the most arcane ways and are the least capable of addressing public political issues that continue to be centrally urgent in our culture. I see that as a truly major problem. I want to feel that there's a broad social mission for feminist studies, queer theory, gender studies, and all of the other spin-offs of the intellectual revolutions that shook academia to its foundations a few decades ago. I want to feel that we have a social impact, that we make a difference in the world off campus. And it begins to feel sometimes that the world on campus isn't just a microcosm of the world off campus, it's a different universe – and that upsets me.   (*Professions* 252–3)

Gilbert certainly has a point about the need for academics to remind themselves (*our*selves) that speaking to each other within university classrooms, committees, and conferences, is only part of (a *small* part of) a process of social change, that political work within the "ivory tower" does not automatically resonate beyond its walls without individuals moving deliberately outside of those walls to speak to a larger population.

Yet theorist Lee Edelman also makes an important point in his preface to *Homographesis*, his own queer theoretical intervention that certainly uses difficult terminology and the language of "high theory":

> If "jargon" names . . . merely the vocabulary of a particular discipline, the following pages do not present, or even desire, to be free of it.

> Metaphor, synecdoche, metalepsis, catachresis: such terms are the "jargon" of a rhetorical criticism that reaches back to Quintilian; cathexis, libido, narcissism, Nachtraglichkeit: these loom large in the jargon – which is to say, the language – of psychoanalysis. The fiction of a common language that can speak of a universally available truth, or even a universally available logic, is the fantasy on which the structures of dominance anatomized throughout this volume rest.   (xvii)

All language is specialized language in that it always encodes the interests of particular groups and is used within discrete communities. His point is well taken. Even so, I disagree with Edelman's claim that "There may come a time when books specifically written for a popular, 'mainstream' audience will be able to make their own versions of the arguments I make in this book now; but for that to occur it will have been necessary for these ideas to have been argued, challenged, refined, and dispersed among the more 'specialized' audiences toward which this volume is largely, though by no means exclusively, aimed" (xvi–xvii). This "top down" model of intellectuals refining ideas and then generously sharing them with nonintellectuals needs further complication. It ignores the fact that important intellectual work and activist struggles over processes of change take place all of the time and among many who do not hold PhDs. "Queer" as a sophisticated and energizing concept came from activists and was appropriated by academics, not the other way around. Granted, there is a process by which intellectuals read and respond to emerging cultural trends and then feed their work back into larger cultural discussions, but no academic should think of himself or herself as unequivocally "necessary." And for that feedback (really, feed back and forth) among academics and nonacademics to occur most productively, we must be able to adjust our language as the context and opportunity demands.

But questions of specialized language are hardly the most important ones to be raised about "queer theories" as practiced and promulgated during the 1990s and later. My next chapter will turn to a host of possible objections to, omissions within, and divergent, fracturing identity positions vis-à-vis the field. As Foucault so memorably theorized in his discussion of the "tactical polyvalence of discourse," every discursive act or set of activities engenders diverse forms of response as well as identification; this is as true for "queer theory" as it was for the fields to which queer theory responded. Thus literary critic Allen Frantzen quotes and responds to one of Michael Warner's foundational statements on "queer theory":

> "'For academics, being interested in queer theory is a way to mess up the desexualized spaces of the academy, exude some rut, reimagine the publics from and for which academic intellectuals write, dress, and perform," writes Warner. Exuding rut (animal sexual excitement, usually male) is certainly a way to sexualize academic space, but it is also a way to gratify professorial ego and remind the profession at large of who is a star with rights to act out, or up, and who is not.
>
> (*Before the Closet* 22)

Indeed, the gender and class obfuscations, among many others, inherent in the "queer" paradigm will take center stage in my next chapter. Before moving on to some "queer" readings of our own, I wish first to "queer" queer, and emphasize the need for a continuing dissensuality in and around the field if it too is to avoid the possibility (inevitability?) of becoming yet another part of the dreary "normal business in the academy."

A Query

In a recent anti-queer theory diatribe (first mentioned in my introduction), gay anthropologist Max Kirsch claims, "Queer theory, much
of which deconstructs collective community, encourages political
apathy as it relativizes all sexuality and gender," and he argues
broadly that "post-structuralism in particular is about ideas rather
than action" (*Queer Theory* 8). Is this true? Is queer theory (or are
queer theories) apathetic and agency deflating?

Frankly, Kirsch's claims are so broad and his selective readings of
and attacks on Judith Butler and others so skewed that his work
hardly deserves mention here. I wouldn't even bother to do so except
that the stereotype of post-structuralist theory as impractical and of
queer theory as simply self-indulgent intellectual freeplay is common
enough to warrant addressing directly. Kirsch reflects the skepticism
of some of my own undergraduates when he condemns post-structuralism in saying, "By taking language and text as a starting point . . .
the person and individual as a subject remain absent and unexplored,
and agency becomes a moot point" (29). As I tell my juniors and
seniors every semester, such objections are based on a mistaken
reading of Jacques Derrida's claim that "there is nothing outside of
the text." In fact, when referencing that assertion, post-structuralists
generally mean that everything *is* textual in the sense of being open to
active forms of critique, reading, and interpretation. This expands the
work of textual critics to include such nonliterary forms as advertise-
ments, films (and even more importantly for our purposes) interpersonal activities, patterns of organization, urban and suburban spaces,
and, of course, the text of political activism itself.

But beyond opening up the possibility of political activism as part
of its critical work, does an engagement with "queer theory/theories"
ever encourage or motivate such work? Kirsch, of course, says "no,"
stating that queer theory actually leads to "a fear of engagement, a
true manifestation of internalized homophobia that rests on the indi-

vidual's rejection of identity and power, [and a] refusal to identify and to engage power" (92). I don't know anything about Kirsch's activist work, but I do know something about that of the "queer theorists" whom he dismisses. As Butler writes in her 1999 introduction to *Gender Trouble*:

> There is one aspect of the conditions of its production that is not always understood about the text: it was produced not merely from the academy, but from convergent social movements of which I have been a part, and within the context of a lesbian and gay community on the east coast of the United States in which I lived for fourteen years prior to the writing of this book. Despite the dislocation of the subject that the text performs, there is a person here: I went to many meetings, bars, and marches and saw many kinds of genders, understood myself to be at the crossroads of some of them, and encountered sexuality at several of its cultural edges.   (xvi)

And as she goes on to mention (and as I referenced earlier), *Gender Trouble* "was taken up by Queer Nation, and some of its reflections of the theatricality of queer self-presentation resonated with the tactics of ACT UP, it was among the materials that also helped to prompt members of the American Psychoanalytic Association and the American Psychological Association to reassess some of their current doxa on homosexuality" (xvii). And it is hardly Butler alone among "queer theorists" who has been intimately involved in activism. Lauren Berlant and Elizabeth Freeman draw on their own activist experiences in Queer Nation, as I quoted earlier; Michael Warner has been highly involved in Sex Panic New York (and especially that group's work in the 1990s to counter the conservative policies of the Rudolph Giuliani administration); and I have been busy for over a decade in AIDS/HIV activism and public awareness campaigns in Los Angeles. The intellectual energy of and perspectives on strategic alliance promoted by "queer theory/theories" have motivated many of us to volunteer our time, to engage in protest marches, and to work strenuously in political campaigns and campus forums to challenge narrow notions of sexual "propriety."

Tellingly, of course, it is Kirsch who ignores sexuality and sexual norms in his own rallying calls and political injunctions. In the concluding list of "strategies" that he offers as a counter to queer theory, he suggests that we confront the policies of "transnational corporations," engage in active recruitment for "unions," and work toward the "formation of a labor party" in the United States, all worthy goals I would say, but out of his eleven calls to action, only in one does he mention anything even barely related to sexual identity, saying that we might engage in "struggles over public curriculums to include discussions of diversity, gender, and sexuality" (121). He offers no specific program for engaging oppression based on sexual nonconformity. Social class is certainly an important arena for political activism, but it is hardly responsible to charge broadly that queer theory – which examines sexuality specifically – is illegitimate because it is not engaged with class issues to the *exclusion* of sexuality.

I write in the introduction to *Professions*, a collection of conversations and interviews on some of the more disturbing "norms" of the academy, that all too often "our function and success as 'critics' seems to be defined by our ability to distinguish our own voice, while dismissing or leaving unexamined consonance and similarity, thereby disabling alliance" (8). We professional critics "seem eager or at least oddly determined to fracture an actually preexisting unity by wholly ignoring or quickly dismissing . . . commonalities; we too often demonize those closest at hand while ignoring broader institutional and extra-professional groups and forces that can be far more divergent and even destructive in their beliefs and agendas regarding the work we do in the classroom, in our writing, and as public intellectuals" (5). Queerly, then, I want to recognize and support Kirsch's work as a Marxist/materialist scholar and, perhaps, activist (though, again, he provides no information about any work outside of his scholarly writing). But it does dismay me that he does not grant the same recognition to the work that Butler and Warner and Berlant and I do. Kirsch could learn some important lessons from other class-interested queer academics. In *Selling Out: The Gay and Lesbian Movement Goes to Market*, a trenchant analysis of how class disparities and market-niche self-identifications have rendered hollow notions of a national gay and lesbian "community," Alexandra Chasin opens by thanking Judith Butler "for all her support and for sorely needed perspective" (xi). Chasin's subtle and well-supported analysis will play a role in my next chapter, and hers is the spirit that I wish to applaud here; she writes generously, "many people have tried to implement their vision for a better society, and I mean to honor such work . . . I am not interested in vilifying individuals, or even groups. I *am* interested in identifying, describing, and understanding institutional mechanisms and systems of practice, for the purpose of changing them for the better" (xvii–xix).

We need multiple engagements with the many ways that current governmental policies and sociocultural norms oppress us today and foreclose options for our future. Queer theories, with their emphasis on changeability over time and on making daily actions and activities a field for disruptive work, provide *one* avenue and motivation for that engagement. If it does not work for you, as it does not for Kirsch and others, then certainly find another – theories of class and race and postcoloniality as singular and powerful statements may do so – but let us at least recognize that we have much more in common with each other than we do with the many who would preserve the status quo or, perhaps, who would have us return to the "golden era" of capital punishment for a host of "crimes against nature."

3 Queering Class, Race, Gender, and Sexual Orientation

What is a body of theory's responsibility to itself? By this, I mean, when theory theorizes *about* something, to what extent must it/should it clearly abide by or incorporate its own skepticism and interrogations? I believe that this self-reflexive move – in which theory (and theoreticians) reflect upon and actively work to remake itself (their selves) to embrace, represent, and live out its (their) own rules and critiques – is something that we in Anglo-American cultural and literary theory have yet to grapple with fully. Too often critics still assume a masterful/objective "outside" position vis-à-vis their subject matter, even when one of their most powerful theoretical points is that such a position is impossible or highly suspicious. Indeed, as I suggested in my introduction, any form of queer theory that is definitively presented, and in thoroughly normal/unqueer fashion, seems hypocritical at best. This chapter will work to grapple with some of the internal problems with and potentials inherent in queer theorization to date. It will work to keep "queer" queer.

I say "we in Anglo-American" theory above because Continental – especially French – forms of theorization have tended to be a bit more ambitious in this regard. Anyone who has struggled with reading the work of Jacques Derrida knows how puzzling his manner of presentation can often be, for Derrida challenges not only "in theory" but also "in practice" the notion of transparent meaning and secure, reliable, masterful communication. This makes for a difficult process of decoding and grappling with the text for the reader, but certainly is a critical writing and reading process that lives by its own rules, so to speak. Derrida risks being dismissed as abstruse or even nonsensical by some readers but he does fulfill a Nietzschean injunction to live bravely and creatively in and through his work. As I remind my students every semester, if you find Derrida infuriating and impossible to understand fully, that is because he is teaching you something about the impossibility *of* understanding fully.

Roland Barthes and Hélène Cixous are among the many other French critics who also work both in theory and in textual practice/presentation to disrupt notions of normality and stable, enduring meaning. Cixous, whom I discussed earlier, will figure again in a later passage of this chapter, but Barthes deserves brief mention here, for he gives us a theoretical framework for considering the question of normal, normalizing modes of thought and expression. Barthes – queer in sexuality, queer in theorization, queer in theoretical self-presentation – was concerned especially in his later texts with avoiding the dogmatic, the fixed, static, and limiting, in theoretical perspective. As Graham Allen has explored in *Intertextuality*,

> The purpose of *The Pleasure of the Text*, and indeed all of Barthes's writings of the late 1960s and 1970s, is to articulate *para-doxa*. As he states in *Roland Barthes by Roland Barthes*: "The *doxa* is current opinion, meaning repeated *as if nothing had happened*". . . . The *doxa* is a stereotypical meaning, a fragment from the intertextual environment of the social text, constituted by established discourses, by the already written and already read. [*Doxa* expresses] the already written as if it were literal, representative, denotative, and, thus, as if it were natural. . . . When politically right-wing people argue for the sanctity of the nuclear family, or for heterosexuality as the only legitimate sexuality, then we are clearly dealing with discursive arguments that Barthes would nominate in terms of the *doxa*. . . . However, when left-wing groups argue that society can only be changed by a revolution of the workers, or that all art which does not reflect working-class conditions is elitist, then we are also dealing with Barthes's *doxa*.
> (91)

The *para-doxa*, on the other hand, is "that which would resist and disturb the beliefs and forms and codes of that culture" (90); it is "anything which is contrary to common opinion and to that which is considered 'natural'" (216). Many of Barthes's later writings – often presented in fragmentary observations, in brief, inconclusive readings, and in unconventional commentaries and linkages – attempt to effect in form and function that work of resistance and disturbance, what D. A. Miller (in *Bringing Out Roland Barthes*) calls a giving up of "self appointed securities" for the "disorienting effects – of intermittence, plurality, violation, exhaustion" (50). I would argue that a singularly important challenge for post-Barthean queer theory, too, is to retain its *para-doxical* status, to avoid falling into the self-satisfaction, stasis, and sterility of the *doxa*.

This is not perfectly realizable, of course. All theories have their presuppositions, their bases of argument and methodology, and their varied and often valuable relationships to standard modes of communication. "Queer" is not chaos; if it were, it would be useless and dispensable. Yet there is a lot of experimentation and unsettling investigation that can be conducted before we reach the point of "chaos." If it is to retain its ability to abrade the "natural," queer must be continuously denaturalized itself. And this means posing and continuing to pose some very hard questions about its omissions, blindspots, normal practices, and nervous avoidances.

Perhaps the easiest place to begin in our consideration of the "doxa" of queer theories is with the objections explored briefly in the conclusion to the last chapter. Here, as earlier, it would be useless to linger in the arguments of those critics who reject "queer theory" wholly and dogmatically for its social constructionist base or because it does not emphasize class (or gender or anything else) to the exclusion of sexuality. But certainly there are thoughtful and important objections to the class ideologies of some forms of queer practices and theorization that warrant attention. Theories of class have long been central to understanding specifically lesbian and gay history and politics. Some of the most important early work in the field was done by individuals who saw sexual identity issues as thoroughly bound up in changes in class consciousness and definition. John D'Emilio's groundbreaking essay "Capitalism and Gay Identity" (first given as a lecture in 1979) explores how previously unknown patterns of social organization arising from capitalism (including urbanization, the rise of wage labor, alterations in domestic arrangements) allowed for new opportunities for homosexual behavior and a new consciousness of specifically homosexual identity during and after the latter part of the nineteenth century. Yet he also asserts, "The elevation of the family to ideological preeminence guarantees that capitalist society will reproduce not just children, but heterosexism and homophobia. In the most profound sense, capitalism is the problem" (474). Thus capitalism both enables contemporary notions of lesbian and gay identity and, inevitably, helps determine its least laudable aspects (consumerism, blindness to class inequities, etc.).

This eagerness to explore the complex relationship between simultaneous forms of empowerment and disempowerment, and among vectors of oppression (sexuality and class here specifically) would appear to be a clear corollary to the "queer" emphasis on coalition building. But certainly it is a path not yet fully taken. To some extent, American "queer theory" has simply followed the broader norms of American middle- and upper-class gay and lesbian culture at it has reflected and reinforced the class disparities of the surrounding American society. We begin to see the intractable nature of the problem here when we inquire into who even has access to education and the types of jobs – academic and professional – that require higher education. Thus Alexandra Chasin remarks that "it is the class position of white men (as a group), relative to the class positions of women and people of color (as groups), that puts a disproportionate number of white men at boardroom tables of for-profit and nonprofit agencies, and on the pages of magazines offered to both straight and gay consumers" (*Selling Out* 224). The academic "queer" table of PhDs and publishing professors at research institutions is certainly no larger or more diverse. And queer theories and practices generally ignore such fundamental, structural inequities. Chasin quotes activist Mab Segrest, who states,

> we have opted for the wrong model. We don't need a queer nationalism – as powerful as the militancy and anti-assimilationist stances of Queer Nation have been. We need a queer socialism that is by necessity anti-racist, feminist and democratic; a politic that does not cut us off from other people, but that unites us with them in the broadest possible movement.   (*Selling Out* 240)

For both Chasin and Segrest, "queer" is not a passé concept. It still offers the possibility of coalition building, critical activity, and consciousness raising that can effectively "dislocate the myth that private consumption can ever do the work of progressive political action" (244). But part of that coalition building must involve making sure that access to the coalition is significantly broadened and that queer academics are committed to seeking out, valuing, and attending to voices and lived perspectives that challenge collusion with an oppressive class structure.

As with Chasin and Segrest, those important voices and perspectives are often those of activists, not academics. This is not to set up a facile "real world" versus "ivory tower" dichotomy, for certainly the nonacademic world has its own forms of bad faith. As "queer" has become commodified and packaged in tantalizing fashion for broad market appeal, clearly it offers a seductive route to spurious forms of quasi-political involvement. Just as with marketing ploys in which corporations offer to donate a tiny percentage of profits to a charitable organization as a way of attracting consumers (who are encouraged to think of themselves as significantly helping the poor, ill, or oppressed by purchasing a greasy hamburger or buying fashionable new clothes), so too is it seductive and somewhat grotesque to think that we are performing important "queer" political work by piercing our noses, purchasing a bumper sticker or t-shirt, or, frankly, by writing a piece of abstrusely worded literary criticism for publication in a scholarly journal. Queer theorization may always have certain class collusions and constraints because it *is* theory that is accessible primarily to those with a university education and that references previous intellectual work which itself is class-inflected. Yet this does not mean that queer theories and theorists (in and beyond their academic pursuits) cannot work more self-consciously and assiduously in the service of economic as well as sexual justice issues. The challenging voices of the activists above should be seen as vital to the continuing dialogue and dynamism of queer theories as ongoing (and never self-satisfied) projects of social critique and political abrasion. They remind us that most queer theories and theorists to date remain silent about or complacent regarding the plight of the world's poor and even those vast numbers within Anglo-American society who do not have adequate housing or health care.

Yet if theories of class and economic oppression can do much to enrich and complicate the field of queer theory, it is equally valid to ask what queer theories can do to or for the broad field of class analysis. Certainly a recognition of the multiplicity of identity positions and positionings, of mutability over time, of skepticism toward any form of calcified definition or dogmatic response, can serve to urge all critics – whether self-identified as "Marxist," "feminist," "postcolonial," or whatever – to move beyond the formulaic and to incorporate into their analysis an awareness of oppression arising from prescriptive notions of sexual identity and activity. A critic may powerfully and accurately analyze economic or gender-based oppression and still be thoroughly heterocentric or even explicitly homophobic. Queer theorists and critics have as much responsibility to point out those biases as other theorists and critics have to point out the omissions and blindspots of queer critique.

And this give-and-take, what one might broadly call mutual challenge, support, and intellectual enrichment, is not only my imagined "ideal" in the relationship between queer and class-based theories, but also for that of queer theories and those examining issues of race and ethnicity. Indeed, "post-structuralist" theories have long been subject to pointed and thoughtful challenge by certain critics working for the recovery and appreciation of works by writers of color. Perhaps the most famous critique is by Barbara Christian, who in "The Race for Theory," decries a climate in which "theory has become a commodity . . . that helps determine whether we are hired or promoted in academic institutions – worse, whether we are heard at all" (225). In her reading of the academic landscape, "some of our most daring and potentially radical critics (and by *our* I mean black, women, Third World) have been influenced, even co-opted, into speaking a language and defining their discussion in terms alien to and opposed to our needs and orientation" (226). "Theory" is a colonizing force, in her perspective, though certainly other forms of oppression remain wholly absent from her analysis. Tellingly, by "orientation," she does not mean sexual orientation, for later she says explicitly, "we need to read the works of our writers in our various ways and remain open to the intricacies of the intersection of language, class, race, and gender in the literature" (227). Sexual identity and sexual expression are lost in her expression of what constitutes valid and useful criticism, a loss that the "alien" theory that she decries might reveal immediately. Indeed, this is a loss of both scope and nuance that Michael Awkward notes in a response to Christian (in "Appropriative Gestures: Theory and Afro-American Literary Criticism"), when he says that post-structuralist theory specifically "offers a provocative means of discussing the texts of non-hegemonic groups" (240), and in particular offers the means to effect "a clear and consistent critique of heterosexual institutions" (241).

Yet beyond dissents, such as Christian's, that wholly reject (as racially or ethnically "alien") the very bases and methods that constitute queer forms of theorization, certainly the field has its respondents who usefully critique its continuing problematic relationship with the analysis of race and ethnicity. In his complex and provocative study *Are We Not Men? Masculine Anxiety and the Problem of*

African-American Identity, Philip Brian Harper makes male homosexuality a central analytical topic and even cites Butler's *Gender Trouble*,
but at the same time he explicitly rejects the use of the adjectives
"gay" or "queer" in his study, in recognition of "the limited degree to
which many men of color feel identified with these latter terms" (205).
In particular, he notes that they conjure up "images of a population
that is characteristically white, male, and financially well-off" and
thus "can actually efface, rather than affirm, the experiences of
women and of men of color" (205).

This loss of specificity that attends any movement toward a broad
collective – such as that which "queer" invites – is certainly a legitimate concern. Just as we saw earlier, theories that examine oppression arising out of sexual activity and identities will never do precisely
the same work of theories that examine, in concentrated, powerful
fashion, class- and race-based oppression. Those analytical, interpretive, and critical tasks are often quite different, even if at other times
related, and even if they *should* work always to be as mutually
supportive as possible. Indeed, saying that they are often discrete critical tasks does not mean that omissions and collusions should not be
challenged aggressively. José Muñoz makes a clear and valid point
when he writes in *Disidentifications*:

> Most of the cornerstones of queer theory that are taught, cited, and
> canonized in gay and lesbian studies classrooms, publications, and
> conferences are decidedly directed toward analyzing white lesbians
> and gay men. The lack of inclusion is most certainly not the main
> problem with the treatment of race. A soft multicultural *inclusion* of
> race and ethnicity does not, on its own, lead to a progressive identity
> discourse. . . . The field of queer theory . . . is – and I write from expe-
> rience – a place where a scholar of color can easily be lost in an
> immersion of vanilla while her or his critical faculties can be frozen
> by an avalanche of snow.   (10–11)

Obviously, the present work might be similarly charged with "soft"
multiculturalism. Yet I am not so sure "hardness" should be our ideal
either. Rather, that ideal might be to value and insist upon in our very
definition of "queer theories," a dynamic of dialogue in which discussions of race and ethnicity are necessary components of the field,
even if we never forget that a critique of sexuality cannot always and
only do the work of challenging racism and ethnocentrism in their
many manifestations. Queer theories can do a much better job of

talking about race and ethnicity, but today they comprise an ever-broadening field that includes voices such as Muñoz's, Harper's, and others whose work on race and ethnicity vitally (and increasingly) complicate hegemonic understandings of sexuality.

Indeed, one of the most important recent challenges to the norms of "queer theory" has been issued by Robert F. Reid-Pharr, whose provocative essay "Dinge" (reprinted in his *Black Gay Man: Essays*) calls for an explicit "queer" discussion of cross-racial sexual desire. I will quote him here at length, because his injunctions are timely and compelling:

> Why, I have asked, do we see so little work by white gays and lesbians that directly addresses the question of cross-racial desire? . . . We do not escape race and racism when we fuck. . . . We must refuse to allow the production of a queer theory so reified that it does nothing to challenge the way we interact, the way we think, and the way we fuck. We must insist on a queer theory that takes the queer body and what we do with it as a primary focus, lest we allow for the articulation of a queer subjectivity that never recognizes the differences we create and carry in our bodies, including not only race but gender, health, and age, to name only the most obvious categories. We must not only think as we fuck but also pay close attention to all the implications, good and bad, of those sometimes startling thoughts.   (97–8)

This call to interrogate continuously, to engage critically our incorporation of identities and the desires that flow from and back into our identities, points us to the future of the field of queer theories, as I will discuss later in this chapter and in my Afterword. To discuss sexuality in sterile and "nice" terms, and with only passing or nervous reference to sexual acts and sexually active bodies, is *not very queer* theory. And nervously avoiding a discussion of racism among queers and racially inflected interactions in our own queer lives is at best intellectually shallow and at worst actively racist.

Yet as above, if queer theories must continue to complicate and enrich themselves through attention to issues of race, so too do queer theories have implications *for* discussions of race. In multiplying and complicating essentialist notions of identity, queer theories urge us to examine critically all claims to simple and singular identity categories. Thus Gregory Conerly in "Are You Black First or Are You Queer?" calls for a "multiplicity of nonoppressive black lesbigay identities that takes into account the diversity among us" even as "black-identified lesbi-

gays and lesbigay-identified blacks must be aware of and deal with
the paternalism, racial essentialism, and other kinds of power relationships that exist – both among themselves and the larger black and
lesbigay communities within which they are marginalized" (21). This
questioning of all forms of essentialism – sexual, racial, or gender-
related – is part of the project of Siobhan B. Somerville's *Queering the
Color Line*, in which she examines Jean Toomer's "refusal to position
himself according to the available categories of 'black' and 'white'"
and links that refusal to the "antinormative project of queer theory"
(137). She imagines a queer theory in which "disrupt[ing] naturalized
constructions of racial difference involves simultaneously unsettling
one's relationship to normative constructions of gender and sexuality
as well" (137). It is a move toward complexity and multiplicity in identification that Gloria Anzaldúa explores in *Borderlands/La Frontera*
when she writes about the plurality of her own identity:

> What we are suffering from is an absolute despot duality that says we
> are able to be only one or the other. . . . But I, like other queer people,
> am two in one body, both male and female. I am the embodiment of
> the *hieros gamos*: the coming together of opposites within. . . . For the
> lesbian of color, the ultimate rebellion she can make against her
> native culture is through her sexual behavior. She goes against two
> moral prohibitions: sexuality and homosexuality. Being lesbian and
> raised Catholic, indoctrinated as straight, I *made the choice to be
> queer* (for some it is genetically inherent). It's an interesting path, one
> that continually slips in and out of the white, the Catholic, the
> Mexican, the indigenous, the instincts. In and out of my head. It
> makes for *loqueria*, the crazies. It is a path of knowledge – one of
> knowing (and of learning) the history of oppression of our *raza*. It is a
> way of balancing, of mitigating duality.   (41)

While genetic inherence is not the specific interest of social
constructionist theories such as those explored here, certainly
Anzaldúa's thorough interrogation of binaries of race, sexuality,
gender, and national identification are "queer" in name, practice, and
theory.

Indeed, the repudiation of any "natural" or assumed, uninterrogated link between identity and genetic inherence has driven another
recent set of energetic interrogatory moves in the broad field under
discussion here: namely, interrogations of gender identity and biological sex. Even predating the advent of specifically "queer" theory in

the early 1990s, the French novelist and theorist Monique Wittig, in an essay from 1981 ("One Is Not Born a Woman"), challenged the utility of the term "woman" vis-à-vis the lives of lesbians, for "woman" is a culturally overloaded term that carries with it so much heterosexual baggage that lesbians, in desiring outside of the heterosexual male/female binary, constitute a category other than "woman." She takes as her starting-point the statement by Simone de Beauvoir, French existentialist and feminist, that "One is not born, but becomes a woman" (quoted in Wittig 103), and argues more broadly that "The refusal to become (or to remain) heterosexual always meant to refuse to become a man or a woman, consciously or not. For a lesbian this goes further than the refusal of the *role* 'woman.' It is the refusal of the economic, ideological, and political power of a man" (105). The point of her argument is that "our survival demands that we contribute all our strength to the ... destruction of heterosexuality as a social system which is based on the oppression of women by men and which produces the doctrine of the difference between the sexes to justify this oppression" (108). Wittig points us toward later interrogations that challenge *any* reliance upon a fixed two-sex model to secure our notions of identity. What has spurred such pointed challenges is not only the performance theory of Judith Butler and others, but also new technologies that make biological sex a potentially changeable aspect of human life. In ways far different from what was the case in de Beauvoir's day, one can indeed now "become" a woman whatever one's biological sex at birth.

This is hardly to say that diverse challenges to the categories of fixed biological sex are new to the late twentieth and early twenty-first centuries. Not only has cross-dressing existed throughout the history of most cultures, but also intersexed individuals, who at birth possess biological characteristics of both women and men, have also always existed to (and almost invariably been oppressed because they) challenge our notions of a simple two-sex division of all human life. And in making these broad statements, I do not mean to conflate, simplistically, sex and gender. Cross-dressing (or transvestism), intersexuality, and transsexuality are distinct and certainly have differing identity implications and affiliations. Yet at the same time all have in common the ability to undermine any sense of a "natural" basis for gender identity and the stability of the relationship between sexuality and biology. As Susan Stryker argues in her introduction to "The Transgender Issue" of *GLQ: A Journal of Lesbian and Gay Studies*:

"Transgender phenomena" emerge from and bear witness to the epistemological rift between gender signifiers and their signifieds. In doing so, they disrupt and denaturalize Western modernity's "normal" reality, specifically the fiction of a unitary psychosocial gender that is rooted biologically in corporeal substance. As such, these phenomena become sources of cultural anxiety and semiotic elaboration. Transgender phenomena have achieved critical importance (and critical chic) to the extent that they provide a site for grappling with the problematic relation between the principles of performativity and a materiality that, while inescapable, defies stable representation, particularly as experienced by embodied subjects.

(147)

For Stryker, "queer" represents a useful identificatory move and self-chosen base for further exploration:

I named myself queer in 1990. In doing so, I felt I could complete the statement "I am a –" for the first time in my life without adding any caveats. The term allowed me to align myself with other antiheteronormative identities and sociopolitical formations without erasing the specificity of my sense of self or the practices I engaged in to perform myself for others. By becoming queer first, I found I could then become transsexual in a way I had not previously considered.

(151)

While Stryker acknowledges fully that what she terms "'queer' utopianism" could be highly problematic in its "erasure of specificity" and its "moralizing teleology" she still finds energizing "the rhetoric of queer inclusivity and gender diversity" (153). Judith Halberstam, too, in *Female Masculinity*, argues that the relationship between transgenderism and queer theory is a very dynamic one, as she "uses the topic of female masculinity to explore a queer subject position that can successfully challenge hegemonic models of gender conformity" (9). For Stryker, Halberstam, and others, the field of queer theory, with its emphasis on mutability and disruptability through differing performances and embodiments, has been rich and rewarding in their efforts to probe gender and sexual diversity.

Yet others in the still developing field of transsexual/transgender theory have been far more critical of queer theories to date. Activist Viviane K. Namaste blasts "queer theory" for its "absolute neglect of everyday life for transgender people," arguing that "queer theory as it is currently practiced needs to be rejected for both theoretical and political reasons" (*Invisible Lives* 9). Namaste takes Judith Butler and others to task for wholly ignoring the many ways that queers (i.e. gays and lesbians) have often oppressed gender nonconformists within their own community. Butler's utopianism and philosophical/intellectual interrogation of identity categories is, for Namaste (a sociologist and social worker) far too removed from the violence perpetrated against many transgendered individuals. Namaste argues that queer theory "exhibits a remarkable insensitivity to the substantive issues of transgendered people's everyday lives," it "robs transgendered people of dignity and integrity," and it objectifies them "in precisely the same way" that traditional social science does (23).

This call for attention to lived experience and the violence of life *within* queer communities is important and certainly a vital part of a dynamic of dialogue and challenge in and surrounding queer theorization. Yet obviously Namaste's broad charges ignore the fact that numerous individuals "within" queer-identified theory are speaking out of transgendered subject positions and clearly out of their own experience of everyday life as transgendered individuals. Namaste, writing from her specific experience in French-speaking Quebec, actually seems more intent on indicting the universalizing moves of Anglo-American transgendered queers who use a term ("queer") foreign to the lives and self-identifications of most of the world. Thus Stryker and Martine Rothblatt (whose *The Apartheid of Sex* argues that the oppression of sexual nonconformists can be theorized as similar to the oppression of nonwhites in South Africa) are first commended, for they "clearly affirm transsexual identities in their work," but then are dismissed, for "they simultaneously create a vision of the world that limits itself to the United States, and that perpetuates a rather dangerous and solipsistic nationalism" (130). Again, these are useful correctives to the inevitable limitations of any theorist who – or theory which – necessarily speaks out of limited knowledge, a race/class/national positioning, and, of course, ignorance, sometimes greater and sometimes lesser, of the complexity of others' lives (especially on the international scale). Namaste reminds us that we should "recognize that there is not one large 'transgendered community,' but rather several small networks of transsexual and transgendered people, as well as many TS/TG people unaffiliated with other individuals like them" (266–7), and that we should pay particular attention to "the lives of prostitutes, immigrants, and the working poor" (270). While I would never fold Namaste's articulations into the field of "queer theories" against her wishes – an act of rhetorical and theoretical violence that would be inexcusable – I will urge those who do not object so clearly and forcefully to queer theories and identity terms to consider and learn from her contributions, even if you do not agree (as I do not) with all of her characterizations and broad dismissals. Here, as elsewhere, academics have much to learn by listening to activists.

Yet this is certainly not to dismiss all "high theoretical" contributions and complications. As the boundaries between the "real" and the technologically constructed become ever blurrier, the feminist scientist and theoretician Donna Haraway has suggested a complex and provocative model of "cyborgism" to link a wide variety of challenges to the "natural," including and beyond those posed by transgender and transsexual identities and embodiments. Haraway's work urges feminists and queer theorists to view technology not as (simply) a necessary evil or as (only) a destructive force within the contemporary world, but also as engendering a myriad of new identity models and possible positionings. In a chapter entitled "A Cyborg Manifesto," in *Simians, Cyborgs and Women*, she proclaims:

> By the late twentieth century, our time, a mythic time, we are all chimeras, theorized and fabricated hybrids of machine and organism; in short, we are cyborgs. The cyborg is our ontology, it gives us our politics. . . . This essay is an argument for *pleasure* in the confusion of boundaries and for *responsibility* in their construction. . . . The cyborg is resolutely committed to partiality, irony, intimacy, and perversity. (150)

Her points are several, including that "the production of universal, totalizing theory is a major mistake that misses most of reality," that "taking responsibility for the social relations of science and technology means refusing an anti-science metaphysics, a demonology of technology," and finally, that we should work towards a "powerful infidel heteroglossia, toward many languages, including voices of abrasion and challenge, of dialogue out of sometimes discrete and sometimes overlapping identity positions" (181). In calling for the "building and destroying [of] machines, identities, categories, relationships, spaces, stories" (181), Haraway confounds and confuses – *queers* – us all in pointing out that everyone today meshes with, incor-

porates, utilizes, and depends upon the nonhuman (animal, techno-
logical, machinic). For Haraway, the question "who am I?" must be
answered in ways that acknowledge our individual interactions with
and dependence upon computers, medical technologies, and the
technologically impacted environment. Hers is a very queer theory in
its challenge to traditional and entrenched binaries of identity formation.

Indeed, it is stunningly clear that technology has thoroughly
complicated what constitutes sexuality and our mechanisms of sexual
identification or identifications. Through web searches for queer
community information, through online chatrooms for the exchange
of personal stories and sexual gratification, through easy access, via
the web or videos, to a myriad of erotic images and narratives,
through phone sex lines and dating services, technology has altered
fundamentally our experience of sexuality and our possibilities for
new and shifting affiliations. In the query that follows this chapter I
pose some particularly difficult questions about how sexual identity is
or is not connected to our fantasy or masturbatory lives, but certainly
the ways that sexuality has moved beyond the hushed experience of
conjugal bedroom behavior for many people clearly prods us to
examine the very terms we use. Is our cyborg sexuality fundamentally
a "preference" or an "orientation"? The former term implies something chosen and changeable, and would allow conservative judgments that queers "choose" to live a deviant or sinful lifestyle and
therefore should be punished or at least considered morally culpable
for that choice. The latter term, however, implies a fixed, perhaps
binary, mapping of sexual identity, and is a clear holdover from the
nineteenth-century social scientific drive to classify and render
perfectly knowable.

Both terms are problematic, though often the phrase "sexual orientation" is used by social progressives because it serves to legitimate
one's sexual identity as outside of one's conscious control and therefore as no more appropriate for state regulation than hair color or
height. Queer theories, in their wide diversity, are sometimes struggling openly and vigorously with the limitations and baggage of such
basic terminology and sometimes are wholly avoiding the issue.
Nowhere has this been played out more tellingly than in the halting
discussion of what I will term (for the sake of convenience) "bisexuality." Indeed, I have argued elsewhere (and still believe) that the possibly morphic and multidirectional (rather than fixed "orientational")

nature of sexual desire poses some of the most interesting and complex challenges for queer theories to consider. They are so complex, in fact, that they are often conveniently ignored.

It would be easy here simply to rehearse the many ways that queer theories often (and queer theory anthologies almost invariably) ignore "bisexuality" or its implications for sexual identity. But others and I have already catalogued those omissions in various publications. In particular, my and Maria Pramaggiore's *RePresenting Bisexualities: Subjects and Cultures of Fluid Desire* and Steven Angelides' *A History of Bisexuality* investigate the subject of "queer theory's" avoidance of "bisexuality" at length. But those silences are already being broken, in the above works, as well as in Marjorie Garber's *Vice Versa* and in *Bisexuality: A Critical Reader*, edited by Merl Storr. The most important implication of these works generally is that "bisexuality" challenges queer identity and queer theorization in ways far more complex than would be addressed by simply adding self-identified "bisexuals" to the list of those subsumed under the "queer" rubric.

I should add that I have placed "bisexuality" in quotation marks here neither to question its existence nor that of the inherent right of many activists and individuals to self-identity accurately as "bisexual." Rather I do so because it is clearly a problematic term *if* we use it to talk both about the mutability of sexual desire over long periods of time and the multiplicity of how desire manifests itself, is piqued and impacted, diffusely at moments in time. Indeed these are two very different challenges, ones that I will discuss separately.

As I discussed briefly in my first chapter, George Chauncy notes that theorists of sexuality have yet to grapple fully with the implications of Kinsey's research (published half a century ago), that some men participate casually in broadly defined "homosexual" contact with other men (receiving oral sex, for instance) while maintaining continuing, satisfying sexual relationships with their wives and other women (70–1). These men never identify as "homosexual" or "bisexual," and "repressed" hardly captures the complexity of their identity positions. In fact, there is no evidence that a "heterosexual" man receiving oral sex from another man is "repressing" anything; he could just as easily be considered less "repressed" than others since he is allowing a rather wide field for possible sexual gratification. Indeed, we have no "queer theory" to date that would even account for the unremarkable experience of "situational" or "circumstantial" homosexuality, such as that which occurs in prison and other single-sex environments. Certainly if we limit our discussion of sexual "identity" to the standard definition encouraged by identity politics – that of self-identification – the point is moot. A "heterosexual" male prisoner receiving oral sex from another man poses no challenge to us or to our theories because he does not self-identify in any way other than though the first term in the polarity hetero/homo.

But my point here is that self-identification, explicit or potential, should *not* limit us in the ways we theorize about desire, that self-identification is a potentially powerful political position, but that it is also an intellectual problem. The fact that many (if not most) young women and men have some form of erotic contact with a member of the same sex, even if they later self-identify firmly as heterosexual, should serve to disrupt and complicate our understanding of the mutability of desire over time (as should the fact that many "homosexuals" have had orgasmic sex with members of the "opposite" sex). While Freudian theory suggests a certain type of diachronic analysis, of "heterosexuality" as a state achieved and maintained (albeit precariously) after a long developmental process – that it is a "culmination" for many individuals – I am skeptical about our need to continue to reference the Freudian paradigm. While "experimentation" during adolescence may be theorized as a sorting out, by trial and error, of what one "truly" (for whatever reason) desires, desires do not necessarily *remain* true. This is not to say, simplistically, that we are "all" really bisexual. The point of queer theories generally is that we are not all "really" any one thing. Nor am I saying, as Altman implied in 1971 in *Homosexual: Oppression and Liberation*, that the point of queer politics should be simply (*over* simply) to liberate our polymorphous sexual potential. Rather, I am suggesting that queer coalition building can be furthered by expressing and exploring more vigorously the many ways that "heterosexual" and "homosexual" are terms that do not capture the complexity of most human lives when viewed diachronically for past behaviors and always inherent future potentials.

And one further point needs to be made regarding such diachronic analysis. We do not even yet have a "queer theory" that looks at how sexual desire and erotic charges change, wane, and are piqued by variation, by "newness" in response to repetition or sameness. One does not have to be a jaded old libertine, à la the Marquis de Sade, to know that routine can (though not always) breed a desire for change.

While I am hardly so naïve that I would celebrate consumerism and its broad commodification of "light" sexual transgression (sex toys, erotica, etc.), I am also unwilling to discount or ignore it completely. Altman, 30 years after *Homosexual: Oppression and Liberation*, expresses his disappointment with what has happened in the intervening years:

> those of us caught up in the radical enthusiasms of the period underestimated the extent to which sexual "liberation" could be successfully co-opted by commercial consumerism. As mainstream publishers produce glossy erotica and sex toys are sold in mall-like sex emporiums, the hope that freedom from sexual restraints will lead to revolutionary change seems increasingly utopian. (*Global Sex* 160)

Granted, we have not seen "revolutionary" change as it might manifest itself in economic justice for the underclasses and a true cessation of discriminatory practices that favor men, whites, and heterosexuals. But, if we complicate the starkness of the liberation/revolution model and recognize gradations of progressive social existence in increased access to sexual identity affiliations and resources, and greater discussion (though certainly not "perfect" freedom of discussion) on sexual diversity issues in the media, have we not had a mini-revolution or epistemic metamorphosis of sorts in the past quarter-century?

And if we follow John D'Emilio and recognize that capitalism in the nineteenth century "created the material conditions for homosexual desire to express itself as a central component of some individuals' lives [and recognize that] now, our political movements are changing consciousness, creating the ideological conditions that make it easier for people to make that choice" ("Capitalism and gay Identity" 474), then are we not in a period of time where material conditions allow for numerous choices, explorations, and expressions beyond that which is captured in a simple, fixed hetero/homo binary? Allowing for the fact that desire outside of that binary exists at points in time in most peoples' lives and that new opportunities exist for re-explorations of such desire through (anonymous, "safe") web-based and telephone-based sexual encounters, do we not have the material conditions today for differing identity patterns that should shift our conceptualization of sexuality yet again, much as it was shifted in the nineteenth century? At the very least, queer theories need to explore these questions more aggressively.

This does not even touch the myriad of issues that attend a more concentrated focus on what sexuality actually *is* or how desire multiply, indescribably, manifests itself in bodily sensations and fleeting mental images or unarticulated desires. This may seem like a discussion that takes us far away from the practical, "real," and mundane, from the harshness of daily life that Viviane Namaste reminds us of above, but, even so, we should not let ourselves off the hook of grappling strenuously with such issues in our theoretical explorations. I would never argue that our sole or primary task is to theorize "queerly" about the implications of what George Castanza from the television show *Seinfeld* grapples with, that "it" (his penis) may have moved as he received a massage from another man, or how some sadomasochists identify themselves sexually by certain activities *regardless* of the biological sex of the person involved. But the fact that queer theories generally avoid wholly the messiness of these issues is telling. Admittedly, those are the "margins" of most individuals' or our collective notion of sexuality or sexual identity. But if post-structuralist theory has taught us anything, it is that what is "marginal" is actually central to understanding the means by which we value, define, and cognitively process. As Robert F. Reid-Pharr states bluntly: "It is surprising . . . that so little within queer theory has been addressed to the question of how we inhabit our various bodies, especially how we fuck or, rather, what we think when we fuck" (*Black Gay Man* 86). Frankly, however, I am not surprised by that avoidance, only dismayed that the relative silence continues and, through that silence, that what should be passé in my opinion – namely, the hetero/homo binary – is further enabled in its power to structure our perceptions and identity designations.

These are hardly new questions. As we saw, Cixous asked over a quarter of a century ago for "a reconsideration of *bisexuality* . . . evident and insistent in different ways according to the individual, the nonexclusion of difference or of a sex, and starting with this 'permission' one gives oneself, the multiplication of the effects of desire's inscription on every part of the body and the other body" ("Sorties" 84–5). Such lingering questions and theoretical articulations can still point us in different (not necessarily "correct," only usefully different) directions. In looking back to Guy Hocquenghem in *Homosexual Desire*, from the early 1970s, we find a usefully provocative model in which the fundamental "polyvocality of desire" (50–1) is taken as a starting point for imagining a future in which a different "system" is "in action," a "system in which polyvocal desire is plugged in on a non-exclusive basis" (131). Hocquenghem references his contemporaries Gilles Deleuze and Félix Guattari in seeing in "the homosexual pick-up machine, which is infinitely more direct and less guilt-induced than the complex system of 'civilised loves'" the model for a "mechanical scattering [which] corresponds to the mode of existence of desire itself" (131–2). And rather than posit any simple notion of "bisexuality" as a telos, he argues instead for a "concrete disintegrative process" abrasive toward the "entire subject-object system which constitutes an oppression of desire" (139).

Hocquenghem in thus referencing Deleuze and Guattari points us toward a paradigm that does not take as its fixed terms of reference the "givens" of Freudian or other nineteenth- and early twentieth-century theory. Deleuze and Guattari hardly provide simple, final answers to complex questions, but certainly they offer important additions to the conversation that constitutes queer theories as ongoing processes of cultural analysis and progressive political work. In focusing specifically on "desire" as multidirectional and productive, rather than binarily-defined and motivated by lack (what they term a "molar" paradigm), Deleuze and Guattari point us toward a "molecular" view of relations among humans of whatever sex or sexes, nonhuman beings and entities, technologies and everything else with which we interact. Even more expansively than Haraway's theory of cyborgism, theirs is a thorough repudiation of a simple model of subject/object relations, focusing instead on the dynamism of our "desiring" connections and interactivities. Deleuze and Guattari argue in *Anti-Oedipus* that "desire does not take as its object persons or things, but the entire surroundings that it traverses, the vibrations and flows of every sort to which it is joined, introducing therein breaks and captures – an always nomadic and migrant desire" (292). As Elizabeth Grosz notes, in her consideration of the utility of Deleuzean theory for feminist critique, "If molar unities, like the divisions of classes, races, and sexes, attempt to form and stabilize an identity, a fixity, a system that functions homeostatically, sealing in its energies and intensities, molecular becomings traverse, create a path, destabilize, energize instabilities, vulnerabilities of the molar unities" (*Volatile Bodies* 172).

As Grosz fully admits, "this is politically dangerous ground to walk on, but if we do not walk in dangerous places and different types of terrain, nothing new will be found, no explorations are possible, and things remain the same" (173). Deleuze and Guattari reject the very terms by which we define our selves and others. To this extent, and as Grosz notes, "They explain that they are not advocating the cultiva- tion of 'bisexuality,' which is simply the internalization of binarized sexuality, the miniaturization of the great molar polarities of the sexes without actually stretching or transforming them" (176). In *A Thousand Plateaus*, Deleuze and Guattari argue that sexuality "is badly explained by the binary organization of the sexes. . . . Sexuality brings into play too great a diversity of conjugated becomings; these are like *n* [the indefinite number] sexes. . . . Sexuality is the production of a thousand sexes, which are so many uncontrollable becomings" (278). Theirs is a view and an imagining in which desire flows in so many ways that identity is never wholly stable, sexuality is never firmly fixed, and possibilities are never foreclosed. They argue expan- sively,

> The truth is that sexuality is everywhere: the way a bureaucrat fondles his records, a judge administers justice, a businessman causes money to circulate; the way the bourgeoisie fucks the proletariat; and so on. And there is no need to resort to metaphors. . . . Hitler got the fascists sexually aroused. Flags, nations, armies, banks get a lot of people aroused. A revolutionary machine is nothing if it does not acquire at least as much force as these coercive machines have for producing breaks and mobilizing flows.   (*Anti-Oedipus* 293)

Indeed, Deleuze and Guattari's complex theories are well worth exploring at length for the student and critic interested in a wholly different model for examining desire and imagining a sexuality of interrelationships without traditional and moralizing limits. Indeed, their transgressions and withholdings of judgment even include passing references to such "taboo" topics as "bestialism," which they describe as "interesting," though not really insofar as it is a "question of making love with animals," rather more so in the breakdown of identity that sexuality involves – what they call "*the becoming-animal of the human*": "that which suddenly sweeps us up and makes us become – a *proximity, an indiscernibility* that extracts a shared element from the animal far more effectively than any domestication, utilization, or imitation could: 'the Beast'" (*A Thousand Plateaus* 278–9).

And this passing reference to "bestialism" does bring us face to face with the question of what forms of sexual desire still remain wholly off-limits for discussion in "queer theories" as currently practiced. While the "question of making love with animals" may not be the most pressing one out there from the perspective of identity politics or practical political responses to oppression, it does force us to acknowledge that most queer theories today confine themselves to discussions of sexuality rather safely adjacent to current norms and definitions of the legitimate and/or legal. Michael Warner's recent work has challenged this silence to a certain extent. In *The Trouble with Normal* he discusses nonmonogamous sexuality and explores "dangerous" (from the perspective of possible HIV transmission) sexual practices in order to call for more funding for and different approaches to AIDS prevention programs. Nonacademic writers, who are not confined by the proprieties of scholarly discourse, are also willing at times to talk about potentially disturbing sexual practices. Pat (now Patrick) Califia in *Public Sex* and other works tackles, from the standpoint of an activist, much more inflammatory issues – S&M practices and sex with and among minors – than academic theorists seem willing to broach.

Indeed, "age of consent" and questions of children's/adolescents' sexual "rights" are particularly, nervously avoided among queer theorists. Although Hocquenghem raised the issue briefly in *Homosexual Desire* – of young people affirming "their right to dispose of their own sexuality" (141) – and even though Gayle Rubin in "Thinking Sex" (from 1984) scorns the hysteria over child pornography and speaks even of the need to sympathize with "the community of men who love underaged youth" (7), no sustained discussion of the topic has followed. I am neither defending nor condemning anyone or any perspective here, only saying that the field of queer theorization has generally avoided issues of age-of-consent laws and intergenerational desire, and perhaps for understandable reasons. Even with the protection of "tenure" and the shield of "academic freedom," queer theorists are usually employed by institutions – often publicly funded universities – that put many forms of overt and covert pressure on them to avoid discussing topics that might engender hysterical (often media-driven) public reactions. And even if that pressure is not palpable, certain silences exist that simply derive from the internalization among even self-styled "queer" academics of broader social designations of the acceptable and unacceptable. We – and I certainly include myself here – are as acculturated and discursively formed as any other members of society, even when our theories and critical musings involve some limited perspective on processes of acculturation and discursive formation. Thus to my knowledge, it is still Rubin alone (again in "Thinking Sex") who openly questions the need for adult "incest statutes" and sees incest as a topic legitimately within the "thinkable" realm of sexuality studies. And she was writing *before* "queer" became a term that, one would imagine, allows and even encourages all sorts of startling avenues of transgressive inquiry.

This payoff has not yet been realized. As much as "queer theorists" may position or regard themselves as being in the vanguard of radical thought, activists – the very individuals who first reclaimed "queer" in highly visible fashion in the late 1980s – are often still the ones raising the most difficult topics. They are, therefore, a vital and necessary component of the dialogue that must constitute queer theories as ongoing, open-ended processes. Thus the "Declaration of Sexual Rights" adopted at the National SexPanic Summit (of activists and academics) held in San Diego, California in 1997 encourages bravely a more sustained discussion of "an end to harassment of sex workers and legal sanctions against paid sex," "the right of youth to sexual freedoms and self-determination," and "an end to the prohibition and stigmatization of public sex," among other issues. These queer, dissensual, nonacademic articulations can add new possibilities to the "unimaginable future" (132) that Annamarie Jagose references in the final words of her *Queer Theory: An Introduction*, help encourage the development of "inventive terms through which we can share differences and respect distinctiveness" (228) that Bristow prophecies at the end of *Sexuality*, and stoke a possible new hyperactivity in contesting codes of "sexuality and gender" in "our politics, in our scholarship, and in all our relationships" (200) that William Turner calls for in his conclusion to *A Genealogy of Queer Theory*.

Thus the point to which I return in concluding the "theory" section of this book is that for any dynamic of queer dissensus to operate successfully, for a model of energetic dialogue, challenge, intellectual articulation, interrogation, and clarification to work as optimally as possible, it must involve numerous individuals from a very wide variety of discursive positions, critical methodologies, and divergent sexual desires and agendas. As Sinfield notes in his conclusion to *Gay and After*, this is not to say that all "diversity is good. We experience among ourselves serious racism, misogyny, ageism, snobbery" (199). But only in the process of active intellectual and political exchange are those often unspoken norms and lingering prejudices highlighted and, just possibly, altered through the very activity of exchange. And this is *not* to imagine or desire that divergent queer theories become *a* queer theory through some form of grand move toward consensus. Quite the opposite. It is to imagine queer theories proliferating and to see that proliferation as itself valuable. It is to hold as our highest priority a respect for and understanding of multiplicity – of identities among and identities within. And while recognizing that speaking is not "liberation," it is to ask immediately, "what silences persist and why?" For as limited as "speaking" may be, silence is far more so. Indeed, that fundamental recognition and continuing belief is perhaps our best motivation to political activism and critical writing.

A Query

Jagose offers various observations on the relationship between "queer" and "identity" in the final paragraphs of *Queer Theory: An Introduction*: "Queer . . . is an identity category that has no interest in consolidating or even stabilizing itself," and then, "queer is less an identity than a *critique* of identity," followed by, "Queer is always an identity under construction, a site of permanent becoming," and then concluding, "Instead of theorizing queer in terms of its opposition to identity politics, it is more accurate to represent it as ceaselessly interrogating both the preconditions of identity and its effects. Queer is not outside the magnetic field of identity" (131–2). The seeming confusion of these observations is not that of the commentator, it is that inherent in the very field she and I discuss. So I cannot clarify for you the relationship between thorough interrogations/denaturalizations of identity and identity itself. As Jagose points out, one cannot move with pseudo-scientific confidence and objectivity "outside" of identity in order to critique masterfully the specimen "of" identity. The challenge of queer theorization, in my opinion, is to return often to those "sites of becoming," and more importantly, *un*becoming, wherein identity is temporary constructed, solidified, and then threatened or rendered inadequate in its explanatory power.

For me, one of those hopelessly complicated and therefore highly intriguing sites is that of the relationship between solitary or masturbatory sexuality and the question of identity. We know (or think we know) through standardized language and accepted points of reference, how to "define" people by their interpersonal activities (even though those definitions are themselves wholly inadequate, even if necessary, fictions). I have had tactile sexual contact with many more men than women; I am socially defined as "gay" for that reason and rarely do I contest that categorization for a host of political and personal reasons. But counting up the number of sexual partners and attempting to quantify or value the intensity of my "desire" for men (generically) or women (again generically) is so wholly reductive that it would be laughable if identity itself was not taken so very seriously. I feel no sexual desire toward the great majority of men or women. My desire is determined as much by a certain wiriness of body type as it is by any specific genitalia present or absent. And certainly my masturbatory life – which is as important to any understanding of my sexuality as my sex life with my partner(s) – takes fantastic rides through a host of possible identities, activities, transgressions, bodies, objects, and substances. Robert F. Reid-Pharr asks, as quoted above, "What do we think when we fuck?" (*Black Gay Man* 96). That begins to get at the problem of how ideas, images, and fantasies contribute to – perhaps are fundamental to – sexuality, but doesn't even approach the issue of what we even mean by "fuck" and why any reliance on interpersonal contact should be the primary means by which we determine sexual identity or delimit the forms of desire that identify us. A much more identity-complicating and revealing question might be: "What do we think when we masturbate?"

I won't bore you (or amuse you) by describing here all of the many thoughts or things that may occur to me as I do so. Other opportunities may arise for that discussion. Nor will I rehearse the arguments I have made elsewhere concerning why, I think, solitary sexuality is so scorned socially and avoided as a topic of inquiry (see my "Private Pleasures" and "Graphic Sexuality" essays listed in the bibliography, or the recent book *Masturbation: The History of a Great Terror*, by Jean Stengers and Anne Van Neck). Instead, we might take a rather pedestrian example, of a "heterosexual" man masturbating to an X-rated video. We obviously do not – cannot – know what thoughts may run through his shifting consciousness, as his visual field encompasses not only images of sexually available women but also sexually active and available men (available for viewing, for identification with or envy of, for fantasized physically proximate sexual activity with, etc.). But one point worth making here is that we do not have to "know" what he thinks. Absolute, comprehensive "knowledge" has never been the prerequisite for theorization. Feminist analysis might legitimately and very astutely examine the gender politics of a masturbatory "site" involving an adamantly "heterosexual" man and, let us say, his choice of a video showing two or three men simultaneously penetrating a relatively docile woman. Such analysis, while never "knowing" what that viewer is thinking, might explore and reveal much about the desire to dominate and control women that appears to constitutes that individual's and perhaps many other men's sexuality and social relationships with women. My point is that "queer" analysis might well take a different, if still highly speculative trajectory. In their interrogation of all adamant (or even halting) claims of sexual identity, applied queer theories might focus very profitably on the same "site's" visual and fantastic involvement of numerous male bodies and body parts (and not just penises, but usually in such videos, revealed and visually available anuses and open mouths), body fluids, and shifting body contacts, and explore what these can tell us about the thoroughly queered forms of desire existing just under the surface of even adamant identity claims.

As I indicate above, we don't know how to talk about, how to analyze in sustained fashion the complex, multiple identity implications of solitary, fantasy-involved, or erotica-involved sexuality. So many things may run through our minds as we masturbate that such topics would render hopeless any set of conclusions or confident interpretations. But rather than allowing such complexity to silence or paralyze us, it can (and should) energize us to continue the theoretical and applied critical investigation of the inherent muddle that always is sexuality. While we may never know precisely what is running through the mind of that "heterosexual" man masturbating to video images of the double or triple penetration of a porn actress, or through the minds of some adamantly lesbian friends of mine who masturbate to porn showing gay men anally penetrating each other, or for that matter, through the mind of the reader of narratives involving sexual contact with a grandmother or house pet, such "marginal" questions and sexualities are in fact central to the broader discussion of how we identify ourselves only by suppressing and maintaining silence on a host of complicating sexual factors. "What do we think when we masturbate?" is a question that takes us down an analytical road of thorough confusion; indeed, the metaphor of a "road" doesn't even begin to capture the three-dimensionality of the interpretive possibilities that such a question engenders. But, I will always insist, such confusion should present us with a myriad of opportunities rather than represent a simple and simplistically (conveniently) defined "roadblock."

Part II

Queer Readings

4 The Queerness of "The Yellow Wall-Paper"

As we move into this section of brief, provocative applications of the theories discussed in earlier chapters, the first issue that we confront is the fundamental question of what texts or sorts of texts lend themselves to queer analysis. Are some poems, short stories, novels, etc. appropriate and others inappropriate for this particular avenue of interpretation and theoretical investigation? As with many of the questions that queer theories generate, there is no simple answer to that query. Of course, texts often lend themselves in rather obvious ways to certain methodologies. For instance, a novel such as Charlotte Brontë's *Jane Eyre*, which concerns the plight of a woman struggling to find satisfying employment and companionship in a patriarchal society, seems tailor-made for feminist analysis. But for the student interested in writing about such a text, the fact that many previous critics have already written about the novel from such a standpoint certainly makes the process of finding one's own perspective and adding uniquely to the conversation about the novel a particularly daunting task. And beyond considering that practical aspect of reviewing and adding to previous scholarship, it is vital to see that other concerns and relationships in the novel, embedded in and adjacent to gender relationships, can be just as important to consider in understanding the text and its context. A skillful and imaginative critic can generate a detailed exploration of the class, colonial, and/or sexual ideologies that exist at or just below the surface of the narrative. A thematically rich and complex text such as *Jane Eyre* can support many different avenues of inquiry and interpretation well beyond the one that is most obvious.

Thus in asking which texts are appropriate for "queer" analysis, we might discern some obvious choices, but with further reflection discover some less obvious possibilities as well. Later chapters will examine some clearly "queer" texts. *Giovanni's Room* and *Dr. Jekyll and Mr. Hyde*, for example, contain explicit or thinly veiled explorations of sexual desire beyond that which was deemed "normal" in the social context portrayed in those novels. But is it possible to generate queer analysis when a text does not even mention sexual desire? Or what if it does contain vague references to sexuality but has no manifestations of specifically homosexual desire? This chapter will answer those questions with a "yes, it is still possible" but offers first a caveat: in selecting a text for queer analysis that contains few sexual implications or references to differing social valuations of desire, the critic is certainly taking on a very difficult project. I would never say that it is impossible to generate a sustained act of queer analysis vis-à-vis Ezra Pound's imagist poem "In a Station of the Metro" ("The apparition of these faces in the crowd; / Petals on a wet, black bough") – other critics may be far more inventive than I – but the poem certainly does not offer much textual material with which to work, and I would not wish to take on that particular critical project. As you mull over possibilities for queer analysis, always make sure that you have *some* textual detail with which to work.

The subject of this chapter, Charlotte Perkins Gilman's short story "The Yellow Wall-Paper," may not be an obvious choice for queer inquiry, but it does offer textual material for queer interpretation. Its concerns, if not explicitly sexual, certainly touch on the sexual and more broadly on the notion of the oppressive nature of the "normal." It invites us to ask provocative questions but at the same time offers no pat or reassuring answers. It emerges from a crucial time period in the construction and contestation of gender and sexual norms but does not imagine or delineate a clear and preferable alternative to its harsh context. It is a text that one might say "queers" the reader in the discomfort it causes us, and queerly refuses to assuage our discomfort even in its final words and images.

So where do we begin a project of queer analysis? When exploring a literary text, we begin with the words on the page. As we will see throughout this section, queer readings are always close readings. In fact, an inattention to nuance and difference, a glossing over of complexity and distinction, and the broad generalizations that such willful or learned blindness to specificity supports and furthers, is precisely what queer theories – and others influenced by post-structuralism – aggressively challenge. Jacques Derrida is famous for his detailed and complex readings as he teases out the underlying structures and meaning-making mechanisms of a given text and then reveals their contingency and instability. *Il n'y a pas de hors-texte* is the famous dictum of Derrida – there is nothing outside of the text – which directs us to textual detail immediately and with the express purpose of finding clues to the making and possible contestation of meaning therein.

With that in mind, then, let us turn to the opening lines of Gilman's narrative:

> It is very seldom that mere ordinary people like John and myself secure ancestral halls for the summer.
>
> A colonial mansion, a hereditary estate, I would say a haunted house, and reach the height of romantic felicity – but that would be asking too much of fate!
>
> Still I will proudly declare that there is something queer about it.
>
> (3)

Thus from its first words, we find a tension in the story between the "ordinary" and the "queer," between a heterosexual couple that is identified as quite common and "something" – unnameable, it seems – that is excessive and unusual. But how ordinary is the narrator, the speaking "self," if she (and she alone) recognizes the "queer" as "queer"? Does it not "take one to know one?" In fact, in the third sentence above we even find the surprising connection between "something queer" and an instance of proud declaration. Secretly (though to her readers explicitly) she seems to have started a process of a very queer form of self-assertion. How far away are we then from the proud declaration that we encountered in previous chapters, "We're here, we're queer, get used to it"?

We are over a century away, of course. "The Yellow Wall-Paper" was written in 1890 and published in 1892. The "I" of the short story is a historically situated "I," something a queer reading would also never forget. Indeed, our knowledge of its late nineteenth-century context directs us immediately to consider its relationship to the rise of the social sciences and the forces of pseudo-scientific normalization charted in my first chapter. And those are not simply contextual forces, but textual ones as well. The "ordinariness" mentioned in the first sentence of the story is clearly that only of the husband, John, not the speaker (as her "proud" declaration to us immediately indicates, of course). However ordinary this heterosexual couple may appear because of his socially sanctioned, defining presence, she is quickly revealed to be secretly aberrant. And in the sentences that follow the lines above, the tension between her queer subjectivity and his imperious, if highly tendentious, "objectivity" is further established:

> John is practical in the extreme. He has no patience with faith, an intense horror of superstition, and he scoffs openly at any talk of things not to be felt and seen and put down in figures.
>
> John is a physician, and *perhaps* . . . that is one reason I do not get well faster.
>
> You see he does not believe I am sick!
>
> And what is one to do? . . .
>
> My brother is also a physician, and also of high standing, and he says the same thing. . . . Personally I disagree with their ideas.   (4)

Immediately, then, we are thrust into the realm of "identity politics," where the "personal" is revealed to be thoroughly "political." As many insightful feminist readings of the story have pointed out, the brutal and insensitive imposition of a pat, "objective" medical reading onto the narrator – her husband John's treatment of her "case" – serves as a pointed indictment of all-too-common contemporary "cures" for (in her husband's words) "a slight hysterical tendency" (3), cures that involved bed rest, isolation, and other forms of confinement, without mental stimulation, within a domestic sphere and space. As we traced in earlier chapters, psychologists, social scientists, and sexologists of the era sought eagerly to impose diagnoses upon aberrant individuals as a way of delimiting and maintaining social order. And as the story reveals, this was explicitly framed as a process of getting individuals to exercise forms of "proper self-control" (4) that was really a form of control of the aberrant "self" being exercised by social scientists and medical personnel. In the story, the complexity, individuality, and expressiveness of the narrator is thus reduced to the sterility of a "case," a "slight" problem to be solved. A multi-faceted human being is thus turned into a "thing" which an interlocking system of familial/medical/psychological authority determines to "cure" efficiently, to normalize thoroughly.

This system of authority appears to carry overwhelming weight as it works to bring the narrator back into line with social expectations and definitions of proper roles and self-expression. She is, in fact, imprisoned for her "slight hysterical tendency," her incarceration captured symbolically in the bars that line the windows of the nursery that she is forced to call her bedroom. And this explicit bedroom setting of much of the story raises the question of whether or not the story's indictment exceeds its scathing treatment of the gender politics of the era and touches on the sexual as well. As discussed earlier, queer readings differ from feminist readings in their specific attention to sexuality and the weight of definitions of "normal" sexuality. And we certainly find that the narrator manifests some interesting behaviors that not only contest the gender ideologies of the day (in her self-assertions to us, for example), but that also "queer" certain broad sexual ideologies of the era. The long "smooch" (15) that runs around her bedroom wall, as she physically rubs her body against the "sin"-ful wallpaper (5), and her explicit claim that there is a "woman behind it" (13), against which she presumably rubs herself, hint at a very queer sexuality. To call this tactile contact "lesbian" would probably exceed the evidence base in the text. But since most readings of the story see the trapped women behind the wallpaper as the narrator herself, the "smooch" and continuous rubbing in the bedroom could be credibly interpreted as masturbatory, another form of abnormal sexuality that abrades late nineteenth-century designations of the proper and properly controlled. The text offers some textual support for such a "queer" reading: the narrator's rubbing "over and over" and her exclamation of "Round and round and round – and round and round and round – it makes me dizzy!" (15) certainly suggest forms of self-directed sexual pleasure that challenge the "norm" confining sexuality to heterosexual coupling alone. Of course, if we as readers and critics pathologize masturbation, then her activity may seem neurotic, even pathetic. But if we read (queerly) masturbatory activity as legitimate sexual exploration and expression, then her actions could be considered resistant and even brave. The fact that the narrator's clothes are stained with the yellow traces of her rubbing seems to bespeak of a visible provocation to the proprieties represented by her husband, an outward sign that she will not exercise the "self-control" that he demands.

Other, specifically generic aspects of the story offer further support for a "queer" reading. "The Yellow Wall-Paper's" "gothic" qualities – the isolation, the "haunted" nature of the house, the impending madness that hangs over the tale – are all in line with a history of that genre's explorations of social deviance. From Lewis's *The Monk* though LeFanu's "Carmilla" and Stoker's *Dracula*, gothic fiction creates "supernatural" spaces to linger in titillating explorations of the "unnatural," and quite often in explorations of unnatural sexuality. But generally gothic conventions allowed for that transgression of the proprieties of "normal," realistic fiction by containing within their narratives a moralizing, socially acceptable conclusion. Evildoers are punished and social order is reasserted by the story's end. Of course, even in such instances of containment the broadest implication of gothic fiction is that order is, in fact, quite fragile, that beneath the "surface" of daily life and social conventions lies disorder and a host of erotic and other desires that are only barely contained.

"The Yellow Wall-Paper," however, queerly refuses even a nod in the direction of convention and containment. The "queerness" of the house and the narrator is and remains highly contagious. By the middle of the story we are told that John too "seems very queer some-times," (13) and slightly later that "John is so queer now" (16). As we discussed in earlier chapters, one of the chief fears driving the rise of nineteenth-century social "science" was that of impending social dissolution, of lawlessness and aberrance no longer checked by religion and tradition. "The Yellow Wall-Paper" lingers in that possibility. Even the narrator's normal/normalizing sister-in-law Jennie seems affected; after discovering that the narrator has stripped off sections of wallpaper, "Jennie looked at the wall in amazement, but I told her merrily that I did it out of pure spite at the vicious thing. She laughed and said she wouldn't mind doing it herself, but I must not get tired. How she betrayed herself that time!" (17). This is hardly to say that the "system" of control represented by John and Jennie is seriously compromised or jeopardized by the activity of the narrator, but certainly it cannot help but be touched by her queerness. As much as their delineations of health/illness and normality/abnormality are socially entrenched and supported by the discourse of science and rationality, those binaries are, after all, social constructs, with all of the endurance and also inherent fragility that attends such constructs.

We might say, then, that the story presents us with a field of skirmish and tactical engagement. And one important site for this struggle is in its probing of the multiplicity and contingent nature of perception. Let us consider for a moment the story's overt use of symbol in its very title. The "yellow wall-paper" is of course that covering the walls of the narrator's bedroom. She writes, "It is the strangest yellow, that wall-paper! It makes me think of all the yellow things I ever saw – not beautiful ones like buttercups, but old foul, bad yellow things" (14). What does "yellow" mean? Rather than fix a single and simple denotation or narrow set of connotations to it, the story and narrator "queers" the term, destabilizing it and opening it up to multiplicity. "Yellow" has no inherent meaning, no essence, rather it is whatever the perceiver ascribes to it, many things, "all" things at once and existing in unresolved conflict. And because "yellow" is open to so many subjective interpretations within the text, it has also evoked a wide array of readings outside of the text. Susan Lanser, in a provocative critique ("Feminist Criticism"), relates the color to a deep-seated anxiety during its time period over nonwhite races, asking "Is the wallpaper, then, the political unconscious of a culture in which an Aryan woman's madness, desire, and anger, repressed by the imperatives of 'reason,' 'duty,' and 'proper self-control' are projected onto the 'yellow' woman who is, however, also the feared alien?" (239–40). She suggests that the answer is "yes," though at the same time she does not foreclose other readings of the story.

Even more pertinent to our project here is Ann Heilmann's suggestion in "Overwriting Decadency" that "yellow" evokes a queer sexuality related to "the image of Oscar Wilde, self-styled 'Professor of Aesthetics,' carrying sunflowers and a yellow silk handkerchief in lieu of aestheticism to the America of the 1880s, and responding to hostile newspaper reports by quipping, 'If you survive yellow journalism, you need not be afraid of yellow fever'" (177). Of course, there is no way of arguing definitively that "yellow" here *means* Wildean sexual identity any more than it is possible to argue that it *means* Asian racial identity. "Yellow" supports all of these speculations, and, in fact, does not even confine itself to its standard usage and quality as a color; in the narrator's queer usage of "yellow," it describes also "a peculiar odor," "the subtlest, most enduring odor I ever met," "A yellow smell" (14–15). Language, denotation, and even perception here is individualistic, unstable, and multiple, which is equally true of the pattern of the paper itself: "there is a lack of sequence, a defiance of law, that is a constant irritant to a normal mind" (12). As signaled in its opening lines, we find a continuing clash throughout "The Yellow Wall-Paper" between that which is ordered and ordinary, and that which actively challenges or exists in defiance of established order.

Of course, we saw in earlier chapters just how heavily weighted that struggle was toward those individuals and forces with social power behind them. Constructions of normality are certainly difficult to resist effectively or overturn wholly. Yet at the same time, Gilman's story does reveal the "normalizers" to be quite obtuse in their exercise of power and even easily duped. The narrator writes, "I get unreasonably angry with John sometimes. I'm sure I never used to be so sensitive. I think it is due to this nervous condition. But John says if I feel so, I shall neglect proper self-control; so I take pains to control myself – before him, at least, and that makes me very tired" (4). As much as it tires her, the narrator plays a role that for the duration of the story fools substantially both her husband and her sister-in-law. She knows well how to manipulate appearances to "perform" for them even as it is clear that such performances are only that – roles assumed for tactical purposes – not unmediated expressions of her own needs, desires, or conception of her "self."

Thus we find that from its first paragraphs and throughout, the primary source of tension in the story is over who/what exercises power over that "self." This is not to imply that there could ever be perfect freedom of self-construction and self-expression; we are all "subject" to our social context. And certainly the story does not indicate that the narrator is imagining some form of facile "liberation" from others' definitions of her. It does suggest, however, that she/we can be more flexible and open to change than are the stark "orderers" represented by John. Indeed, the narrow and destructive ways that her husband dictates to her – how she should act, where she should sleep, what she should do with her time – and his demand that she internalize these, that his dictates should form part of her mechanism of "self"-control, allow us to see just how connected to the practical and quotidian "queer" analysis can be. In applying queer theories here, we are not dealing with the abstruse and academic, rather we are probing the story's interest in who has the right to impose definitions of selfhood on others and how those definitions manifest themselves in and through the body.

This is the reason why the story has been of such enduring interest to feminist critics. Granted, Ruth Robbins makes an important point in her *Literary Feminisms* that the overall pessimism and final tragedy of the story hardly make its narrator a feminist heroine: "We've had the diagnosis that women are sick because they are oppressed and repressed, and because they lack the means of self-expression. But that is not the end, the sole aim, of feminist theories. There are more spaces to conquer than attic rooms" (258). That may be the case if we look at feminism or any other manifestation of identity politics over time, but certainly by foregrounding the historical situatedness of the story, we cannot ask more of it than what it offers: a window onto a specific clash between unruly selfhood and the forces that wish to normalize and control that selfhood. That the narrator's struggle is finally futile or very problematically realized is itself a statement about the weight of the forces represented by her husband and the medical establishment generally in 1890. The fact that she struggles and negotiates with the very terms offered to her – of capitulation, of sickness, of hysteria – shows how individuals within contexts of oppression/repression are "subject to" the discourse generated by the powers that be, even if they can (as Foucault suggests) use that discourse polyvalently and in ways antagonistic to the empowered.

Thus the story ends in very queer fashion, not with the explicit reestablishment of social order but also not in the "liberation" of its heroine. Her husband breaks into the bedroom, finds her creeping along the wall, and faints dead way; she then asks, "Now why should that man have fainted? But he did, and right across my path by the wall, so that I had to creep over him every time!" (19). Husbands and doctors are certainly not supposed to faint; her queerness unmasks the fragility just behind the veneer of control that he maintains in both of his social roles. The last sentence and the narrator's activity place him in the position of the weak, feminized patient, while she resumes her activity, reversing the gender dynamics for the moment. Granted, he will certainly return to his senses and she will, no doubt, be incarcerated in an asylum, if we project past the end of the narrative, but the disruption and exposure of the ease with which social power can be upset lingers. This is hardly a successful revolution against the "system" of doctors and husbands, but is a very revealing skirmish with it.

So even as I agree with Robbins that there are "more spaces to conquer than attic rooms" (*Literary Feminisms* 258), we always have to remember the heavy social constraints against which the narrator is struggling. Throughout the story we find intimations of possible suicide: "There is a recurrent spot where the pattern lolls like a broken neck and two bulbous eyes stare at you upside down" (7) and "All of those strangled head and bulbous eyes and waddling fungous growths just shriek with derision!" (18). In the battle for control of the "self" – between institutional discourses that wish to define and normalize the self and an aberrant narrator who struggles to defy those weighty impositions and definitions – there is no clear victor. But rather than destroying her "self" through suicide, the narrator does find a compromised space for a "different" self that is, admittedly, mad and pathologized, but that at the very least continues to exist. And as Sandra Gilbert and Susan Gubar suggest, "John's unmasculine swoon of surprise is the least of the triumphs Gilman imagines for her madwoman. More significant are the madwoman's own imaginings and creations, mirages of health and freedom in which her author endows her like a fairy godmother showering gold on a sleeping heroine" ("From *The Madwoman in the Attic*" 121). She remains a speaking, writing, and defiant subject at the story's end, still seeming to "proudly declare that there is something queer," much as at the tale's beginning.

Of course, madness is not "liberation," but as we discussed in earlier chapters, liberation is a highly problematic construct. One can only work within, even if against, the discourses available. As Foucault and other theorists following him have pointed out, the social construction of madness – its marginality and the sequestering of the "mad" for the discomfort they cause society – reveals much about the variety of mechanisms necessary for normality to maintain its shaky hold. John Brannigan argues in his "New Historicist" reading of "The Yellow Wall-Paper," that the story reveals how "confinement was a method necessary to a discourse which conceived of madness as requiring the demarcation and means of controlling the excessive passion and force of madness" (158–9). He goes on to suggest, "The issue which is really at stake in the story is the power relationship between medical discourse and the insane, between the physician and his patient" (160–1). At the very least, we must recognize the disruptive agency evinced by the narrator even at the story's end, for while John calls for "self-control" and the figures in the wall-paper hint at the likelihood of self-destruction, the narrator finds a form of self-expression, albeit a heavily compromised one. And this is what queer theories and social constructionist theories more generally ask us to recognize, that successes are always complex and imbricated within preexisting terms. And even the binary of success/failure needs deconstructing in a queer reading. Yes, we are disappointed if we want the heroine to meet standards of self-realization or self-expression that are of our own day, but not hers. This story must be allowed to queer our expectations and definitions; the narrator defies us as well as those around her.

But to call "The Yellow Wall-Paper" "queer" in this way is not to offer a final and definitive judgment upon it. There are many aspects of the story that queer theories simply do not help us critique. As a story firmly set in upper middle-class life, "The Yellow Wall-Paper" has implications about class privilege and material wealth that queer theories are ill equipped to analyze in extended ways. While the narrator's failed struggle to be allowed to work (in her case, to write) are tragic from the perspective of middle-class women's struggle for equality and self-realization, certainly from the perspective of "Mary," the cursorily mentioned, working-class woman who was, perhaps, cleaning her floors and doing her laundry, her horrible "rest cure" might sound like a blissful vacation. Indeed, from the perspective of a housemaid or laundress, this mad woman stripping off and tossing about wall-paper and getting endless yellow stains on her dress does need "normalizing," but not for the same reasons that John might offer, simply because she is causing them endless amounts of work. To focus on her struggle means excluding to a large extent their struggles. And similar exclusions are pointed out in Lanser's commentary on the racial "unconscious" of the text, for the story, "calls upon us to recognize that the white, female, intellectual-class subjectivity which Gilman's narrator attempts to construct, and to which feminists have also been committed perhaps unwittingly, is a subjectivity whose illusory unity, like the unity imposed on the paper, is built on the repression of difference" (246). Indeed, a "queer" reading that focuses on the social construction of selfhood might do well to look at the specificity of its own analysis, what it does and does not call its own "subject," and how it sets up its own margins and norms.

And part of what queer readings do generally exclude is the narrowly "biographical." When Barthes famously proclaimed the "death of the author," he makes a larger point worth reiterating here:

> We know now that a text is not a line of words releasing a single "theological" meaning (the "message" of the Author-God) but a multi-dimensional space in which a variety of writings, none of them original, blend and clash . . . .
>
> Once the Author is removed, the claim to decipher a text becomes quite futile. To give a text an Author is to impose a limit on that text, to furnish it with a final signified, to close the writing. ("The Death of the Author" 1468–9)

Indeed, "The Yellow Wall-Paper" has been analyzed often from the standpoint of its author's own life story and her supposed "intent." While useful from a certain perspective, biographical linkages also can constrain readings unnecessarily. Roland Barthes urges us to see through the text to the context and ongoing social conversation. In fact, we might even see a critical move to "decipher" a story solely along the lines of "intent" and "biography" as roughly similar to the reduction of the multiplicity of the narrator herself to a "case" with a simple diagnosis. That Gilman suffered her own trials at the hands of men like "John" is well documented, but her personal experience would not delimit a queer reading. The "clash" of which Barthes speaks is that of social power systems that may have had terrible consequences for the work's "author," but that must also be seen as larger than that individual. To open up the text in this way is in fact a way of politicizing it even more aggressively, of making it potentially relevant to and reflective of a wide variety of struggles and discrete situations. Queer readings would not necessarily deny that there is a writing author who experienced poignant, even tragic, circumstances in her life, but "Gilman" cannot be the center of our reading or we impose a limit both on its import and impact.

In sum, a Barthean acknowledgement of the "multidimensionality" of the text could be considered the *sine qua non* of queer analysis. Which is why "The Yellow Wall-Paper," as far removed as it may seem at first glance from lesbian and gay experience or struggles for civil rights, is still appropriate for a queer reading. Yes, there are other spaces, beyond attic rooms, to conquer for those who are oppressed by John and the various medical/domestic/gendered forces that he represents, but certainly Gilman's story has been used often to raise consciousness in classrooms and among readers and as a starting-point for heated discussion. It has its own polyvalent aspects. Indeed, the fact that I am writing about it here demonstrates the generative quality of its scathing indictment of "normality." It has entered and affected the discourse on gender relations and the credibility of diagnoses of deviance, and one cannot read it even in the twenty-first century without recognizing and confronting the social construction of familial and doctor/patient relations. Our brief encounter with it thus provides us with a solid set of analytical skills and piqued skepticisms with which to continue our queer analyses in our next chapters.

A Query

"Aren't we reading too much into it?" I have heard that question many times – with "it" variously meaning a story, poem, play, or other text – and "we" often referring to a class of undergraduate, non-English majors, but occasionally a group of majors or even graduate students. And the question is legitimate. At what point does any critic cross the line between well-supported analysis and wild speculation? This question is especially pertinent to the field under discussion here, because the charge of "reading too much into it" is an easy one to level against a queer reading that challenges norms, normal practices, and critical precedent.

Social constructionist readings always work to tease out clues to the presuppositions, biases, and naturalized, historically contingent categories and definitions that pervade and underlie a text. Often those are the ones still lingering in the reference systems of contemporary readers and critics. It is an easy response, when someone feels that cherished beliefs and frames of reference are being challenged, to claim that the offending critic is exceeding her or his authority, is "making too much" out of something or "reading too much" into a text or situation. Indeed, that response often means that the critic is in dangerous and therefore *very interesting* territory, that which readers and other critics wish to protect. Perhaps this involves core beliefs regarding religion, gender roles, sexual norms, national interests, or critical authority. Indeed, these are some of the bedrocks of "culture," and provide the very organizing principles (often binary-based) that post-structuralist critics in particular wish to interrogate intensely. And certainly when such critics reject the notion that they must reference or consider authorial "intent," then they are always open to the facile charge that the writer simply did not "mean" what is being found in the text. Indeed, such skeptical – or worse, fundamentally hostile – responses may come even from professors grading student essays and examinations.

It is best to assume a skeptical audience for all of your writing, and to remember that in any act of interpretation or application of theory a heavy burden of proof always lies with the writer. Even if the critic is doing a close reading of form or theme, she or he must provide ample textual detail to support the reading. And the same is true for the critic doing "queer" or other iconoclastic readings. The words on the page (or other textual detail), the words of the theorists being used, and the words of relevant historical documents and other resources must provide the substance of such readings. Wild, unsupported speculation is never acceptable in critical writing, and that rule is one that even queer analysis does not break. I have given as many failing grades for unsupported or poorly argued "queer" readings as I have to much less ambitious projects. And I am hardly the most "skeptical" reader one might imagine.

But what about those audience members who will never accept a queer reading, no matter how ample the evidence? Queer theories, as I am describing them here, do not ask you to martyr yourself. When I was a student, I had professors whom I knew would reject wholly a reading of homoeroticism or nonconformist sexual desire. I did not risk my grade in the class and graduation prospects to do battle with entrenched homophobia when I knew that I could not possibly win that particular skirmish. Other classes, other professors, and other projects provided less hostile terrain and I had ample opportunities to do "queer" work in those instances. Indeed, I have colleagues now whom I know will react hostilely to students who deploy post-structuralist theory, no matter how strenuously I lobby them or how brilliant the student's work may be. I always urge the student to think of the audience and choose a critical project more appropriate for that particular class and readership. As careful readers of "texts," broadly defined, we have to be able to read the texts of our classes, audiences, and writing contexts. This is not to minimize the legitimate outrage of a student victimized or constrained by a homophobic (or racist or sexist) professor, but it is to urge a continuing and careful attention to strategy when our goals must be long term as well as short term, must stretch beyond the end of a particular class or situation and which therefore demand care and complexity – a "queer" perspective.

But to reiterate an important point, such readerly hostility certainly does not account for why I sometimes give low grades to acts of self-styled "queer" analysis. I invariably do so because there is far too little textual detail provided to support the conclusions drawn. Sometimes the problem originates in a very poor choice of text for such analysis. You *can* read "too much" into a text if the text does not have enough in it to warrant or support your analysis. On the other hand, other choices may be quite appropriate and the poor realization of the project can be attributed to poor research, scanty citation of theory, or infrequent reference to the words or images that comprise the text under consideration. This is not reading "too much" into a text; it is not drawing enough out of it. All acts of critical interpretation ask their audiences to spend time and energy reading and considering the interpretation being offered. Make it clear to your readers why they should devote that time and energy to your work, and make sure that they finish your interpretation without profound doubts as to your intent, your evidence base, or your writing abilities.

Of course, none of this is to warn you away from doing "queer" or other provocative, iconoclastic readings. It is simply to urge you to approach your writing with awareness – of your context, your responsibilities, and your short- and long-term goals – and to use all of your reading skills to enhance your chances of success at writing. Instead of reading "into" a text, you should think always of reading "out of" texts. The words, images, and meaning-making details that fill their pages must fill the pages of your analysis as well.

5 Queering the Self: *Dr. Jekyll and Mr. Hyde*

I concluded my last chapter with the statement that "a Barthean acknowledgement of the 'multidimensionality' of the text could be considered the *sine qua non* of queer analysis." That is true is several ways. Certainly the multidimensionality of the text as it appears on the page (in the case of a literary text) would involve its relationship to both a social context and one of previous literary and nonliterary articulations. That multidimensionality would also include its complicated usage by readers, who may use it as a basis of identification, reaction, or some other response that becomes "textual" in and of itself. Indeed, by opening up dramatically what we mean by "text" the queer insistence on "multidimensionality" takes us immediately to the multifaceted, textually complicated, and contextually involved nature of "selfhood" itself. And that is the textual terrain that the present chapter will examine: how "queer" notions of selfhood might elude definitive representation and yet proliferate nevertheless, and how the tenuous, easily attenuated self is always contextually engaged and yet also possibly resistant.

In musing on these issues we continue our exploration of some of the difficult questions raised in the previous chapter and by queer theories generally. Do queer readings hinge necessarily on the location of a specific "homosexual" content in the text being examined? I maintain that they do not, and that in fact, queer multiplicity often exceeds any simple designation or static location within the historically specific heterosexual/homosexual binary. This is not to preclude from queer relevance the discussion of latent or overt "homosexual" content, but it is to expand our definition of queer relevance to discuss the variability and instability of sexual selfhood beyond such content. Yes, this thorough complication may render definitive judgments about such selfhood impossible, but that lack of definitive closure is itself part and parcel of queer reading and response. In the coming pages, Robert Louis Stevenson's *Dr. Jekyll and Mr. Hyde* will provide us with some exemplary instances of such thorough defini-tional instability – within and beyond the print text – and this allows us to continue to explore some of the many possible applications of queer theories.

Yet it is equally important to reiterate that such an acknowledge-ment of the impossibility of definitive closure in our own readings and responses is also to insist that agency – political, critical, etc. – is still quite possible even in a state of, or with a consciousness of, ambi-guity and instability. As I discussed in previous chapters, social constructionist theories argue generally that selfhood has no "essence" prior to a being's immersion in/creation through language and the various value-laden differences that society recognizes as "real": ones of gender, race, class, and sexuality. Yet certainly any one individual can demonstrate a greater or lesser degree of critical consciousness vis-à-vis those differences and the values assigned to them. In fact, if we were only and simply "determined" by language and reified differences, there would hardly be any reason for me to write this book. It is always possible to engage in an active critique of those discursive forces that religion, science, art, media, political institutions, and parents tell us are "real" and "true." Indeed, individ-ual experience of complexity, variability, and complication as it exists in excess of and in implicit or explicit challenge to the starkness of narrow social categories and valuations means that the evidentiary base for critiquing those categories and valuations is often at hand. In fact, the suppression of that complexity – itself – can be difficult to achieve, can depend upon a fragile and anxious set of processes and individual (and certainly group-reinforced) decisions.

Before discussing sexuality specifically, let me offer a stark example or two. Racist designations of "higher" and "lower" races, with ascrip-tions of degrees of intelligence and innate ability, were common for centuries throughout much of Anglo-American (and European) culture and cultural production (literary writings, "scientific" theories, art, etc.). Taking as a given here that such valuations are appalling falsehoods used to justify economic and other forms of exploitation of groups of peoples (through slavery, colonization, and relegation to the ill-paid forms of labor that privileged classes depend upon), it is undeniable that the suppression of clear and/or implicit evidence undermining these falsehoods was certainly more easily achieved when groups were geographically or otherwise separated or segregated. Simply put, it is much easier for me to maintain a lie about your abilities or basic human complexity (indeed, basic humanity) if I rarely see you or never interact with you in the workplace, schoolroom, or other social or political venue. Once, however, we commingle in urban spaces, in work or social situations, and in cultural exchanges, the lies and fictions become harder to maintain. They *are* maintained often – racism, sexism, and other differential valuations of peoples certainly persist – but the suppression of complicating and contradictory information certainly requires more energy and its achievement is rendered more fragile. Indeed, the energy of baldly hypocritical suppression often engenders a physics of startlingly violent confrontation.

Admittedly, the schema above does not take into account how individuals are socialized – partially or largely – into believing certain "lies" about themselves, nor does it consider the heavy weight of lingering, inherently skewed cultural evidence that allows us to persist in our designations of "higher" and "lower," worthy and unworthy, normal and abnormal. Even if women during the nineteenth and twentieth centuries clearly proved their abilities and capacities in ways that rendered thoroughly bankrupt notions of "natural" spheres and roles (i.e. domestic, singularly emotive, solely maternal), centuries of literature, religious writings, and other "evidence" persisted and persist today to allow individuals and/or groups of individuals to suppress or ignore the evidence before them. Indeed, the heavy valence of that "evidence" helps account for the very, very slow nature of social change. Yet it is my (admittedly optimistic) contention here that complexity wins out over time, that mounting evidence of variability and different value-*ability* slowly erodes simplistic, tendentious categories and the institutions that enforce and reinforce them. This process is never linear or neat, and rarely peaceful or proper, and often it is barely discernible over the course of an individual's lifetime (though, of course, it may be). Yet to ignore social changes that reflect such processes of complication is, potentially, to choose defeatism. Indeed, a social progressive today actually would have to engage in a very energetic suppression of evidence to argue that social roles, definitions, and opportunities have failed to change significantly for women over the past 200 years.

This process of changing valuation and destabilization of hierarchized binary definitions, begins with, and is furthered by, evidence of inherent complication, and is accelerated by confrontation with the fact that what is possible in you is also possible in me. To be sure, that we are all capable of "sin" has long been the core belief of the Christian church and has led to energetic rules and violent institutional devices to suppress the enactment of that capacity. Even so, it certainly has not led to stasis. And the recognition of that polyvalent, if always unpredictable, generative potential of "queered" and complicated selfhood brings us to the specific text of this chapter. Robert Louis Stevenson's *Dr. Jekyll and Mr. Hyde*, from 1886, hardly represents a clarion call for tolerance of social deviance. In many ways it is a deeply conservative work in its valuation of and response to explicitly identified "queerness." But it is a text that critics have returned to often for its intriguing implications and contextual imbrications, as it unsettles thoroughly any facile notion that any of us is any one thing, solely and forever. And in that revelation it opens up the possibility for a host of challenges to facile categorizations and binary definitions.

As with other works discussed here, this work's "text" is also clearly that of its context. Much as with "The Yellow Wall-Paper," *Dr. Jekyll and Mr. Hyde*'s publication near the end of the nineteenth century clues us immediately into its connection to a vexed set of contemporary questions regarding social identity. Its thematic concerns – the eruption of uncontrolled and wildly deviant desires from beneath the thin veneer of social decorum – have made it of great interest to critics interested in the rise of psychology as well as others intent on probing contemporary controversies concerning social "normality" (even before the advent of specifically "queer" forms of analysis). Martin Danahay (in *A Community of One*) echoes the psychoanalytic interests of numerous critics in pointing out that the tale "reveals an underlying suspicion that the autonomous, private self is an antisocial force that, if given public expression, would erupt in violent and criminal acts. The story of *Dr. Jekyll and Mr. Hyde* suggests that to repress the autonomous self is a social duty, but one that is achieved at great cost" (137). In fact, it is now a critical commonplace to interpret Mr. Hyde as representing the Freudian "id," that violent and wildly desiring "base" of human identity that is just barely kept in check and that always has the potential for wreaking havoc if let loose. Thus the "horror of *Dr. Jekyll and Mr. Hyde*," in Danahay's words, is its "imagining a double life in which the repressed other returns with redoubled force and takes over the respectable public persona" (144).

I certainly have no quarrel with such a reading, for it comes directly

out of the text itself, which was written during an era that also saw
Freud's early work and a new attention to the "inner life" of human
beings, as well as a clear desire to chart that inner life. Queer theories,
as explored throughout this book, would never deny that a text such
as *Dr. Jekyll and Mr. Hyde* might reflect in such a way a specific historical understanding of social and sexual identity. But they certainly
would insist that such a one-to-one correspondence is not the only
avenue for interpretation, especially when the text itself lingers in
definitional crisis and ambiguity. While we know from first-hand
reports of two "crimes" committed by Mr. Hyde – the trampling of a
child and the murder of an elderly member of Parliament – almost all
of his degenerate and deviant behavior remains out of sight and
unnamed. As Danahay remarks, Hyde "is a sign of the repressed half
of the Victorian male's double existence, but a sign without a specific
content. We can fill in the other with a range of impermissible desires
from homosexuality to masturbation" (144), and indeed, many critics
have filled in that blank in pertinent fashion.

One of the most influential readings of the tale is that of Elaine
Showalter in *Sexual Anarchy*; she relates the story's concerns to the
specific anxieties of the *fin de siècle* and that era's fears of social and
specifically sexual chaos. She notes that "In January [1886], just as
Stevenson published his novel, the Labouchere Amendment criminal-
izing homosexual acts went into effect, and Krafft-Ebing's
Psychopathia Sexualis offered some of the first case studies of homosexual men" (106). She goes on to argue that the tale is a veritable
"case study of male hysteria, not only that of Henry J., but also of the
men in the community around him. It can most persuasively be read
as a fable of fin-de-siècle homosexual panic, the discovery and resistance of the homosexual self" (107). Yet is there more to say about the
tale? While Showalter usefully picks up on the tale's explicit use of the
term "queer" to refer most specifically to the possibility of blackmail,
but also, perhaps, to raise the hint of homosexuality – for as "a
number of scholars have noted, the homosexual significance of
'queer' had entered English slang by 1900" (112) – a "queer" reading
of the tale might do much more than simply locate its possible or
likely homosexual implications. The tale also has generative, as well
as reflective, aspects. Not only is it locatable specifically in a context of
contemporary Freudian and sexological discourse, but is also inter-
pretable through the lens of Foucauldian notions of polyvalence and
proliferation – during and beyond the late nineteenth century. In fact,

such generative potential has been pointed out in a supple reading by M. Kellen Williams, which departs from Showalter's in examining "how Hyde's indeterminacy works in relation to Stevenson's own contestation of the shared affinities between realist tactics of representation and late-nineteenth century medical and scientific configurations of social and sexual deviance" ("Designating Deviance" 413). Williams argues persuasively that "Hyde's capacity for eluding language is precisely what makes him so outstanding a menace" (417). For Williams, "Hyde's deviance [which] doesn't seem to make itself linguistically available" (421), is part of a social context that listens eagerly to the descriptions of the indescribable: "rather than representing his deviance, the tale in fact disperses and multiplies it" (416). We are never told directly what Hyde's crimes consist of, but we do know that the variability and transgressive potential inherent in Jekyll is that potentially of all human subjects. The tale suggests rather emphatically that there may be "something queer about" all of us (*Dr. Jekyll* 68), that we all live in some form and fashion on "Queer Street" (33).

As discussed earlier, Foucault's major point in his introductory section to the first volume of *The History of Sexuality* – entitled "We 'Other Victorians'" – is that the Freudian model of "repression" – as widely circulated and subscribed to as it is – is wholly inadequate (though also not wholly erroneous). Thus to embark on a Foucauldian, "queer" reading of *Dr. Jekyll and Mr. Hyde* would not be to reject necessarily the tale's reflection of and contributions to late Victorian notions of repression, but it would be to recognize at once that the tale participates in a dynamic of voluble discussion of sexuality and deviance that belies any theoretical model dependent upon the idea of Victorian "silence" or "prudishness." Foucault writes:

> [It] is not a matter of saying that sexuality, far from being repressed in capitalist and bourgeois societies, has on the contrary benefited from a regime of unchanging liberty; nor is it a matter of saying that power in societies such as ours is more tolerant than repressive. . . .
>
> I do not claim that sex has not been prohibited or barred or masked or misapprehended since the classical age; nor do I even assert that it has suffered these things any less from that period on than before. I do not maintain that the prohibition of sex is a ruse; but it is a ruse to make prohibition into the basic and constitutive element from which one would be able to write the history of what

has been said concerning sex starting from the modern epoch.
(10–12)

Here as always, a queer reading would emphasize "both/and" rather
than "either/or" in its perspective on a text and that text's contextual
imbrication and effects. And even "both/and" too simplistically
encodes duality, when, in fact, multiplicity – "and" and "and" and
"and" – might be the more supple and queerly appropriate paradigm
here.

Let us glance then at a few of those multiplicities. As mentioned
earlier, the tale only hints at the many perverse activities of Hyde. In
Jekyll's own recounting,

> This familiar that I called out of my own soul, and sent forth alone to
> do his good pleasure, was a being inherently malign and villainous;
> his every act and thought centred on self; drinking pleasure with
> bestial avidity from any degree of torture to another; relentless like a
> man of stone. . . . Into the details of the infamy at which I thus
> connived (for even now I can scarce grant that I committed it) I have
> no design of entering.   (86–7)

Bestial avidity, infamy, silence. The story remains tantalizing in its
withholding of "details." Yet Foucault again queers our perspective on
that dynamic, reminding us that

> Silence itself – the things one declines to say, or is forbidden to name,
> the discretion that is required between different speakers – is less the
> absolute limit of discourse, the other side from which it is separated
> by a strict boundary, than an element that functions alongside the
> things said, with them and in relation to them within over-all strate-
> gies. There is no binary division to be made between what one says
> and what one does not say; we must try to determine the different
> ways of not saying such things. . . . There is not one but many
> silences. . . .   (*History of Sexuality* 27)

In declining to enter into details, Jekyll is not simply participating in a
silence "about" homosexuality, however much the gay or gay-affirm-
ing critic may wish to read homosexuality into/out of the text (and
certainly there is evidence to support such a reading, as Showalter
demonstrates). In fact, Jekyll's silence does not "repress" meaning at
all, rather it proliferates possible meanings. The indescribable nature

of Hyde's indulgences and pleasure-seekings is open fully to any reader's wishes or desires for (among other possibilities) scapegoating, validation, or castigation. Whether Hyde goes out at night to indulge desires for murder or opium use, or for sex with men, prostitutes, animals, vegetables, or baked goods before they are sold at market the next morning – indeed in any form of perversity imagined or unimagined in Krafft-Ebing's *Psychopathia Sexualis* – the text's silence allows for the possibility. In offering blanks which the reader must fill in, the variety of infamies is as various as those among all readers.

Certainly the lawyer, commentator, investigator Mr. Utterson – whose perspectives dominate the narrative – is one reader/viewer/voyeur who fills in those blanks to meet his own needs and desires. And this is one reason why "homosexuality" is read into the text so often. Utterson offers titillating clues to what might happen if something let loose his own Hyde. He has a dream in which

> he would see a room in a rich house, where his friend lay asleep, dreaming and smiling at his dreams; and then the door of that room would be opened, the curtains of the bed plucked apart, the sleeper recalled, and, lo! there would stand by his side a figure to whom power was given, and even at that dead hour he must rise and do its bidding.   (37)

We know almost nothing about Jekyll-and-Hyde's terrible activities and transgressive desires, but do know that Utterson dreams of men and beds and having the power to make a man in a bed do one's bidding (or having a man tell one what to do while one is in bed). But that, of course, is only one possibility among many that a Hyde-like individual might indulge in.

Yet if Utterson's ill-concealed, homoerotic desires do structure so many readings and responses to the text, there is certainly good reason for that fact. His is the vision and perspective with which the reader is most often in contact, is the touchstone against which Hyde's horrors are held in implicit contrast. Yet at the same time, it is hardly one to which the tale simply lends its unequivocal support. Indeed, as easy as it has been for critics to see the tale as structured thematically around the binary of Jekyll/Hyde, we might explore queerly what happens when we replace "Jekyll" with "Utterson" in that hierarchized binary, and conflate Jekyll-and-Hyde into the same person (for they are, of course). Such a queer recasting of tension reveals much about a process of potential proliferation and social destabilization enacted in/through the tale. While in some ways the story can be read as a moralizing exploration of the contrast between a "self-centred" Hyde (as quoted above) and a socially benevolent Utterson, in fact, we see that the latter desperately needs the former to center him/his "self."

We are told from the tale's opening line that Utterson, "the lawyer," is "lean, long, dusty, [and] dreary" (29). In the same paragraph we discover that he "was austere with himself," and

> had an approved tolerance for others; sometimes wondering, almost with envy, at the high pressure of spirits involved in their misdeeds; and in any extremity inclined to help rather than to reprove. . . . In this character it was frequently his fortune to be the last reputable acquaintance and the last good influence in the lives of down-going men.   (29)

He is clearly cast as a normalizing influence, not only the center of the narrative but also a (would-be) centering influence on others. But what has received little attention is the fact that he is also obviously a wholly ineffective influence, given his explicitly noted history of inter-actions with "down-going men" and lack of any impact on Jekyll-and-Hyde. If Utterson is the dusty, dreary "norm" and Jekyll-and-Hyde the queer and various "other," what does this tale reveal about the power, fixity, and stability of the "normal" self?

The "wondering," envious Utterson uses – and may, in fact, desper-ately need – his succession of "down-going" acquaintances to keep himself "up," to fix and delimit temporarily his own sense of normal selfhood, even as this dynamic reveals a very fragile construction. Post-structuralists generally would read the glorified first term of a hierarchized binary as inherently unstable, fixed only, and only temporarily, through an insistence on the degraded nature of the second term (whether that term is "woman," "black," or "homosex-ual"). Utterson "frequents" down-going men, ending with Jekyll-and-Hyde, as he over and over again inflates himself – reassures, reasserts, and stabilizes meaning (though certainly we would not want to read "down-going" as "going down on" – giving oral sex to – which opens up intriguing but anachronistic interpretive possibilities). Even though the tale attributes this activity to benevolence, it is productive to read the repetition as constituting a late Victorian enactment of a dynamic we explored in Chapter 2 in our discussion of Judith Butler's theories: of repeated performance and underlying fragility, of the "norm" needing again and again to instantiate itself and prove its "reality." Eve Sedgwick, among many others, has pointed out that the tale explores the seductiveness and degradation of Jekyll's substance abuse, arguing that "drug addiction is both a camouflage and an expression for the dynamics of male same-sex desire and its prohibition" (*Tendencies* 135). But Utterson too could be read as addicted to his queer men and a certain eager voyeurism concerning their lives. Indeed, his frequenting of Jekyll-and-Hyde and other degraded men actually reveals more about him and what he stands for, than them and their otherwise dismissible, idiosyncratic antics and deviancies. If *Dr. Jekyll and Mr. Hyde* is a tale concerning one drug-addicted sociopath then it is certainly interesting and spooky, but if it is a tale about how such abnormality underlies all human behavior and has the potential always to proliferate, then of course it is much more unsettling and revealing.

And that is the point, of course, of psychoanalytic readings of the text, which again see Hyde as the "id" that underlies the veneer of social control. But my own queer point here has to do with processes and interactions between as well as within individuals. Certainly it is intriguing that Jekyll finally loses control over Hyde, but Utterson appears to need such queer men to stabilize himself – his self – over and over again because he is already thoroughly queer. Though we are told that he is a "lover of the sane and customary sides of life, to whom the fanciful was the immodest" (35), his own thoughts reveal otherwise, as he lingers over Hyde's "black secrets.... It turns me quite cold to think of this creature stealing like a thief to Harry's bedside" (42). "[T]he face of Hyde sat heavy in his memory" (41):

> Mr. Hyde was pale and dwarfish; he gave an impression of deformity without any namable malformation. . . . – all these were points against him; but not all of these together could explain the hitherto unknown disgust, loathing and fear with which Utterson regarded him. "There must be something else," said the perplexed gentleman. "There *is* something more, if I could find a name for it." (40)

This unnamable, which is emphasized time and again, raises an interesting series of half-thoughts in Utterson:

> And the lawyer . . . brooded awhile on his own past, groping in all the
> corners of memory, lest by chance some Jack-in-the-Box of an old
> iniquity should leap to light there. His past was fairly blameless; few
> men could read the rolls of their life with less apprehension; yet he
> was humbled to the dust by the many ill things he had done, and
> raised up again into a sober and fearful gratitude by the many that he
> had come so near to doing, yet avoided.   (41–2)

That nearness of doing the same, the lingering possibility of the
Hyde within himself, of the unnamable, of the queer, helps the queer
reader account not only for Utterson's "disgust," but also for the
perpetuation of homophobia and other normalizing social power
dynamics over time. Indeed, given the fact that Utterson – the hypocritical oppressor and repressor – represents explicitly "the law," we
see immediately how and why that "law" must seek out, investigate,
and judge transgressors to reify itself repeatedly. Inherent instability
and continuing queer possibility must be held at bay through violent
outward action.

And that queer "threat" to normality is nowhere rendered more
apparent than in the death of Dr. Lanyon. His proximity to Utterson is
made clear, for the two "were old friends, old mates both at school
and college, both thorough respecters of themselves and of each
other, and, what does not always follow, men who thoroughly enjoyed
each other's company" (36). If their "normal" homosocial bonding
always carries within it the seed and unnerving potential of the homosexual (which is Sedgwick's broad thesis in *Between Men*), then
certainly an overt manifestation of the queer bursting forth from the
normal would be particularly unsettling. Indeed, when Lanyon sees,
firsthand, that his friend Jekyll is in fact able to metamorphose from
and into the lascivious Hyde with the quaff of a drink, that the two are
one and the same, the proof of such queer inherence quickly kills him:
"My life is shaken to its roots; sleep has left me; the deadliest terror
sits by me at all hours of the day and night; I feel that my days are
numbered, and that I must die" (80). And equally intriguing is the fact
that Jekyll-and-Hyde's own narrative ends the tale as a whole. We
know that Utterson is reading it, but there is no frame to indicate his
reaction, only the silence of the end of the tale. Does Utterson himself
survive the revelations of Jekyll-and-Hyde? We cannot know, but the
indications are that the dusty, dreary norm is easily shaken by proof
of its own queer potentiality, shaken even to death.

And it is that thoroughly unsettling dynamic that might be of great-est interest in a queer reading. While the murderous confrontation between Hyde and the old man, Sir Danvers Carew, is hardly one to celebrate, it certainly points to a deadly struggle among social forces, when the Uttersons of the world are so intent on using others for their own purposes. The elderly Member of Parliament who accosts the other "with a very pretty manner of politeness," full of "old-world kindness" (46) is a clear representative of "maturity," "propriety," and, of course, the governmental system. The "younger," and clearly improper and ungoverned, Hyde is infuriated by the old gentleman, breaks "out of all bounds," clubs him to death, and wildy tramples the body. This queer, furious eruption of violence against an embodiment of everything normal, controlled, and proper is certainly meant to shock and disturb, as it does everyone in the tale, but might also be read as pointing toward confrontations in the twentieth century between a hypocritical "normal" society and angry queer radicals, refusing to "take" the bald and ubiquitous hypocrisy any more. Indeed, Hyde could be interpreted queerly as a raging member of a marginalized sector of society, haunting the parks at night, visiting unnamed dens of vice, and suffering always the judgments of men like Utterson and Carew. That he kills is hardly laudable or justifiable, but it is certainly as explainable as similar activities among oppressed and degraded groups in other contexts. Indeed, the question is never one of justification, but rather one of what social dynamics produce such fury and violence.

Indeed, blatantly oppressive forces engender multiple responses, and not all of them are laudable. This is true even in the tale's oft-explored interest in drug use. In Jekyll's own words, the potion that he takes shakes "the very fortress of identity" and opens up new possibilities:

> There was something strange in my sensations, something indescrib-ably new and, from its very novelty, incredibly sweet. I felt younger, lighter, happier in body; within I was conscious of a heady reckless-ness, a current of disordered sensual images running like a mill race in my fancy, a solution of the bonds of obligation, an unknown but not an innocent freedom of the soul.   (83)

While I would not want to promote or apologize for substance addiction, and agree with Sedgwick's point about the pathologizing of homosexuality though its connection to drug use in the tale, we can still understand the lure of intoxication and all such temporary escapes from the bondage of constricted, controlled identity when social forces are so dusty and dreary. Like the violence manifested in the text, its representation of addiction can help us trace down some fundamental social inequities. Yes, alcoholism, drug abuse, and other potentially self-destructive activities are widespread among oppressed groups (including queers), but it is important to ask what broad social forces make that route the only mechanism for escaping the confines of "normal," day-to-day existence. The problem is the narrowness of the norm; addiction itself is only a symptom.

Thus to recognize in this text a Foucauldian, polyvalent potential is to see in its classification of queer evil in Hyde a possible starting-point for resistance. As Foucault notes,

> There is no question that the appearance in nineteenth-century psychiatry, jurisprudence, and literature of a whole series of discourses on the species and subspecies of homosexuality, inversion, pederasty, and "psychic hermaphrodism" made possible a strong advance of social controls into this area of "perversity"; but it also made possible the formation of a "reverse" discourse: homosexuality began to speak in its own behalf, to demand that its legitimacy or "naturality" be acknowledged, often in the same vocabulary, using the same categories by which it was medically disqualified. There is not, on the one side, a discourse of power, and opposite it, another discourse that runs counter to it. Discourses are tactical elements or blocks operating in the field of force relations. . . .   (101–2)

Thus in shameless ways, a queer reading might work to do exactly what Foucault points to above. The queer reader/critic cannot change – and must acknowledge – the discourse on Jekyll-and-Hyde presented by the tale. In my reading, I am as constrained by the words on the page as other critics, but I can use those words differently and abrasively vis-à-vis the interests represented by the moralizing of the text and its characters. In seeing this tale of hidden, barely hinted-at subcultures and a legal system intent on tracing down abnormality and bringing it to light and justice, of men like Utterson who are full of queer desires but eager to punish those who act on desires (a nineteenth-century J. Edgar Hoover, we might say), and of violent response to the hypocrisy of such men of the era, as one of queer potential for challenge and change, this reading is not arguing for a particular action plan. Nor is it seeing such challenge and change as easy to effect. But the fact that Jekyll-and-Hyde die at the end of the tale also does not point to easy closure, which is why it continues to thrill and interest readers even today. We receive tantalizing hints that there is a hidden, unnamed subculture that Hyde has been visiting every night, vices that he has been participating in with others (his "strange associates" [56] in the words of the tale), that persist even past his death. Urban London in 1886 already presented possibilities for anonymous, transgressive existence, which clearly elicited concern, investigation, and (in and through the text) condemnation. Thus even though the Stonewall Riots were over 80 years away, this tale hints that there was already a marginalized urban population and, perhaps, a slowly simmering rage against normality that would one day burst forth. I opened this chapter by saying that proximity breeds change. Indeed, geographical proximity means that intellectual, behavioral, or in this case libidinal proximity can become startlingly clear. When an eagerly moralizing (though secretly, inherently queer) Utterson/Carew meets up with a blatantly "immoral" (defiantly queer) Hyde, dynamism – not stasis – is the result.

Thus the queer multiplicities of this tale abound, over and beyond the clear implication that there is more than one "self" to any of us. That synchronic multiplicity inherent within the constrictions of normal social selfhood and the tale's implication of diachronic mutability (with the aid of a magical potion or powder) serve as powerful disturbances to the rigid classification systems of the late Victorian era. And, of course, the Freudian emphasis on the structure of human consciousness, with its Hyde-like "id" and necessary, controlling "super-ego" is itself a classification system that works in the service of contextual notions of propriety and normality. That is why queer readings, while never untouched or unaffected by the classification systems of the text, would challenge or at least react skeptically to the "reality" of those at work within it. If we read Utterson's law-driven inquiry into Jekyll's private affairs as a method of surveillance and control, then certainly a quasi-Freudian probing and delineation of health and normality is not necessarily less restrictive, only differently so. A queer reading would question aggressively the "self"-assurance of all such systems of categorization and social ordering.

Obviously, the tracings and provocations above are just a few of the many queer possibilities suggested in and through *Dr. Jekyll and Mr.*

Hyde. Many others will no doubt occur to you, as you interact with the text and your own context of reading and research. Jekyll refers to Hyde "alone, in the ranks of mankind, [as] pure evil" (85). To be sure, that is the contextually approved response, with Lanyon and Jekyll representing the scientific/medical establishment and Utterson the law, all in full agreement. But that textual/contextual classification need not be ours. The queered self of Jekyll-and-Hyde – both internally various and socially transgressive – is compelling for what it reveals about hypocrisy and insufficiency of the "austere" norm. Indeed, Jekyll-and-Hyde continue to thrill and appeal to us because Utterson and Lanyon are so very unappealing when offered as points of comparison. And the fact that Utterson and Hyde operate as extremes – spurious ones at that – certainly challenges the queer reader to imagine alternatives that are neither murderous nor imperiously moralizing. As I will continue to explore in the next and final chapters, the binaries of the text and its context do not have to be ours if we choose to read queerly.

A Query

So is there a "queer" ethics or is that phrase an oxymoron? In other words, when we challenge the "norm" and confront its advocates, when we repudiate "essential" values and definitions, are we led inevitably to wholesale chaos, murder, and mayhem, as Hyde enacts? Or is there a possibility for imagining a supple, interpersonal sense of responsibility that at once minimizes "normalization" and at the same time allows for continued exploration and various enactments of desire and selfhood? These are questions well worth musing on, for certainly one of the most common charges against lesbians, gays, and self-styled queers, is that their activities portend or would bring about the collapse of civil society, that their "self"-indulgence leads to a free-for-all that means anything goes, including (in some conservatives' wild imaginings) widespread riot, rape, and slaughter.

The question of "ethics" is always controversial, of course, for any call to think first of the needs of other human beings is open to a charge of conservative, status-quo-reinforcing restriction. Identity politics demand a certain recognition and validation of self-interest. And certainly if one speaks of a common social "obligation" that moderates or necessarily offsets individualized action and desire then one does run the risk of setting up a transcendent ideal of "good," something that post-structuralist theory treats with fundamental and thorough skepticism.

Yet I would argue that critically assumed conventions do not mean necessarily uninterrogated transcendent notions. Even the most skeptical post-structuralist uses (perhaps strategically and self-consciously) certain social conventions – of language, of copyright, of traffic laws, of passport requirements – while retaining a critical stance toward the motivations behind, and consequences of, such systems of social interaction and normalization. We do not exist within – do not have to interpret our existence by way of – a facile binary of "conformity/anarchy," as much as those who wish only to enforce the former may wish to scare us into believing that it is an either/or situation. It is possible to use strategic notions of inter-personal responsibility to achieve and even further a measure of health and well-being among disparate and diverse groups of people without locking ourselves into narrow and traditional forms of "morality."

The late-twentieth century philosopher Emmanuel Levinas points us in an interesting and useful direction. I have explored this topic before in a brief dialogue published in the journal *Victorian Poetry* in 2000 and I wish to reiterate some of my points here. While queers and other oppressed individuals may well wish to question Levinas's pointed emphasis on self-sacrifice for the "other" as the bedrock of ethical behavior (given that oppressors would be all too willing for queers and others to sacrifice themselves for the "good" of society), at the very least we must recognize a placing of concern for others – within or without a queer community – as a prime ethical considera-tion always potentially restricting and certainly rendering problem-atic any self-willed desire or selfish action. Levinas suggests in "Ethics of the Infinite":

> For me, the freedom of the subject is not the highest or primary value. The heteronomy of our response to the human other . . . precedes the autonomy of our subjective freedom. As soon as I acknowledge that it is "I" who am responsible, I accept that my freedom is anteceded by an obligation to the other. Ethics redefines subjectivity as this heteronymous responsibility in contrast to autonomous freedom.   (192)

In Levinas's words, "I become a responsible or ethical 'I' to the extent that I agree to depose or dethrone myself – to abdicate my position of centrality – in favour of the vulnerable other" (192). This emphasis on responsibility does not mean sacrificing or martyring oneself, but it does mean always complicating one's activities by recognizing one's interpersonal ties. Rebellious action and anguished, even violent, reactions may be discretely necessary, but certainly they must be problematized – critically engaged – in and through an ethical self-conceptualization.

Here, as elsewhere, we are under no compulsion to accept any construct wholly and uncritically, even if we find some of Levinas's reminders very useful. Seyla Benhabib in *Situating the Self* argues for an ethical model that is "reflexive, it allows the non-dogmatic questioning of its own presuppositions; it is pluralistic and tolerant, in that it promotes the coexistence of all ways of life compatible with the acceptable of a framework of universal life and justice" (45–6). Behabib and other postmodern ethicists define "ethics" in explicit ways as an aggressive practice of questioning and self-questioning, a repudiation of the validity of universal maxims and reliance upon unilateral power, but with an allowance still of limits on the self and its enactments of desire and self-centered interest.

Indeed, a queer emphasis on variety, multiplicity, and aggressive questioning can include – I would argue, must include – points of reference and responsibility outside of self-interest. Thus postmodern ethicist Zygmunt Bauman disagrees with those commentators who complain about the death of morality today; he says, instead, that:

> One might say that postmodernity is an "era of morality". . . . It is possible now, nay inevitable, to face the moral issues point-blank, in all their naked truth, as they emerge from the life experience of men and women, and as they confront moral selves in all their irreparable and irredeemable ambivalence. . . . It is only now that actions appear to the moral selves as matters of responsible choice. . . . The denizens of the postmodern era are, so to speak, forced to stand face-to-face with their moral autonomy, and so also with their moral responsibility. This is the cause of moral agony. This is also the chance the moral selves never confronted before.   (*Life in Fragments* 42–3).

This excruciatingly difficult, yet intellectually riveting and compelling, moral labor is one of the greatest challenges facing queer theorists and activists today. It drives queer theory to self-critique as well as to critique others, and to remain vigilant so as never to set up its own narrow and normalizing practices that disallow variety or condone violence against others who exist in a state of variance or dissent. Mr. Hyde is neither a role model nor is he an inevitability. Queers can haunt dens of "vice" that would appall some Utterson-like commentators, they can explore their multiple selves wildly and exuberantly, they can even experiment with intoxication in a variety of ways, but they do not necessarily kill old men or run down children. After careful consideration, *Dr. Jekyll and Mr. Hyde*'s moralizing warnings are, finally, queerly dispensable, for there is no reason why there cannot be a queer ethics of conjoined concern and resistance.

6 Reading for Excess: The Queer Texts of *Orlando*, *Giovanni's Room*, and *The Color Purple*

In this last chapter of readings, I want to suggest an analytical category that may be of use to students interested in deploying the "queer theories" discussed earlier. In raising the possibility of the rubric of the "queer text" I want to remind (and, of course, remember) that it is just as vital to discuss always the limitations of such a rubric (and, indeed, the project of rubric-building), as it is to discuss its parameters and utilities. Even so, delimitations, thoughtfully explored and (self-)critically assumed allow for discrete interventions and powerful, because carefully circumscribed, arguments and interpretations. As I have suggested throughout this book, "queer" is not chaos; it is always implicated within and impacted by surrounding definitions, norms, and rules of engagement. Yet it – *we* – can certainly question and abrade those definitions, norms, and rules forthrightly and with overt (and covert) political intent.

Thus to explore thoughtfully here the rubric of the "queer text" is neither to suggest a hard and fast distinction nor a set of litmus tests. All texts have certain queer internal aspects, traces, and resonances, and, of course, all texts can be used "queerly" by any reader or set of readers who wish to do so. Thus nowhere in this chapter or book am I arguing for a new "queer" canon. My purposes are much more open-ended than that. What I will do in the coming pages is point to a few texts that have characteristics clearly amenable to queer analysis as this book defines that type of inquiry, ones in which substantial evidence exists that might make a particular text attractive and readily available to students interested in pursuing such work. In doing so, this discussion should help students locate other provocative texts with which to pursue their own queer projects.

The title of this chapter points to "excess" as a quality that one might look for in a "queer" text. Yet many texts could be considered "excessive" in wording, imagery, or sexual representations, and have little connection to the "queer theories" discussed in this book. It is a particular type of "excess" that I will focus on in the coming pages: that which complicates the binary of heterosexuality/homosexuality (and below I explore how *Orlando, Giovanni's Room,* and *The Color Purple* are, indeed, "excessive" in this regard). If, as I have suggested throughout preceding chapters, "queer theories" are themselves positioned abrasively toward notions of the normal – and specifically tendentious categories of "normal sexuality" – a "queer text," as I am defining it here, would provide evidence of the limitations, exclusions, and biases inherent within the process of delimiting sexual normality. Many texts do so, which is why critics so often and profitably "queer" texts that may or may not have an *explicit* theme that is wholly supportive of such queer work. Indeed, the "queering" of ostensibly "straight" texts is particularly important from a critical and political perspective for it helps locate the always inherent instabilities at work within processes of identity formation and performance.

Yet the queer interests of this chapter are more narrowly circumscribed, for the most pervasive organizing principle at work today in our notions of "normal" sexual identity is that of the heterosexual/homosexual binary which arose during the second half of the nineteenth century. And while much lesbian/gay and even some self-styled "queer" analysis has attempted aggressively to challenge the hierarchized nature of that binary (specifically, the clear and often violently enforced degraded status accorded the second part of the conjoined term), too little critical activity has been focused on resisting, repudiating, or even aggressively questioning the binary itself, however one might reweigh its value ascriptions.

Certainly there are ample opportunities to do so. Once you begin looking for relevant textual evidence, it is really not difficult at all to locate texts that explicitly or implicitly denaturalize notions of sexual normality and that provide evidence of the mutability and variability of human sexual desire and performance in excess of the hetero/homo binary. Such "queer" texts offer characters, themes, plot situations, narratorial expressions, and symbolic representations that undermine the fixed, "natural" status of the identifiers "heterosexual" and "homosexual," and thereby expose the reductiveness and constructedness of binarily defined sexual identity, "orientation," and/or classification systems. Yet whatever a text may express or expose, your work as a reader/critic is equally important, for clearly a "queer text" must be met with a corresponding "queer reading" or "queer interpretive" practice or it is easily recuperated back within the very binaries that it abrades. And that is why, as I indicated in my introduction to this book, my desire to "queer" you is a particularly urgent one. In helping to foster and support queer reading and interpretive practices, in working to realize more fully the potential of often abstract "queer theories" as described earlier, I want to proliferate a form of queer work that I believe is vital and intellectually dynamic, one that invites innumerable queer possibilities rather than describes or delimits any single, simple queer telos (a fixed image or narrowly defined form of social/sexual liberation).

Yet at the same time, and in a way that demands acknowledgement, this does mean being purposefully exclusive in our discussion. To focus on the queer text in its work on sexual epistemology and ontology is often to repress its meanings regarding other aspects of identity – racial, national, class-related, and even at times gendered. Yet our "inside/outside" move as described in my introduction means that it is possible to reflect on those exclusions and acknowledge resonances among identities and social positionings, even as those exclusions are clearly necessary for cogent and compelling analysis. We cannot all do all forms of socially progressive or radical work at all times. We choose our limits and projects even as we might always more carefully see those choices *as* choices that are neither "natural" nor more valuable than ones that others might make.

Indeed, other critics have suggested rubrics that are similar (though differently inflected), ones that students may wish to examine as they construct their own interpretations and analyses. Particularly relevant here is Jonathan Dollimore's supple theory of "dissidence" and his concern with

> several of the binaries which powerfully organize our cultures: natural/unnatural, masculine/feminine, hetero/homosexuality; with what hold[s] them in place socially, and what is necessarily disavowed in their political effectiveness – with, in other words, what

enables them to endure and yet also renders them unstable.   (*Sexual Dissidence* 65)

Alan Sinfield, adding his own inflection to this concept, describes the "dissident text" as one that "may embarrass the dominant by appropriating its concepts and imagery" but that also implies a "refusal of an aspect of the dominant, without prejudging an outcome" (*Faultlines* 48–9). Indeed, Dollimore turns even more directly to the hetero/homo binary in his *Sex, Literature and Censorship.* Imagining in oblique fashion a possible future in which what "will seem strangest of all is our current obsessive binary division between heterosexual and homosexual: the classification of people according to the sex/gender of their partners, or desired partners" (18), he goes on to decry the failures of sexuality-related theories generally to address adequately the "terrifying *mutability* of desire" (56), and to point out many other lapses. I certainly echo that concern, and hope to confront the issue directly in the coming pages. Indeed, as intriguing as Dollimore's dissidence model is, its meta-theoretical, even meta-social, aspirations do deflate its use value in attacking the binary that he so accurately pinpoints above as ubiquitous. Thus my advice always to the present book's readers concerning the theories of Dollimore (as well as those of Butler, Warner, and others) is to take them and apply them aggressively and brashly. If a queer text provides us with an evidence base for provocation and change, then it is our responsibility to use it appropriately rather than linger simply in the omissions or the missed chances of others.

So how might we identify a "queer text" and also approach it in appropriately queer fashion? In looking at a novel such as Virginia Woolf's *Orlando* from 1928 and asking to what extent it is "queer," the first question that arises concerns the extent to which it foregrounds identity and desire as static, naturally occurring, and firmly fixed, or mutable, contingent, even arbitrary. In that regard it is a very queer text indeed, even when we limit our definition of text to the print document of the novel and not that of its author's biography (thus the often-discussed queerness of Woolf – and Baldwin later – is intriguing but beside the point of this book's specifically post-Barthean perspective). In fact, *Orlando* highlights the synchronic multiplicity, the historical contingency, and the diachronic mutability of selfhood as its major thematic concerns. Thus in its last pages, long after its title character has abruptly changed biological sex and lived through centuries of historical changes, the narrator writes that

> if there are (at a venture) seventy-six different times all ticking in the mind at once, how many different people are there not – Heaven help us – all having lodgment at one time or another in the human spirit? Some say two thousand and fifty-two. . . . [T]hese selves of which we are built up, one on top of another, as plates are piled on a waiter's hand, have attachments elsewhere, sympathies, little constitutions and rights of their own, call them what you will (and for many of these things there is no name) so that one will only come if it is raining, another in a room with green curtains, another when Mrs. Jones is not there, another if you can promise it a glass of wine – and so on; for everybody can multiply from his own experience the different terms which his different selves have made with him – and some are too wildly ridiculous to be mentioned in print at all.   (308–9)

If we examine this passage closely, we find a remarkable series of reflections on selfhood, even before we come (in the paragraph that follows the above) to some specific reflections upon Orlando's own varied and various selfhood. While the text indicates that there are vast numbers of possible selves within every human being, our own agency over those selves is quite limited; all are contingent and dependent to some extent upon contextual circumstances. At the same time, and even if one's ability to call forth a specific self is questionable, this passage implies clearly that there remains always the possibility of active reflection upon selfhood, its variety and its interconnectivity, which is, to my mind, some of the most compelling work that queer theories today can perform. Such critical self-reflection is not perfectly realizable, of course; the thinking "self" or "selves" cannot know it/themselves with clarity and absolute precision, as we will see in a moment, but the ability to denaturalize selfhood and render it multiple should not be discounted as a major intellectual, critical feat.

But the necessity for a queer dialogism, for an active give and take upon selfhood beyond the reflecting "I" is indicated clearly in the passage following immediately upon the one above. Here as always, a queer text must be met always with an equally queer reading practice that does not fail to challenge the text's own exclusions and blindspots. As Orlando attempts to call forth "Orlando" – asking "who am I?" – we find that

> she had a great variety of selves to call upon, far more than we have
> been able to find room for, since a biography is considered complete
> if it merely accounts for six or seven selves, whereas a person may
> well have as many thousand. Choosing then, only those selves we
> have found room for, Orlando may now have called on the boy who
> cut the nigger's head down; the boy who strung it up again; the boy
> who sat on the hill; ... or she may have wanted the woman to come to
> her; the Gypsy; the Fine Lady; the Hermit; the girl in love with life; the
> Patroness of Letters. . . .   (309)

Granted, as the text tells us, "all of these selves were different and she
may have called upon any one of them" (310), still not one of those
selves would likely have challenged the grotesque insensitivity of the
representation (from the text's first pages) of a Moor's ("nigger's")
head being hung from the rafters and being batted about as a game.
Yes, we are told,

> Orlando was strangely compounded of many humours – of melan-
> choly, of indolence, of passion, of love of solitude, to say nothing of
> all those contortions and subtleties of temper which were indicated
> on the first page, when he slashed at a dead nigger's head; cut it
> down, hung it chivalrously out of his reach again and then betook
> himself to the window-seat with a book.   (73)

But other disruptive and oblique (from the perspective of the novel)
voices are needed to challenge the limitations of the text's own representations. The Anglo-centrism, class, and racial biases, inherent in
these and other passages throughout the text (including scenes "with
the Gypsies") are not ones to lead to some blanket condemnation of
the text as simply racist (or any other single thing), but they do point
immediately to the limitations of any one thinking "self" or conglomeration of "selves" (even Woolf's) in its/their ability to self-critique
and challenge its/their own standpoint epistemology. I have had
numerous students point out immediately the underlying racism of
some of Woolf's passages. Only by openly and energetically exchang-
ing those perspectives on selfhood(s) and the inevitable insensitivities
of the inevitably limited self can we acquire greater critical knowledge
of our (perhaps many connected) selves.

And this is in no way to denigrate the intellectual achievement of
Woolf in and through *Orlando*. It is a remarkable text in its exploration of the impact of historical context and even historically specific

clothing on gendered, and sexually inflected, performance. Indeed, the text opens with the scene of the batting of the head of the Moor as a way of reflecting in its own way upon a certain thoughtlessly self-confident performance of masculinity, one that is complicated over time and, of course, as Orlando changes sex (which leads Jaime Hovey, perhaps over-generously, to term the early scenes a "sarcastic rendering of . . . racialized masculinity" [398]). Orlando is discursively programmed, we might say, in a remarkable variety of ways, as a man, as a woman, later as an expatriate, and, as the Renaissance is succeeded by other ages, with widely varying expectations of "proper" gender performances. And pertinent to our analysis is the fact that the ambiguity that often surrounds the transsexual Orlando certainly complicates any notion of fixed sexual orientation or evocation of desire(s) for and from others. Thus Hovey suggests, "The theatrical, campy staging of the protagonist's gender mutability . . . points to performativity and queerness" (399). Indeed, at one point Orlando, the man,

> beheld . . . a figure, which, whether boy's or woman's, for the loose tunic and trousers of the Russian fashion served to disguise the sex, filled him with the highest curiosity. The person, whatever the name or sex, was about middle height, very slenderly fashioned, and dressed entirely in oyster-coloured velvet, trimmed with some unfamiliar greenish-coloured fur. But these details were obscured by the extraordinary seductiveness which issued from the whole person. (37)

Since much of sociosexual conditioning and reception depend upon clothing in this text, when that clothing is ambiguous the possibility of desires that exceed heterosexuality are raised in tantalizing fashion. Critic Adam Parkes points out that "the process of theatrical self-transformation offers potential freedom from the historically assigned social roles which often censor present and future possibilities" ("Lesbianism, History, and Censorship" 451). And Elizabeth Meese has argued more pointedly that "Androgyny [in *Orlando*] is a way out of the either/or trap through substitution of a both/and relationship" ("When Virginia Looked at Vita" 104). Thus the text raises queerly (and in ways students may wish to explore aggressively) the possibility that our desires are piqued, perhaps even determined, by "gender," not biological "sex," that we react erotically to the surface trappings of self-presentation in ways that exceed (and therefore call into question) any necessarily fixed reactions to biological difference. Students might explore how ambiguous genders and gender performances in *Orlando* point to different explanations for why we feel desire when seeing another person. *Orlando* suggests that our erotic response may be to the most superficial forms of gender presentation, not to genitalia or other biological differences that account for our assignment to a specific biological sex.

And indeed, when Orlando is living in Constantinople, we are told, "he possessed, now that he was in the prime of life, the power to stir the fancy and rivet the eye. . . . He became the adored of many women and some men" (124–5). Compelling personal attributes and powerful performances raise the possibility of evoking both homosexual and heterosexual desire, though the novel certainly remains clear in its commitments only to representations of explicit expressions of piqued desire within a heterosexual context, however Orlando's biological sex may vary. Here, as elsewhere, this text from 1928 reflects its own historical context and that context's limitations on the explicit representation of homosexuality. We cannot demand that it be other than what it is.

Yet what "it is" is certainly queer in its own way. Christy Burns (in "Re-Dressing Feminist Identities") has argued that *Orlando* "informatively examines the tensions between notions of *essential* personal identity and *contextually re-defined* subjectivity" (344), without ever resolving those tensions. The text straddles both multiplicity and unity of selfhood; without ever indicating that there is an *essential* self, it still argues that selfhood is synchronically coherent and has continuing diachronic aspects (after all, this is not a novel about multiple personality disorder or schizophrenia). At the text's end,

> when she had ceased to call "Orlando" and was deep in thoughts of something else ... the Orlando whom she had called came of its own accord. . . .
>
> The whole of her darkened and settled, as when some foil whose addition makes the round and solidity of a surface is added to it, and the shallow becomes deep and the near distant; and all is contained as water is contained by the sides of a well. So she was now darkened, stilled, and become, with the addition of this Orlando, what is called, rightly or wrongly, a single self, a real self. And she fell silent. For it is probable that when people talk aloud, the selves (of which there may

be more than two thousand) are conscious of disseverment, and are
trying to communicate, but when communication is established
there is nothing more to be said.   (313–14)

This is a coherence that always contains multiplicity within and the
continuing possibility of internally disruptive communication. Yet the
metaphor of the "sides of the well" indicates clearly that such variability and fluidity is always bounded, is potentially very deep, but still
narrowly delimited and contained. Interestingly, this fluidity "within"
leads to the possibility of a certain responsiveness to variability in the
external world too, for in the state described above, Orlando takes in
avidly the variety of changeable nature: "All this, the trees, deer, and
turf, she observed with the greatest satisfaction as if her mind had
become a fluid that flowed round things and enclosed them
completely" (314). Indeed, this tension between a recognition of such
complexity and a desire to enclose it and make it understandable and
one's "own" is that between what Dollimore calls "terrifying mutability" and our continuing drive to order and fix. Our naturalized
hetero/homo binary is one manifestation of that very drive. Yet
certainly *Orlando* remains open to exploring such tensions, and this
queer state of openness – not epiphany, but exchange and change – is
key to this text's queer work of denaturalizing gender, sex, and sexuality, even as its clear, though often fragile, coherence renders its own
boundaries as noteworthy as its internal variety.

   That revelation of the mutability and contingency of sexual selfhood is the central characteristic of the "queer text" as I am defining it
here. James Baldwin's *Giovanni's Room* allows further exploration of
this rubric. Indeed, while Baldwin's text (when it is actually discussed
– and it is often simply ignored) has been read variously as a text
about its narrator's repressed homosexuality, about its own repression of racial difference (all of its characters are white), and about
confining American constructions of masculinity, I want to consider it
more specifically as a text about the tension between fixity and fluidity in sexuality. In this sense it is an exemplary "queer text."

   Certainly the few discussions to date of the novel's representation of
"bisexuality" come closest to recognizing this tension. Marjorie Garber
suggests that "Bisexuality functions in *Giovanni's Room* as a metaphor
for exile, for marginality, for not belonging" (*Vice Versa* 128). In it,
Brett Beemyn adds, "Baldwin sought to foster meanings that move
beyond narrow identity categories" ("Sexual and Gender Fluidity" 58).

Yet, rather than "fix" the novel in terms of a specific identity construct – bisexuality – that is not even mentioned in it, I want to reference a metaphor that does appear repeatedly in the novel, to make a case for its interest in a specifically queer mutability in sexual desire and a potential lack of fixity in sexual self-identification.

Clearly, the novel concerns two individuals – David and Giovanni – who are capable of maintaining physical, sexual relationships with both men and women, at different times in their lives and with different degrees of emotional satisfaction. Yet the chief difference between the two is how they process such diachronic variability. Its narrator, David, longs for fixity and socially sanctioned sexual identity. He refers repeatedly to a certain sense of "moored" identity that he hopes to find with women: "I supposed this is why I asked her to marry me: to give myself something to be moored to. Perhaps this was why, in Spain, she decided that she wanted to marry me. But people can't, unhappily, invent their mooring posts, their lovers, and their friends, anymore than they can invent their parents" (5). "Mooring" is an intriguing metaphor for sexual relationships and identity builiding, for inspite of David's wishes it indicates only a temporary fixity or anchorage in a general dynamic of movement and change. A mooring may be useful and even necessary at times, but is defined precisely because of its contrast to a continuing and defining state of motion. A "boat," let us say, is not a "boat" because it is moored, it is a boat because it generally floats and moves despite temporary moorings. David desires the impossible and his own activities reveal this quandary. His early sexual encounter with another boy, Joey, and the way that encounter haunts his sense of any fixed and socially sanctioned sexual definition, leads to his literal flight from America to Paris, "remaining, in effect, in constant motion" (20), as he enacts in literal fashion the un-mooredness that he remains terrified of both epistemologically and ontologically.

Indeed, it is revealing that David holds the highest contempt for individuals whom he identifies as fluid and unfixed. Thus "les folles," the cross-dressers of the bars that he visits in Paris, "turn" his stomach because of their lack of clear, moored definition. One such individual, whom he repeatedly terms "it," receives a verbal blast of David's scorn, but reveals accurately the payoff for David's own inflexibility and hypocrisy: "You will be very unhappy. Remember that I told you so" (40). David seeks a form of fixity that belies his own desires: "I wanted a woman to be for me a steady ground, like the earth itself" (104). In his search for such an impossibly permanent mooring he callously uses Hella and finally destroys Giovanni.

But before discussing Giovanni, it is important to note that Hella too seems desperately to search for such a mooring through traditional, socially sanctioned sexual/gender definitions. Though she is independent and unconventional in her lifestyle, she finally demands a very traditional domestic relationship with a man to give her life a fixed meaning: "I'm talking about my life. I've got you to take care of and feed and torment and trick and love – I've got you to put up with. From now on, I can have a wonderful time complaining about being a woman. But I won't be terrified that I'm *not* one" (126). Her fears are expressed more pointedly later in the novel: "if women are supposed to be led by men and there aren't any men to lead them, what happens then? What happens then?" (165). Neither she nor David seems willing or able to accept changing and always changeable social and sexual definitions.

But Giovanni does. David points this out upon their first meeting when he repeats the common perception "that the Italians are too fluid, too volatile, have no sense of measure" (36), which elicits Giovanni's derision: "I do not like to offend your ears by saying all the things I am sure these people measure before they permit themselves any act whatever" (36). While Giovanni is no paragon of progressive beliefs (there is much in this novel that deserves pointed feminist critique), he is clearly comfortable with multiple, contingent, and mutable sexual relationships. From the beginning, he assumes that the men in the gay bar where he works have wives who "are waiting at home" (29). He has had a wife, whom he sexually desired and loved, and fathered a child in Italy, yet falls in love with David without hesitation or epistemological/ontological anguish because he does not demand fixed sexual identity. He is therefore wholly untroubled that David is involved with a woman, even assumes that David's "other woman" may also have a husband or another lover, and admits that he too may have a mistress "again one day" (79). When David begins to pull back from their affair because "People have very dirty words for – for this situation" (81), Giovanni is mystified at the power David grants such words, "If dirty words frighten you . . . I really do not know how you have managed to live so long. People are full of dirty words" (81). And that is one of the most powerful themes running throughout the novel, that too often we give categories and words the power to define and finally destroy us.

Jacques, an acquaintance of both men, thus offers David some pointed advice (that he, of course, wholly ignores):

> Love him . . . love him and let him love you. Do you think anything else under heaven really matters? And how long, at the best can it last? since you are both men and still have everywhere to go? Only five minutes, I assure you, only five minutes, and most of that, *helas!* in the dark. And if you think of think of them as dirty, then they *will* be dirty – they will be dirty because you will be giving nothing, you will be despising your flesh and his. But you can make your time together anything but dirty; you can give each other something which will make both of you better – forever – if you will *not* be ashamed, if you will only *not* play it safe. . . . You play it safe long enough. . . . and you'll end up trapped in your own dirty body, forever and forever and forever – like me.   (57)

This is pointed commentary on the tension between personal desire and social definition. Jacques here does not predict that David will be able to repudiate social categories and valuations simply and forever. Five minutes may be the longest that he and Giovanni can maintain a happy relationship when society deems their love "dirty." However, Jacques does insist that David has the ability to resist imposed values, categories, and meanings long enough to garner transient forms of happiness with Giovanni and also to alter forever his own perception of one's inherent *ability* always to resist contextual forces, even if in that transient fashion. And that agency – however tenuous and limited – is the novel's best hope for social and interpersonal change.

To be sure it is a hope that is unrealized in this novel because of David's upbringing, his fears, and, also, his own decisions. Thus Stephen Adams argues that David "seeks a refuge in the conventional" as the novel itself dramatizes "the sacrifice of personal fulfillment to the gods of conformity" (133). Giovanni makes clear David's responsibility for the way he capitulates to or resists social categories:

> You love your purity, you love your mirror – you are just like a little virgin, you walk around with your hands in front of you as though you had some precious metal, gold, silver, rubies, maybe *diamonds* down there between your legs! You will never give it to anybody, you will never let anybody *touch it* – man *or* woman. You want to be *clean*. . . . You want to despise Giovanni because he is not afraid of the stink of

> love. You want to *kill* him in the name of all of your lying little morali-
> ties. And you – you are *immoral.* You are, by far, the most immoral
> man I have met in my life.   (141)

One's "morality," as the novel defines that term, reflects the degree
to which one capitulates to skewed social definitions and categoriza-
tions or resists them. Indeed, this capitulation or resistance falls
within the realm of "morality" because, the novel insists, it *is* finally a
question of personal decision making and responsibility. Thus
Giovanni's social commentary is broad when he says to David, "You
lie so much, you have come to believe all your own lies" (140). And the
distinction between them is clear when he says to David, "You are the
only one who keeps talking about *what* I want. But I have only been
talking about *who* I want" (142). Giovanni asks David to shift his
frame of reference, but to no avail.

But certainly the lingering possibility that individuals can resist by
living and loving in excess of preexisting social categories does make
this text a thoroughly queer one. It suggests that desire can manifest
itself in the most surprising ways and in nonexclusive terms. It
suggests mutability in sexual relationships over time and also in ways
that exceed a simple hetero/homo binary. It suggests strongly that
individuals have the ability and responsibility to allow for human
complexity outside of the starkness of received social definitions and
valuations, even as it does not deny the power of those contextual
forces. It evokes the possibility of a different set of sexual relationships
and definitions without prescribing exactly what the future might hold.
But clearly it reserves its most pointed condemnation and contempt
for those individuals who cling to received notions of normality and
propriety when their own desires are so manifestly improper and
abnormal. "I'm sort of queer for girls myself" (30), is one of David's
early claims, but he finally refuses to allow for the messiness of any
form of "sort of" and certainly runs in terror of his own queer desires.

But that is not the case with the last text that I wish to mention here.
The Color Purple, by Alice Walker, is a text much studied for its
scathing portrayal of sexual, physical, and emotional abuse (familial
and specifically marital), and its explorations of entrenched, brutal
racism. Yet it is also a text deeply interested in eroticism and possibilities for finding and allowing sexual satisfaction outside of the socially
sanctioned structures of "normal" heterosexuality. Indeed, *The Color
Purple* is a very queer novel as it demonstrates how a single text can

critique numerous vectors of oppression and offers some surprising possibilities for response.

From its opening pages the novel offers scathing analysis of sexual violence and its terrible legacy. The repeated rape of the novel narrator, Celie, by her stepfather, and the similar violent usage of her by "Mr.," her husband, leads to her total disconnection from her own desires and any sense of possible sexual pleasure. The novel suggests that heterosexual marriage and "conventional" domestic arrangements are constructed on principles of violent male ownership of the bodies of women and an absolute disregard of their needs, desires, and basic rights to safety, economic security, and emotional support. If the larger, brutal system of race relations treats African-American men as property in this novel, that system of degradation and usage is replicated, even intensified dramatically, in the gender relationships within their own homes.

Yet the novel does not simply reveal and condemn such abuse, it is also clearly concerned with discovery and recovery – of supportive familial relationships, of economic independence, and of emotional and sexual fulfillment. Indeed, in one sense, *The Color Purple* portrays the sexual self-discovery of a lesbian – Celie – who for the first time in her life finds sexual pleasure and a sense of erotic selfhood in the embrace of another woman, the blues singer Shug. This is the compelling point made by Linda Abbandonato in an essay ("Rewriting the Heroine's Story") that explores how the novel "expos[es] and oppos[es] a powerful ideological constraint, institutionalized or 'compulsory' heterosexuality'" (296). Indeed, from the time she first hears of Shug and sees her picture, Celie's erotic interest begins to grow. And Shug eventually does become Celie's erotic partner and teacher, encouraging her exploration of her own body and its possibilities for generating pleasure: "In loving Shug, Celie becomes a desiring subject, and in being loved by Shug, she is made visible to herself as an object of desire" (ibid. 304). Celie falls in love with Shug and finds through their relationship not only the first (and only) satisfying sexual experiences of her life, but also much of the emotional support that she needs to stand up to "Mr."

Yet even if this is a novel that seems tailor-made for traditional studies in lesbian "identity" and self-discovery, it also suggests that sexual selfhood is variable in ways that exceed the hetero/homo binary. Shug embodies and lives that excess. Mae Henderson has related Shug's characterization importantly to the rich historical context of the "high-living, adventurous, independent blues singer, whose life-style gives her greater freedom than Celie's more conventional status" (72). Indeed, that blues "life-style" has an historical association with unconventional activity, because as Marjorie Garber argues, "Among the female blues singers who made Harlem the musical showplace of the twenties were Bessie Smith and Ma Rainey, both bisexual" (*Vice Versa* 119). Abbandonato too argues that, "as polymorphously perverse as a child, [Shug] pursues her pleasures without guilt or repression. Her sexual pluralism reminds us that sexuality is the site not only of regulation but of subversion" (304). Shug is an exuberantly sexual being: "One thing my mama hated me for was how much I love to fuck" (115). Even when the community condemns her, she pursues pleasure, "Us fuck so much in the open us give fucking a bad name" (116). The "us" in the previous sentence is Shug and "Mr." Yet her love of sex also comes to encompass Celie, a husband named Grady, and finally (when she is near 60) a 19-year-old named Germaine. Shug's sense of erotic and emotional potential is nonexclusive, confining itself to neither side of a hetero/homo binary, nor seeing anything wrong with or impossible about multiple simultaneous connections. And while Shug's "polymorphousness" may cause pain for Celie and is hardly held up as a simple ideal in the novel, it does present us with an alternate system of variability and multiplicity that is far more attractive than the "normal" sociosexual relations portrayed in the novel. Indeed, Shug seems to live the multiplying flowing and variously engaged desires suggested by Delueze and Guattari, as I discussed in Chapter 3. Her exuberance puts into practice Hocquenghem's "system in which polyvocal desire is plugged in on a non-exclusive basis" (*Homosexual Desire* 131). And her characterization also points to the possibility that such transgressions of spuriously "civilised loves" are not the prerogative solely of male homosexuals, as Hocquenghem's analysis would seem to suggest.

That openness to change and difference, without defining a precise telos or a new set of "normal" restrictions, resonates thematically throughout the novel. Shug herself evokes possibilities for disrupting rigidly confined and tensely controlled selfhood in her love of music and dance:

> I tell you something else, Shug say to Mary Agnes, listening to you sing, folks git to thinking bout a good screw.
> Aw, *Miss Shug*, say Mary Agnes, changing color.

Shug say, What, too shamefaced to put singing and dancing and fucking together? She laugh. That's the reason they call what us sing the devil's music. Devils love to fuck.   (111)

In fact, Shug has a very relaxed sense of morality that challenges received notions and that centers primarily on pleasure; thus she happily tells Celie:

I is a sinner, say Shug. Cause I was born. I don't deny it. But once you find out what's out there waiting for us, what else can you be?
Sinners have more good times, I say.
You know why? she ast.
Cause you ain't all the time worrying bout God, I say.
Naw, that ain't it, she say. Us worry bout God a lot. But once us feel loved by God, us do the best us can to please him with what us like. . . . There's a lot of things I can do that I speck God likes. . . . I can lay back and just admire stuff. Be happy. Have a good time.   (176)

This hedonism, of a sort, abrades notions of sexual propriety and is also part and parcel of Shug's rejection of received notions of who and what "God" is – in this novel neither male nor white. "It" – God – is for Shug "inside you and inside everybody else. You come into the world with God. But only them that search for it inside find it" (177). While the metaphysics of her commentary may seem far afield from "queer theories" as discussed earlier, certainly it allows for a disruption of the status quo in a way that "queers" received morality, propriety, and proprietorship. In ways that thoroughly abrade contextual notions, Shug finally equates religious devotion with sex: "It sort of like you know what, she say, grinning and rubbing high up on my thigh.... Oh, she say. God love all them feelings. That's some of the best stuff God did. And when you know God loves 'em you enjoys 'em a lot more. You can just relax, go with everything that's going, and praise God by liking what you like" (178). Thus Lauren Berlant (in "Race, Gender and Nation") has argued convincingly that "Celie's religion . . . is transformed from a social, institutional enterprise to an aestheticized . . . sexual practice. Admiring the color purple is equated with what Celie calls 'making love to God'" (226).

So while the novel hardly holds up Shug as its spokesperson for a new, absolute "truth," and certainly her spiritualized hedonism causes Celie pain when Shug falls in love with Germaine, Shug does lead Celie to critique received notions and to learn to exist in and live with a state of nonexclusivity that pays off in equanimity by the novel's end. Celie has learned to find happiness in her community of women and even to make her peace with "Mr.," who, importantly, has also learned many lessons from Shug about loving others and letting "folks do together with they bodies" (236) as they wish and without judgment. That calm existence with the variable needs and actions of others seems to be the self-described "lesson" that Celie decides she "was suppose to learn" (248). While this references Buddhist belief systems, and the novel as a whole relies upon a sense of divine imma-nence that are hardly "queer" in that term's connection to thorough existential skepticism, it does abrade notions of fixed subjectivity and morality in ways that are queer-relevant. If we allow for variability and nonexclusivity, as the book itself suggests, then certainly there is no need to set up hard and fast rules about what is and is not "queer." *The Color Purple* is, to my mind, clearly and queerly relevant to our discussion of putting queer theories into queer practices.

So what queer qualities might you look for in a text, as you think about generating analysis informed by the queer theories covered here? In the following summary, I want to offer a few possibilities, but at the same time affirm that the queer-interested critic will no doubt generate her or his own revisions and significant reinterrogations of the queer engagements and qualities I suggest.

1   Queer texts politicize and/or allow the critic to politicize the interplay of sexuality and identity

All of the texts that we have discussed in the "Readings" section of this book – "The Yellow Wall-Paper," *Dr. Jekyll and Mr. Hyde, Orlando, Giovanni's Room,* and *The Color Purple* – reveal in explicit and implicit ways the myriad of connections between the erotic desires that individuals may feel and the ways those desires are classified, categorized, and valued socially. Those classifications, categoriza-tions, and valuations have a *political* resonance not in the sense of becoming necessarily the explicit topic of debate by politicians but rather in how they reveal the ways that certain groups of people (white, male, heterosexual, etc.) have the social and political power to further a narrow set of interests and enforce a justifying mind-set or belief system. The term "ideology" is often used to indicate such justifications and to signal clearly that they carry social and political consequences, even when termed "natural" or "normal" in ways that are supposed to foreclose further discussion. Of course, a queer text may or may not reveal political self-consciousness among characters concerning the interplay of sexuality and identity; that politicization may be implicit in the text and may be done explicitly only by the reader or critic. Thus it is quite possible that the queer critic must do the work of revealing the differential valuation of sexualities within the text and the queer reading will be the primary vehicle for politicizing identity.

2 Furthermore, queer texts abrade or refuse the naturalized binary of hetero- and homosexuality

As we have explored throughout much of this book, heterosexuality and homosexuality have been used as structuring categories since the nineteenth century, and with clear precedents before then. With the rise of social and sexological "science," those two oppositions have been key to differentiating peoples and ascribing to some the designation "normal" and branding others with the condemnation "abnormal." Lost in much of the rush to classify, and even to counter such classifications, has been a critical attachment to the constructed and oversimplifying nature of that foundational binary itself.

Yet the inadequacy of that binary to capture the complexity of human desire as it is manifested in individuals, groups, and interpersonal contacts and mediated encounters is certainly revealed in many texts, from television shows and films suggesting transient forms of "homosexual" desire between ostensibly "heterosexual" characters, to novels and dramas portraying changing and changeable sexual definitions and self-identifications. Yet this remains unexplored by critics who are themselves thoroughly invested in the binary of mutually exclusive hetero- and homosexuality. Thus, as I suggested earlier, a "queer text" that reveals mutability, mutuality, possibilities for exceeding or abrading that binary must be met with a queer reading and critical response practice (or set of practices) that similarly recognizes and allows for such excess. Indeed, this helps us differentiate "lesbian/gay" critical practices from queer critical practices in useful ways. If a reading of *The Color Purple* isolates only the self-realization of Celie as a lesbian and highlights the singularity of that identity position without critically examining the complications offered by Shug, then it is not a "queer" reading as this book defines that term.

3   Queer texts often historicize and localize sexuality and sexual identity assumptions

As I suggested in my discussion of the differences and tensions between essentialism and constructionism, central to the latter perspective is an understanding that beliefs, categories, and identities are always specific to times and places, though they may also proliferate across geographical areas and certainly endure in substantial ways through time. Even so, they are never *precisely* the same as they move temporally or geographically. And some of the most important work that can be performed by the queer critic is to attempt to understand those complexities, rather than isolate a few consistencies as proof of an overall fixity or essential nature.

Again, when the queer text, which may reveal historically specific, local definitions, and which may expose contextual influences and the class-, race-, and/or cultural identity-related interplay of sexualities and subjectivities, is met with queer critical practices similarly interested in variation, complexity, and specificity, then supple and sophisticated readings can be generated. Many writing challenges may arise for the queer critic examining such complexities, but certainly when a text offers ample evidence of historical and geographical specificity and the critical approach taken allows for and pursues research concerning that specificity, then the critic herself or himself has the opportunity to produce a new queer text.

4   Thus the queer *critical* text is one that resists facile closure on questions of sexual identity and that helps propel a continuing queer dialogue on sexuality and desire

And this is finally one of the most important points to remember: that critics and students of literary and other cultural texts are themselves writers, that we produce texts that are themselves queer or otherwise. While all successful critical writing has a sense of purpose and a desire to make clear interpretive points with ample evidence and effective expression, successful queer writing does not have to violate its own assumptions about complexity and contingency. We all speak out of our own sexual, historical, geographical, ideological, class-, gender-, and ethnicity-related positions. Indeed, that specificity and variability accounts for the dynamism of the current conversation in and on literary and cultural studies. As critics, queer or otherwise, we enter a conversation about a text, topic, and/or methodology, and we may change that conversation dramatically through our intervention. Yet the conversation will not end with our intervention. It is taking place and will continue to take place in many locations and with many different inflections. A queer critical practice will allow for, invite, or incite further complications and investigations. "Queer" does not claim or countenance closure.

Indeed, there are innumerable possibilities for the student interested in pursuing queer analysis of literary or cultural texts. Texts that demonstrate some or all of the above qualities will lend themselves easily to investigations of the temporal or geographical specificity of sexual identities, to explorations of the ways that desires exceed or abrade the hetero/homo binary, as well as analyses of the social forces accounting for the entrenched nature of that binary and possibilities for agency in continuing to disrupt its self-assurance.

The student interested in queer analysis may draw on a wide variety of methods and find compatible analyses of gender, race, class, age, and other identity inflections. To center one's critical work on sexuality is not necessarily to ignore other aspects of human existence. Yet certainly, and as suggested in previous chapters, to do queer work is not to ignore, downplay, or denigrate the importance of or insights available through an analysis of sexuality. It is to find in and through sexuality a way of understanding human organization, interaction, and meaning-making.

Thus it is worth concluding this chapter with a reiteration of a few general writing and research tips. To conduct successful queer research means necessarily choosing a discrete line of inquiry and analysis. Many potentially successful research and writing projects go awry because they attempt to do too much, have too little focus, or no sense of clear purpose. To decide to pursue queer analysis is to delimit one's project by way of an investigation of sexuality; to keep that focus intact and to exploit that focus appropriately is key to constructing a successful argument, essay, or research project. All writers who are excited about their work and approach it with a sense of multiple possibilities and supple methodology must make difficult decisions about what *not* to discuss or investigate. But if we give up the notion that we are offering definitive interpretations or bringing closure to a topic then those necessary exclusions will be far less painful and difficult. All readings and responses are partial and tendentious. If we allow ourselves to recognize that fact early in our process of project construction and textual response, then we can also allow for the inevitable choices we must make as we say "this or that aspect of the text" is not germane to the argument or project at hand.

Those exclusions, whether explicitly identified in your writing or carefully signaled through the specificity of your thesis or set of methodological references, are your responsibility and are vital to your success. The base of evidence that you offer – your direct quotations from the text, the theorists whom you cite, the historical or cultural research that you conduct and draw upon – will determine the impact of your reading and its contribution to the ongoing critical conversation. That contribution will be most effective if it is both carefully delimited and fully developed. Indeed, those two qualities go hand in hand.

Yet as I bring this section of readings and textual examples to a close, I hope to leave you with the sense of numerous possibilities and open-ended queer engagements. Certainly you do not have to be "a" queer to do queer-relevant and queer-theoretically informed research and critical work. Of course I might argue that doing such work, destabilizing received notions of sexual normality and differential valuations, seeing diverse possibilities for identifications and affiliations, opening up new questions about how to imagine a future of different sexual expressions and subject positions, is to be a queer agent, is, in fact, to be "a" queer. But that label is, as Sedgwick suggested at the beginning of this book, a decision that must be expressed through a statement in the first person. All I can do is issue the invitation to do the work, to identify as one's impulses may change and one's critical engagements may vary, and to continue the vital, critical work of calling into question all that is assumed to be "natural" and to react skeptically to that which we are told is "true."

A Query

Is there a queer "authority"? In asking this question, I'm really posing two separate queries. One, does a queer insistence on lack of mastery, closure, and definitive answers mean an undermining of any sense of critical authoritativeness? And two, to what extent does the Barthean concept of the "death of the author" pertain to our own sense of "authority?" In musing on these questions, we confront both the responsibilities and the limitations of the writer of literary and cultural analysis who draws on the queer theories discussed earlier.

Without a doubt, the queer theories we have studied clearly undermine any claim to definitive or final authority. Yet we might think of this undermining as one that allows us to distinguish between being "authoritarian" and being "authoritative" in our interpretations and our critical personas. As we have seen throughout previous chapters, queer theories have developed from foundations in social constructionism and recognitions of historical/discursive contingency. Yet as critics, we are just as "constructed" and contingent as those texts that we study. Our norms, practices, professional rules and behaviors are no more "real" in some metaphysical or essential sense than those of the sexologists and religious thinkers whose authority we questioned in preceding chapters. To recognize this is not to deny or ignore the fact that our tendentious and contingent practices are the means by which we communicate effectively. We can both maintain a critical consciousness concerning our roles as critics, writers, and queer thinkers and at the same time operate as agents within a context of expectations and notions of cogent expression and formal argumentation. It is no more a simple "either/or" situation than any of the other binaries that we have discussed here.

Indeed, meeting the expectations and needs of our readers and critical respondents means understanding how one establishes an authoritative critical persona and how one constructs a compelling argument or interpretation. It means care in reading and attention to the text at hand, care in selecting compelling and ample evidence for an argument, and care in organizing and presenting that evidence so that the reader's needs for understanding are met. Whether our particular "queer" work is critical, political, activist, pedagogical, or some combination of all of those, we cannot do that work effectively without a knowledge of "the system," so to speak, even if a particular manifestation of the social/political/sexual "system" is the target of our concerted critical engagement. Thus in no way does our iconoclasm or desire for radical change serve as an excuse for laziness, sloppiness, or a disregard for the basic needs of others (including the needs of our readers for clarity of expression and evidence). In this way, our responsibility for queer authoritativeness is one small manifestation of the queer ethics that I discussed at the end of the last chapter.

And that authoritativeness can coexist even with our knowledge of the "death" of the notion of the author as final authority. We are no more the masterful "creator" of our own texts than are novelists, poets, or dramatists of centuries past. Our own era, its values, definitions, and political conversations and crises speak through us just as previous eras spoke through the works of as Charlotte Perkins Gilman and Robert Louis Stevenson. Indeed, if we acknowledge and understand that fact, we can less anxiously process the responses and opinions of others who come to our work with their own standpoint epistemologies, their own contextual backgrounds, ideological motivations, and perhaps differing set of definitions and agendas. This is not to textualize to the point of irrelevance important political debates over the right to sexually self-define and live a nonconformist life, or the need for AIDS funding or laws protecting queers from violence and discrimination. But certainly it does mean that we can engage in those struggles with a recognition of where others "are coming from," so to speak, and with an understanding that we too are limited in our perspective and partial in our understanding. Here as elsewhere it is to approach the multiplicity and complexity of human life and behavior without resorting to a reductive (and always seductive) binary of "right/wrong," "good/evil," and "truth/falsehood."

If we need to feel absolutely secure in occupying only the first half of those three binaries, we may find ourselves highly motivated through a sense of righteousness and dogmatic zeal, but also easily dismissed and even derailed in our critical work. Indeed, we can anticipate the critical readings of others and work toward convincing even the most profound skeptics without becoming defeatist, paranoid, or paralyzed if we allow our "authority" to be placed always in quotation marks and to see it always as a critical role and writerly performance, one that is as "real" as any other that we engage in on a daily basis and with consequences that can mean failing or passing grades, employment or lack thereof, or even (in extreme situations of healthcare access, etc.) life or death. Indeed, our "authority" can be quite queer in its complexity and its understanding of multiplicity and variability, and it can be particularly effective for that very reason.

Part III

Post Queer?

Afterword: W(h)ither Identity?

The theories and readings that have been covered in the preceding pages raise numerous questions and certainly provide few simple or comforting answers. And perhaps the most intriguing question of them all is the one that is clearly most unanswerable: "What does the future hold?" It is a question that will be answered, of course, in ways that some of us will witness firsthand (in the short run, at least) but that will obviously elude all of this book's readers as years give way to decades and centuries. After all, no one in the Renaissance could have predicted cyber-sex; who knows what new technologies and social possibilities will arise? Yet clearly, one way to motivate ourselves to continue working for change is to imagine an ideal moment or utopian state that we hope to achieve and to which our efforts contribute importantly. Indeed, this delimitation of a clear and powerful telos has helped propel the work of many social progressives and radicals – lesbigay, Marxist, feminist, etc. – as vigorously as it has that of social conservatives and reactionaries – fundamentalists, fascists, white supremacists, etc. The parameters of a group's utopian state will be far different depending upon its politics, of course, but the methods and motivational tactics used to work toward that state are often remarkably similar.

Yet the queer theories overviewed here usually make *other* demands on their readers and adherents. While queer activists and academic theorists certainly choose often to work for discrete and concrete goals – an increase in funding for AIDS research, an end to harassment and employment discrimination on the basis of sexual identity, the addition of queer theories to critical methods courses, etc. – there is rarely a single, simple "ideal" that is articulated as the common social goal for all such work, no queer utopia to which I can point conclusively and say here, "once we have achieved *that*, our work is done." Yet, at the same time, there is a common work that is performed and that will continue, a work that will change significantly and meet unimaginable new challenges, but that can serve as the basis for some tentative, concluding words to the present book.

As we have seen, queer theories generally ask for a sharpened degree of critical consciousness on identity/identities, especially in its/their connection to sexuality, even as queer theorists reiterate often that "sharpened" can never mean "perfect" or "comprehensive." And, of course, this critical consciousness is tied inextricably to an awareness of the historical, cultural, national, even local and directly interpersonal contingency of identity, and therefore its lack of an enduring, essential nature. Such common work among queer theorists is no doubt clear to any reader who has carefully attended to the overviews and analyses of previous chapters. But, we might ask, to what end or ends? Is critical consciousness an end in and of itself? Or is there a certain agency that is implicitly valued as a possible result of such consciousness?

I would argue that there is. Practically speaking, the "denaturalizing" of identity allows for some leverage in arguing for concrete sociopolitical changes – revisions in discriminatory laws, changes in school curricula, specific alterations in the "norms" of interpersonal contacts, relationships, and degrees of respect and tolerance. Yet alongside – and thoroughly connected to – the external and social, is the realm of the internal and personal. As I have suggested often, queer theories ask us to recognize and grapple with the implications of the multiplicity and variability of identities . . . and not only *among* but also *within* us all. And this recognition and critical grappling does imply a degree of agency, not only to effect certain discretely defined sociopolitical changes, but also over our own identity assumptions. The specific degree of agency is a hotly and widely contested issue, as I will discuss below, but implicit always even in the very act of writing with dour pessimism about such agency is the assumption that changes in affiliation and identification can occur through sharpened critical understanding. Indeed, urging an audience to alter its opinion about agency in sexual self-definition, awareness, and potentiality is to urge it to identify differently within the broad realm of the sexual.

To tease out just a few of the possibilities for such queer change and agency, I want to look for a moment at current reflections on subjectivity beyond the realm of self-identifying "queer theories" or narrowly focused commentaries on sexuality. Legal theorist and sociologist Lawrence M. Friedman in *The Horizontal Society* speaks, if not exactly optimistically, then certainly expansively, when he notes that "We live in an age ... in which old forms and traditions seem to be breaking down – forms and traditions that trapped the individual in a cage of ascriptions; that fixed human beings in definite social roles, pinned them like specimens to a given position in the world, no matter how they might wriggle and fight" (vii–viii). "Identity," he argues, "is vastly more fluid than it once was" (229).

> [O]ne even chooses (within limits) a race, a gender, a form of sexuality. One can also choose *not* to be counted as part of any particular group, though this is sometimes more difficult, because the outside society does not always go along with one's choice. . . . I do not ignore the fact that choice is often an illusion. People are firm believers in free will. But they choose their politics, their dress, their manners, their very identity, from a menu they had no hand in writing. They are constrained by forces they do not understand and are not even conscious of. But even the *illusion* of a choice is of enormous social significance. (240)

Indeed, as illusory as such choices often are, Friedman certainly follows numerous other late twentieth-century sociologists and political theorists in noting that the continuing interplay and overt discussion of choice and constraint has led inexorably to increases in the former and an incremental but nevertheless significant waning of the latter as identities become ever more elective and as a form of critical consciousness concerning identity/identities is furthered. Indeed, the broadest goal of his writing is to stoke the very "understanding" and "consciousness" that he laments as still too often illusory in his comments above.

Perhaps the best known recent commentator on the waning of such constraints has been the British sociologist Anthony Giddens. In his books *The Consequences of Modernity, Modernity and Self-Identity,* and *The Transformation of Intimacy* Giddens suggests that we are now in an age of "reflexive" modernity (or "late" modernity) in which individuals are allowed, and in many cases required, to make active choices concerning their identity bases. While Giddens does not suggest we have perfect freedom of choice in creating our "selves" – indeed, he speaks often of the "ontological security" provided by routine and habit (*Consequences* 98) – he certainly ascribes considerable agency to the individual in making choices about how to construct a sense of personal identity. This even extends to the "body [which] is not just a physical entity which we 'possess,' it is an action-system, a mode of praxis, and its practical immersion in the interactions of day-to-day life is an essential part of the sustaining of a coherent sense of self-identity" (*Modernity and Self-Identity* 99). He sums up the provisional and speculative nature of much of our existence with the term "everyday social experiments," ones that extend even to "sexuality" (*Transformation of Intimacy* 8), and through which we test new modes of self-expression and identity affiliations. In Giddens's analysis, "A person [now] 'has' a sexuality, gay or otherwise, which can be reflexively grasped, interrogated and developed. . . . Sexuality thereby becomes free-floating; at the same time as 'gay' is something one can 'be,' and 'discover oneself to be,' sexuality opens itself up to many objects" (*Transformation* 14). He uses as exemplary in this regard the case study of a man whose beloved wife dies and who then, at age 65, falls in love with another man, even though "he had never before been sexually attracted to another man or fantasized about homosexual acts" (14). He sums up optimistically that

> "Sexuality" today has been discovered, opened up and made accessible to the development of varying life-styles. It is something each of us 'has,' or cultivates, no longer a natural condition which an individual accepts as a preordained state of affairs. Somehow . . . sexuality functions as a malleable feature of self, a prime connecting point between body, self-identity and social norms.   (*Transformation* 15)

While Giddens never uses the term "queer," he certainly draws, in queer-relevant fashion, on the theories of Foucault as he points to a newly "plastic sexuality" and "radical pluralism" that offers considerable agency to the individual in making and remaking sexual identity as different inter-personal possibilities arise and as new information comes one's way (*Transformation* 178–9).

While I find Giddens's work quite useful, his emphasis on personal agency does need tempering with a much clearer acknowledgement of the many ways that we are constrained in any attempt to "choose" a new and different sexuality. In spite of Giddens's comments about one's ability to "grasp" and "interrogate" sexuality, we have to recognize that it would be highly reductive to define "sexuality" as simply that which is thereby articulated or articulatable (just as it would be to ignore wholly such verbalization and explicit affiliatory moves). Yes, we may identify a new sexual project and even choose to self-identify in a new way, overtly or covertly, but those linguistic moves do not translate necessarily into different or piqued sexual desire, which must bear some consideration in a discussion of "plastic sexuality." Indeed, just as the nervous claim "I am heterosexual" may not correspond at all to an individual's realized or unrealized desires (which may diverge dramatically from social conventions) so too the affiliatory announcement "I am gay" or "I am bisexual" could be socially or politically motivated but finally have a very murky relationship to the actual vectors of one's bodily desires and physiological responses. Sexuality, in that sense, is not "free-floating." As a stark example, in the Victorian erotic autobiography *My Secret Life* (1888), the male narrator decides summarily that he will experience homosexual sex by anally penetrating another man, but soon finds that no matter how much he wishes to do so out of intellectual and political principles (as a neo-libertine determined to put his philosophy into all imaginable forms of practice), he simply cannot maintain an erection long enough to penetrate his partner. His body repeatedly resists his attempt to choose a new mode of sexual expression. And we hardly have any greater degree of control today. Even Viagra and similar drugs do not create sexual desire in men; they simply help sustain the physical manifestations of already-present desire. And while I would argue that the announcement "I am queer" is different – that it indicates an intensely critical stance toward sexual normativity, not a specific type of sexual desire – I hardly think that bold announcements and bold experiments prove that our sexuality has now been fully "opened up" and rendered "malleable." As untold numbers of women and men have found when trying to "will" themselves heterosexual, orgasmic, or simply aroused, our bodies often belie our best efforts.

Indeed, those limits on one's agency in consciously making and remaking selfhood – sexual or otherwise – have been explored by two of the queer theorists covered in earlier chapters: Diana Fuss and Judith Butler. In *Identification Papers*, Fuss argues that "the most serious difficulty with designing a politics around identification is the fact that the unconscious plays a formative role in the production of identifications, and it is a formidable (not to say impossible) task for the political subject to exert any steady or lasting control over them" (9). Certainly no one familiar with the basic insights of psychoanalytic theory, and its recognition of the always inexpressible and never fully knowable qualities and content of the unconscious, would be foolish enough to assert otherwise. However, Fuss's next sentence should make us pause before we therefore write off agency completely: "Given the capacity of identifications continually to evolve and change, to slip and shift under the weight of fantasy and ideology, the task of harnessing a complex and protean set of emotional ties for specific social ends cannot help but to pose intractable problems for politics" (9). Indeed, as useful as Fuss's reminders are here, a question still lingers: does not that very ability to evolve, change, slip, and shift offer some social and political leverage, even if no grounds for an assertion of "steady or lasting control"? Fuss asserts that "identification is the detour through the other that defines a self" (2). I would agree, but certainly I would pluralize all of the nouns in that sentence, for we multiply identify with others, and our "self" is always a conglomeration of *selves* defined through numerous and changing detours. The fact that we identify with numerous others in ways that can change dramatically over time and that can alter our conscious lives and even, perhaps, our very desires, motivations, values, and valuations, does suggest some leeway for a possible agency-driven "politics" of identity/identities. Frankly, we are setting ourselves up for inevitable disappointment if we choose a verb like "harness" to define our expectation of the relationship between identity and political will or choice.

And while Butler, reacting to the oversimplifications and misunderstandings that drove some readers' usages of *Gender Trouble*, repeatedly emphasizes constraints on agency in later works, the pluralizations just effected also allow us to loosen somewhat her tight reins on the interplay of identity and politics. Granted, there "is a risk in the affirmation of *denaturalization* as a strategy" (*Bodies That Matter* 93), for denaturalizing identity/identities is certainly never solely *sufficient* for radical political change in the realm of sexuality, but, I would argue, it is *necessary* for such change – a key distinction. Butler is wise to remind us that "sexuality cannot be summarily made or unmade, and it would be a mistake to associate 'constructivism' with 'the freedom of a subject to form her/his sexuality as s/he pleases'" (*Bodies That Matter* 94), but making or unmaking "summarily" is – like "harnessing" – an unnecessary overstatement of the expectations one might bring to the interplay of agency and identity. As Butler notes, "Identifications are multiple and contestatory" (*Bodies That Matter* 99), and out of the multiplicity and contestation can come change, enhanced critical consciousness, and, I believe, grounds for optimism concerning the possible effects of our queer work.

And this is my primary rejoinder to the cogent analysis that Butler provides in *The Psychic Life of Power* (1997), a book that tempers to an unnecessary degree the implicit optimism of *Gender Trouble*. As Butler works to construct a notion of "subjectivity" in which she draws on Foucauldian and psychoanalytic principles, "in which the subject emerges both as the *effect* of a prior power and as the *condition of possibility* for a radically conditioned form of agency" (14–15), she always renders the nouns "subject" and "subjectivity" as singular and static objects of inquiry. Yet if we again pluralize and recognize subjectivities within and among us all, of always changing, new, and different interactions among differing peoples and the possibilities and epistemologies that they represent, we can come closer to Giddens's optimism, even with an always tempering recognition of unharnessable desires and energies. While I do not want to make a lengthy detour here through Butler's use and revision of Louis Althusser's notion of "interpellation," which suggests that we are constructed (and, in some ways, seduced) through preexisting categories and imposed definitions of selfhood, she always declines to pluralize that notion of interpellation. She argues cautiously that "we might reread 'being' as precisely the potentiality that remains unexhausted by any particular interpellation. Such a failure of interpellation may well undermine the capacity of the subject to 'be' in a self-identical sense, but it may also mark the path toward a more open, even more ethical, kind of being, one of or for the future" (131). Yet by rendering singular all of her nouns above, she deflates the energy of her own argument.

From my moment of immersion into language, social interaction, and consciousness, I may be "interpellated" – socially identified and defined – as someone of a certain race, gender, class, nationality, religion, and sexuality (along with many other possibilities). However, it is vital to recognize that those interpellations – some of which I may eagerly seek or cling to, others of which may be imposed and imperfectly settle on me – can clash and/or support each other in different ways and very differently at different times. As Gloria Anzaldúa has explored in *Borderlands*, the imposed parameters of one's gender, ethnicity, religion, and sexuality may not coexist comfortably at all, may be irreconcilable in sometimes glaring and fundamental ways. I would argue that out of that discomfort and clash can come a broad critical consciousness and considerable change, particularly if "identity" as a previously "fixed" concept/construct *is* denaturalized and rendered always problematic. At times, we may be asked to choose our primary identity bases and affiliations because of any number of contextual demands placed on us. And, yes, we may choose in conservative or even reactionary fashion, but certainly our common queer work is to discuss why and how that is not the only choice one might make.

And this does not even account for the complexities offered by other dramatic, as well as smaller-scale, changes over time in our contexts: my class standing could alter significantly with the loss or acquisition of a particular job, my social group and daily interpersonal interactions could vary with my move to a new city or even with someone else's move into the apartment next door. New technologies add yet another layer of complexity to this issue of identity/subjectivity. Indeed, because of a simple reorganization of my office environment, effected by an unknown administrator thousands of mile away, I could suddenly find myself at a desk next to a man who was formerly a woman but who has chosen not to undergo phalloplasty (the surgical creation of a penis) and to whom I find myself attracted sexually in ways that I never would have imagined previously. And if he is attracted to me, and we act on our desires and our lives become intertwined, I may find myself among people and with identificatory possibilities that are far different from anything that my earlier experiences would have allowed. Wholesale agency in remaking our "selves" may never be possible, but certainly discrete acts of agency in experimentation and new affiliation are possible as new information and different possibilities present themselves.

Granted, this begs the question wholly of whether or not our capacity to "experiment" differently is set and settled from childhood. There are any number of reasons why the situation just described may never occur or why I might never act on desires that suddenly arise and that disturb my previous identity bases. But my broad point remains: many forms of change do occur in our lives and new possibilities are acted upon at times, but both can be overlooked by overly cautious theorists. My unforeseen move to Los Angeles in 1991 to take a new job led to significant and previously unimaginable changes in my sexuality simply because different people, possibilities, group definitions, and abrasions of normality exist in LA compared to my previous places of residence. To be sure, this is *not* to argue that

wholesale radical change in identities, affiliations, and experimentations happens overnight or in self-controlled fashion. But it is to
suggest that very gradual shifts in identity and identifications occur
often. Indeed, we accept the fact now that "trauma" at any point in
our lives can radically alter our psyches, leading to post-traumatic
stress and other indications of alterations in the very content and
constitution of our unconscious. Queer theorists have not yet
explored if, in fact, nontraumatic and perhaps much slower processes
of change occur all the time in the constitution of our sexual selfhoods
and the unconscious desires that underlie them. None of us is able to
exert control over our sexuality, but neither has it been "proven" (to
my satisfaction) that our sexuality is firmly fixed and our potentials for
future identifications foreclosed from early childhood. Giddens's
anecdote above concerning the man who suddenly falls in love with
another man without any previous inclination or precursor may seem
far-fetched and anomalous, but so is the hermetically sealed notion of
identity and foreclosures of identity change that seem to constrict
some discussions of possible queer futures. Here as always, we need
to complicate any underlying and obviously seductive (because clean
and neatly available for use in our own definitive conclusion reach-
ing) "either/or" binary.

So the questions posed by the title to this conclusion remain open.
Where will our discussion of identity and identities go and will the
notion of constricted identity/identities wither away? I think it would
be absurd to predict some future without identity bases; we need and
will, no doubt, need always to attach ourselves to affiliations and
modes of meaning-making that exclude and severely limit as well as
include and enable, ones that will never be fully conscious or wholly
alterable. There is no queer utopia of absolute freedom and free-play.
But, as I have suggested throughout this book, forms of energetic
intellectual work and creative activity abound and certainly can
continue, taking us . . . who knows where? And even if "queer"
inevitably loses its currency and potential for motivation because of
overuse and appropriation (Butler points out that "it will doubtless
have to be yielded in favor of terms that do . . . political work more
effectively" [*Bodies That Matter* 228]), its basic "work" of interrogating
the norms of identity – whatever arises "post" queer – will remain
important and always timely, even if inevitably, differently inflected.

This has continuing implications for the specifically cultural/liter-
ary critical work that this book takes as its primary subject matter. In

examining texts for the historical, geographical, and contextual variability of (and the myriad of individual inflections given to) identity,
we can better understand how certain patterns of identity formation
came to predominate and take on the heavy weight of the "natural."
While yesterday's structures of power, its terminologies, valuations,
and differentiations, are never precisely the same as our own, exploring both the continuities and the differences between "now" and
"then," and between "here" (wherever that is for you) and "there"
allows us a potential analytical leverage vis-à-vis our own norms and
naturalized notions. This is not to suggest that we can ever move
"outside" of our own systems of reference, our ontologies and epistemologies, yet admitting that fact does not mean wholesale defeatism
or critical complacency. In exploring queer theories and examining
texts of selfhood from the past, we are at the very least (and perhaps at
the very best) empowered by an awareness that what we see before us
today has not always been, does not always have to be, and may or
may not "be" for all people at the present moment.

That may sound like a rather meager and common form of critical
consciousness, but I am not at all sure that it is emphasized and
valued enough. Indeed, if this book does nothing else, it will perform
important work if it encourages you to read critically, generously, but
always attentively the "texts" that you encounter every day, from the
speeches of politicians, to the ads you see for clothing, to the lives and
lifestyles of your family and friends. It encourages you to see the
variety of sexual lives, affiliations, desires, self-identifications, mediated, fantasized, and actualized encounters, as ones without essential
value except that which we ascribe to them. This is not to countenance or apologize for abuse, violence, or interpersonal (or internalized) oppression (even as it is to recognize always the contested
nature of those very terms), but it is to dislodge our sense of the
absolute sanctity of our own definitions even as we may argue for
them with suppleness and acuity.

For clearly a critical attachment to our present texts and contexts
should lead, could lead, to different possibilities in the future. Those
seeking quick radical change will be disappointed, of course (indeed,
"impatience" is a very interesting text itself). Yet if one "payoff," so to
speak, of continuing and proliferating critical attachment to current
sexual norms and notions is simply the ability 20 years from now of
two women to hold hands at a McDonald's in Dallas, Texas, without
fear of harassment or violence, then something significant will have

been achieved. You might argue that many larger questions would still be wholly unaddressed (why only two women, why not three women or two women and a man? why lend support to a socially irresponsible corporate entity like McDonald's?), and I might agree with you, but an even slightly expanded field of potential sexual self-expression is itself something to recognize as valuable. But at the same time, if you are one of those two women now able to hold hands and you foreclose my options to exist and self-express differently, then your own standpoint epistemologies, norms and notions, have been "Real"-ized, so to speak, and the "Real" remains an appropriate target always for concerted critical activity. Any sense of a fixed, narrowly defined sexual utopia (in which all gay couples will marry and have children, or alternatively, exist exuberantly in multipartnered sexual affiliations) is hardly better than any other set of simple social prescriptions and proscriptions. It is that very mechanism of prescribing and proscribing sexual behaviors that must be rendered – in any unimaginable, un-delimited queer utopia – thoroughly suspicious and continuously critically engaged.

In a piece entitled "The Subject and Power," Michel Foucault says,

> Maybe the target nowadays is not to discover what we are but to refuse what we are. We have to imagine and to build up what we could be to get rid of this kind of political "double bind," which is the simultaneous individualization and totalization of modern power structures.
>
> The conclusion would be that the political, ethical, social, philosophical problem of our days is not to try to liberate the individual from the state, and from the state's institutions, but to liberate us both from the state and from the type of individualization linked to the state. We have to promote new forms of subjectivity through the refusal of this kind of individuality that has been imposed on us for several centuries. (336)

In *The Psychic Life of Power* Butler raises several important questions about Foucault's call for "refusal" here, noting that "[w]e cannot simply throw off the identities we have become, and Foucault's call to 'refuse' will certainly be met with resistance." She goes on to ask, "how are we to understand, not merely the disciplinary production of the subject, but the disciplinary cultivation of *an attachment to subjection*?" (102). In other words, how can we refuse identities when others will certainly work to keep us in our places and when we also so desperately need specific "places" by which, through which, to identify ourselves?

Granted, Foucault may be overly optimistic in his rhetoric (of "liberation") in the passage above (much as Butler was in certain sections of *Gender Trouble*, and as I have certainly been many times), but his key verbs above are to "imagine," to "build up," and to "promote," and with the identification of individuality as a "problem," he suggests clearly that "problematizing" is particularly important for all who are politically, socially, ethically, and philosophically engaged today. Indeed that injunction to critical attachment resonates throughout Foucault's final writings and interviews. In a 1984 piece, he writes: "The work of an intellectual is not to form the political will of others; it is, through the analyses he does in his own domains, to bring assumptions and things taken for granted again into question, to shake habits, ways of acting and thinking, to dispel the familiarity of the accepted" (quoted in Gordon xxxiv). In a 1980s interview entitled "So is it Important to Think?" he suggests that "criticism" at its best consists of "seeing on what type of assumptions, of familiar notions, of established, unexamined ways of thinking . . . accepted practices are based. . . . To do criticism is to make harder those acts which are now too easy" (456). In such passages, Foucault does not predict exactly "where" we will go by way of such critical engagement, questionings, and promotions, but he certainly remains optimistic that "thinking" and "critiquing" are potentially very valuable social forces when one refuses to rest comfortably on received notions and accepted definitions. I hope that thoughtful optimism has been communicated to you throughout *Queer Theories*.

Indeed, however its detractors may wish to mischaracterize it in order to achieve their own narrow goals and promote their own orthodoxies, the body of work explored in this volume is finally both optimistic and intellectually/politically invigorating. It finds in the mere *potential* for new and different forms of sexual selfhood, affiliation, and expression the reason to write, to work, to organize politically, and to engage in vigorous conversations. For all of the reasons that Judith Butler has insightfully traced (and certainly for many others heretofore unrecognized), our current sexual "selves," norms, and notions are not simply going to go away. However, we must remember always that they *are* changing, slowly and inevitably, most obviously because everything does change over time, as the history of "sexuality" itself demonstrates, but also because of the intense political and intellectual work of self-styled "queers" and their allies. Indeed, if our current notion of "identity politics" simply gives way to a more complex and supple notion of a politics of "identities," within and among us, we will have in fact done something significant. We will have acknowledged our own, always circumscribed, agency in choosing our affiliations, experimentations, and forms of political/critical work, and our responsibility for choosing intelligently and in ways that validate our right in exist and self-express in our current and potential sexual diversity.

And that holding out of unnamed and unimagined possibilities – indeed, not even needing to name them or to imagine a precise goal – is what drives my teaching, my criticism, my political work, and that has led to my devoting many months of time to writing *Queer Theories*. It is work – applied, political, critical, theoretical – that you too can choose to do.

A Final Query

So what can you do? "I'm just a ____," you might be thinking, with that blank indicating a current identity position arising from geographical location, age, student status, class standing, or some situation of perhaps significant social disempowerment. While I would never deny the real contextual limitations that all of us face in our lives – and that you may encounter in much more severe ways than I do or ever have – I would still suggest that there is always something *to do* arising from the queer theories explored in the preceding pages. Here are just a few ideas.

1 Write a paper in a class, drawing on some of the theories we have discussed, and let your friends, colleagues, and classmates read it

Of course, make sure that any queer-related project or research plan is in line with the expectations of the class – as I mentioned in an earlier query, you are not expected to martyr yourself to make a political point. But certainly your instructor may learn something significant through reading your work, and your friends and colleagues will not only help you hone and polish your writing, but they too may learn about this body of "queer theories," which may invite and incite their own contributions in the future. And certainly in doing more research on the topic of sexuality, you too will be empowered in your perspective on changing sexualities and changing sexual norms and notions.

2   Even outside of formal writing projects, approach the "texts" that you encounter every day – of television, advertising, personal expression, and overt political rhetoric – as ones that demand critical engagement through the theories covered here

The critical work that this book extols is not limited to the classroom and university environment. It is the urgent work of our everyday lives – in our interactions with family and friends, in our voting, in our responses to the rhetorical violence of anti-queer advertising, media stereotypes, and political posturing. Post-structuralist theory generally reminds us that everything is "textual" in the sense of conveying meaning and also demanding analysis and response: verbal, political, and written. Bring an urgent and eager intellectual attachment to bear on the many texts of your life.

3   Let your own norms and notions be challenged and changed through such attachment and the different ideas and provocations that you encounter

Your own positions and paradigms are as limited, textual, and tendentious as any of those you decide to challenge. This is not to suggest that we cannot or should not hold certain beliefs and values tenaciously and in ways that invigorate and motivate us. But those beliefs and values are only vigorous and communally responsible when they are open to examination, are brought into contact with differing opinions and standpoint epistemologies, and are defined and refined through discussion and continuing intellectual investigation. You can offer no final answers or definitive solutions, only additions to continuing conversations.

4   Identify yourself variously and multiply

Recognize the many different and potentially changing identities that you possess (and that possess you) and that can clash and converge in ways that allow a critical engagement on the limitations of any one identity base. If I am at once a labor unionist and a feminist, a citizen of a rural town and a gay man, a born Catholic and a committed supporter of women's abortion rights, those identities in their possible clash and continuing potential for critical conversation have the ability to further my de-naturalization of the notion of identity as fixed, static, and factual. Indeed, we should look for the "queer" aspects of all of our lives.

5   React when you hear "Hey queer!"

As was mine in the first query of this book, your reaction to "Hey queer!" may be internal (though still intellectually and politically dynamic) or it may be external, with a brave and forthright defense of yourself or someone else being targeted with a slur. But remember it is also possible that "queer" is being called out as an invitation to identify your "self" differently.

And only you can now (or later) decide if you will/would answer that greeting, that invitation, that new interpellation, in the affirmative.

Annotated Bibliography

Abelove, Henry et al. eds., *The Lesbian and Gay Studies Reader*. London and New York: Routledge, 1993.

This remarkable and hefty anthology contains a wealth of critical materials on sexuality and gay/lesbian identity, as well as examples of applied analysis in the field. Of particular note for students of "queer theories" – as those theories overlap with the field signaled in the reader's title – are important essays by Gayle Rubin ("Thinking Sex"), Judith Butler ("Imitation and Gender Insubordination"), and John D'Emilio ("Capitalism and Gay Identity"), all of which have been discussed here. This anthology is also noteworthy and commendable for its inclusion of essays on sexualities other than those of white Anglo-Americans (including sexualities among the ancient Greeks, as well as in Chicano and Native American culture). This is a superb compendium of materials on homosexuality published from the late 1970s through the early 1990s.

Altman, Dennis, *Homosexual: Oppression and Liberation*. New York: Outerbridge & Dienstfrey, 1971.

While today the liberationist rhetoric of this early and important contribution to the study of identity and sexual nonconformity may seem dated, it not only demonstrates that questions concerning the fixed "nature" of identity have been intriguing some writers for many decades, but it also speculates in still compelling fashion about the future of sexual identity categories. This is a powerful statement from a place and time (1960s/1970s New York) that seems at once distant and yet very familiar. And for students of queer history, it offers copious data on the micropolitics and organizational activities of the early "gay rights" movement.

Bristow, Joseph, *Sexuality*. London and New York: Routledge, 1997.

This is the best of the current introductory overviews of theories of sexuality and desire. It begins with nineteenth-century sexology, explains thoroughly the work of Freud and Lacan, and covers the influence of Foucault and even more recent theorists on our current work in the field of sexuality studies. Well written and highly detailed, this volume in Routledge's "New Critical Idiom" series provides a solid base from which to begin a study of specifically "queer theories," which only receive brief attention in Bristow's discussion. Its summaries and explanations are both accessible and reliable.

Butler, Judith, *Bodies That Matter: On the Discursive Limits of "Sex."* London and New York: Routledge, 1993.

This is the second of Butler's major works in and on "queer theory." Its introduction tackles the question of "agency" in social constructionist theories; succeeding chapters offer detailed readings of Plato, Freud, Lacan, and, notably, a variety of non-"theoretical" texts: Willa Cather's short stories, Jennie Livingstone's film *Paris is Burning*, and Nella Larsen's novel *Passing*. Butler's last chapter, "Critically Queer," addresses directly the utility of the term "queer" and the various misreadings of her first book *Gender Trouble* that began to circulate after its publication three years earlier. Indeed, that discussion is perhaps the best succinct introduction you will find to the concept of "performativity" and its responsible use in critical analysis.

Butler, Judith, *Gender Trouble: Feminism and the Subversion of Identity*. (1990) London and New York: Routledge, 1999.

This is perhaps the most important book in the brief history of "queer theory" as a discrete field of speculation and investigation, though the term does not appear in the text itself. Much of Butler's discussion is devoted to close readings of and responses to Freud, Lacan, and feminist theorists of the 1980s, including Julia Kristeva, Monique Wittig, and, to a lesser extent, Luce Irigaray. These are important for anyone interested in contemporary debates in feminist and psychoanalytic theories. But it is Butler's last two sections, "Bodily Inscriptions, Performative Subversions" and

"From Parody to Politics," that made this book necessary reading for everyone involved in queer academic and activist movements in the early 1990s. Butler suggests that the repetitive nature of gender performance and identity allows for subversive, politically useful interventions through differing, parodic performances. While some may have read "too much" into the agency that this seems to allow those interested in subverting the norm, it certainly represented a timely and intellectually sophisticated provocation. To the second edition of *Gender Trouble* (1999), Butler adds a preface that cautions care in attending to the limits she places on "parody" as a political strategy.

Chauncy, George, *Gay New York: Gender, Urban Culture, and the Making of the Gay Male World, 1890–1940*. New York: Basic Books, 1994.

This extraordinary book provides a wealth of detail concerning urban life and meaning-making among sexual minorities during the last decade of the nineteenth century and first decades of the twentieth century. It challenges our notion that homosexuals before the civil rights movement of the latter half of the twentieth century were silent, hidden, and self-hating, demonstrating instead that men who sexually desired other men formed communities and support networks, had complex ways of recognizing each other and communicating their "identity," organized at times politically, and even were recognized and commented upon in the general media. While its purview is limited to men and to New York City, its implications for reevaluating the past are much wider. Its use of documentary evidence and its overall methodological sophistication are models for future studies in the history of sexual minorities.

Foucault, Michel, *The History of Sexuality*, vol. 1: *An Introduction*, trans. Robert Hurley. New York: Vintage Books, 1978.

This book dramatically altered literary and cultural theorists' understanding of how power operates and how resistance to power arises. From its first pages, in which Foucault challenges the Freudian notion of a "repression" of sexuality during the nineteenth and twentieth centuries, to its closing statements commenting ironically on our obsession with the "truth" of sexuality, it asks us to reexamine the past two centuries of discussion on sexuality and see not a model of top-down oppression but a give-and-take of definition, response, counter-response, and proliferation. Of particular note is its discussion of the "birth" of the category "homosexual" in the later half of the nineteenth century and its theorization of the tactical polyvalence of discourse in which seemingly oppressive categories and classifications become sites of resistance and struggle.

Fuss, Diana, *Essentially Speaking: Feminism, Nature, and Difference.* London and New York: Routledge, 1989.

This is one of the key works exploring the debate between "essentialism" and "constructionism" and articulating the theoretical interests that would drive the creation of "queer studies" in the 1990s. Fuss's readings of Luce Irigaray, Monique Wittig, and other leading feminists and theoreticians of identity are supple and intellectually stimulating, but her first chapter – "The Risk of Essence" – is particularly useful for its exploration of the possibility of "deploying" essentialism in ways that are self-conscious and politically useful. Her 1995 work *Identification Papers* continues her project of unsettling the terms by which we understand identity issues and the possibilities for and limitations of "identity politics."

Fuss, Diana, ed., *Inside/Out: Lesbian Theories, Gay Theories.* London and New York: Routledge, 1991.

This was one of the first of many essay collections offering a range of interventions in the new field of "lesbian and gay studies" and contributing to the creation of queer studies as an abrasive set of theoretical speculations. Fuss's introduction, "Inside/Out," is an important problematization of perspectives in and on identity politics, and is followed by important theoretical articulations by Judith Butler, Carole-Anne Tyler, and Lee Edelman, and provocative applications of theory by D. A. Miller, Michelle Aina Barale, and Jeff Nunokawa. It concludes with two strong essays on pedagogy and politics by Cindy Patton and Simon Watney. This is a collection that over a decade after its publication still deserves careful reading and consideration by all students interested in the fields of gay/lesbian studies and queer theories.

Halberstam, Judith, *Female Masculinity*. Durham, NC, and London: Duke University Press, 1998.

This exceptional book intervenes imaginatively in the debates over essentialism and constructionism by examining the crises in social definition posed by masculine women. Halberstam examines texts ranging from nineteenth-century sexology through twentieth-century film, music, and performance art. Her overviews of debates among activists working from transgendered and transsexual subject positions, her reading and response to the theories of Judith Butler, and her final chapter on "new masculinities" make this an important book for all critics and students interested in queer theories and their possible future fields of inquiry and modes of application.

Hall, Donald E. and Maria Pramaggiore, eds. *RePresenting Bisexualities: Subjects and Cultures of Fluid Desire*. New York: New York University Press, 1996.

This book provides a wide-ranging set of theoretical speculations and applications concerned with sexualities that do not fall neatly into the heterosexual/homosexual binary. The pluralizations of its title and subtitle indicate its interest in providing numerous complications rather than a set of definitive answers or methodological formulae. Among the various topics that the collection addresses are "queer theory's" all-too-common erasure of bisexuality, the presence of fluid or changing sexual subject positions in pre-Victorian and Victorian erotica, African-American bisexual narratives, and representations of bisexualities in film culture. Its two-part introduction entitled "Epistemologies of the Fence" offers two different readings of the challenge posed by "bisexuality" to cultural critical theorization and identification.

Halperin, David M., *Saint Foucault: Towards a Gay Hagiography*. New York and Oxford: Oxford University Press, 1995.

This is the best introduction to Foucault's theories as they bear specifically on the creation of "gay and lesbian studies" as an academic pursuit and the genesis of "queer theory" as a phenomenon linked to AIDS activism in the late 1980s and early 1990s. Unabashedly celebratory, Halperin's book provides both accessible explanations of key concepts in Foucauldian theory and a reliable survey of the many, sometimes competing biographies of Foucault published after his death in 1984. Halperin also provides a detailed history of queer political activism in the latter decades of the twentieth century and a brief survey of the work of other theorists who draw on Foucault. In effect, this book provides a companion and reading guide to Foucault's *History of Sexuality, Volume 1* for all beginning students of theory.

Hocquenghem, Guy, *Homosexual Desire*. 1972, trans. Daniella Dangoor. Durham, NC, and London: Duke University Press, 1993.

Like Dennis Altman's *Homosexual: Oppression and Liberation*, Hocquenghem's book offers a wealth of historical data from and information about the early years of the "gay rights" struggle. But unlike Altman's book, which focuses primarily on New York, Hocquenghem's is centered in France and owes much of its primary theory base to the influence of Deleuze and Guattari, and the Marxist theories that helped fuel protests by workers and students in Paris in 1968. And beyond its important interventions on the connection between capitalism and desire, this book also provides sophisticated commentary on the relationship between social classifications and identity formation, on the rights of youth to sexual self-determination, and on the role of the psychiatric establishment in the continuing oppression of sexual nonconformists. Furthermore, Hocquenghem is an adept reader of some of his contemporaries' work on sexuality, including that of Sartre. The 1993 reissue of this important book includes the helpful, original preface by Jeffrey Weeks (from 1978) and a new introduction by Michael Moon.

Jagose, Annamarie, *Queer Theory: An Introduction*. New York: New York University Press, 1996.

This was the best and most widely used brief introduction to "queer theory" published in the 1990s. It is succinct, accessible, and reliable. Jagose's particular strengths are her careful relating of the origins of "queer theory" to the feminist movement and her examination of the early years of the "gay liberation" movement. At the same time, her book is limited in its lack of any detailed applications of the theories she overviews, in its hesitation to critique or even mention any lacks or omissions in "queer theory," and in its now somewhat dated quality. Furthermore, it barely mentions the complications to "queer theory" offered by bisexual and transgender theory. Nevertheless, it is still a useful resource for students who desire another introductory guide to the origins of specifically "queer" forms of theorization and the use of the term "queer" in political activism as well as in the academy.

Reid-Pharr, Robert F., *Black Gay Man: Essays.* New York: New York University Press, 2001.

This brilliant set of interrelated essays combines theoretical and autobiographical musings, as well as applied literary analysis and broad cultural critique. It asks questions that few other books are willing to broach: how do we inhabit these bodies that can manifest desire in very disturbing ways, how do we account for the way race inflects our desires, and why do critics so nervously avoid a discussion of their own desires in their too-often antiseptic theorizations *of* desire? In offering a few tentative answers to these difficult questions, Reid-Pharr takes us through readings of nineteenth- and twentieth-century American literature, cultural phenomena such as the "Million Man March," and anti-Semitism and sexism in contemporary culture. Reid-Pharr leads the way into a new set of engagements with sexuality that take "queer theory" as their base, but that remain determined to critique multiple, coexisting forms of oppression and retain always "queer theory's" interest in denaturalizing and abrading notions of "normality," even that underlying queer theory itself.

Sedgwick, Eve Kosofsky, *Epistemology of the Closet.* Berkeley, CA: University of California Press, 1990.

Sedgwick is one of the best known and most incisive of the critics/theorists working in the field of "gay studies" and queer theory (though she rarely discusses lesbians in her work, which is why I use the term "gay studies" here). This book is perhaps her most important contribution to the field, and of particular interest are her "axiomatic" introduction and her first chapter, "Epistemology of the Closet." In these two sections Sedgwick provides a thorough overview of the ongoing discussion about sexuality and identity, and explores the general muddle in current attempts to regulate and legislate expressions of sexual identity. Following those discussions are intriguing and complex readings of a variety of late-nineteenth- and early twentieth-century literary works, from Melville's *Billy Budd* through texts by Wilde, Henry James, and Marcel Proust. Written before the advent of specifically "queer" theorizations, Sedgwick's analysis here remains provocative and important for anyone interested in sexuality studies today.

Sedgwick, Eve Kosofsky, *Tendencies*. Durham, NC, and London: Duke University Press, 1993.

This collection of essays, musings, and autobiographical reflections is Sedgwick's important intervention into specifically "queer" studies. Its "Queer and Now" introduction is one of the best investigations ever published of the origins and implications of the word "queer." Her varied and brash readings of Jane Austen, Willa Cather, and numerous other writers are also intriguing and important. Yet one of the most provocative aspects of this book is its abrasion of the standard literary critical form, with its at times experimental language and bold "inside/outside" move in self-presentation. It remains one of the few books by a major American theorist that attempts to *be* queer as well as discuss queer concepts, even as it retains its intellectual integrity and its commitment to accessible communication. It is a book to return to often and from which one may glean many and varied reading pleasures.

Somerville, Siobhan B., *Queering the Color Line: Race and the Invention of Homosexuality in American Culture*. Durham, NC, and London: Duke University Press, 2000.

Relatively few books have attempted to use the insights of "queer theory" (or theories) and apply them outside of the arena of sexuality studies. This book takes tremendous risks in using its theory base in Foucault, Butler, D'Emilio, and others, to discuss the creation of and abrasions of categories of race during the nineteenth and twentieth centuries. Critics always lose a certain degree of specificity and conceptual consistency when they cross such boundaries, but the risk, to my mind, is well worth taking. Thus in her final chapter, Somerville offers a gutsy and intriguing investigation of Jean Toomer's use of the term "queer" in his writings in ways that undercut notions of static and self-evident categories of racial and sexual identity. Somerville's is hardly the "final" word on discussions of the interplay of race and sexuality, but she certainly takes the conversation in new and interesting directions.

Turner, William B., *A Genealogy of Queer Theory*. Philadelphia: Temple University Press, 2000.

While written more for the use of students of history and philosophy than for students of literature, this book provides a very thorough overview of "queer theory's" roots in Anglo-European philosophy and many of its varieties and disputed concerns today. Turner is particularly good at explaining Foucault's insights and implications for historians, and provides accessible basic definitions of a range of often confusing terms (post-structuralism, discourse, power, etc.). This is a solid summing-up of the field from the perspective of a full decade of theorization and debate. While Turner makes no attempt to look to the future, and barely glances at film, literature, art, and other expressions of culture, he does offer his readers clear insights into the sociopolitical, legal, and academic implications of queer theory/theories as a new and abrasive field.

Warner, Michael, ed., *Fear of a Queer Planet: Queer Politics and Social Theory*. Minneapolis: University of Minnesota Press, 1993.

This collection of essays is the most important set of original articulations yet published that explore queer theory's specific interest in interrogating of notions of "normal" sexuality. Warner's introduction is necessary reading for anyone interested in "queer theory" as a intellectual enterprise, Lauren Berlant and Elizabeth Freeman's "Queer Nationality" is unparalleled in its insight into the "Queer Nation" movement, and Steven Seidman's "Identity and Politics in a 'Postmodern' Gay Culture" is an impressive exploration of possible "queer" sociologies. A decade and more after their writing, the essays published in *Fear of a Queer Planet* are still timely and intellectually dynamic. Indeed, your own "fear" of a queer planet may be piqued and/or assuaged by reading this collection.

Weeks, Jeffrey, *Coming Out: Homosexual Politics in Britain from the Nineteenth Century to the Present*. 1977; London: Quartet Books, 1990.

> What Altman provides for New York and Holquenghem for France, Weeks offers here for Britain: a detailed history of the early struggle for "gay rights" that will be of interest to all students of marginalized sexualities. Weeks is particularly good at covering the rise of the medical and legal regulation of sexuality during the late nineteenth century, and includes a lengthy section tracing the birth of the lesbian rights movement. To the 1990 edition Weeks adds a chapter entitled "Identity and Community in the 1980s and 1990s," which details the impact of the AIDS crisis in Britain and mentions briefly the new radical response tactics of ACT UP. As we have seen, Queer Nation and queer theory were soon to follow.

Bibliography

Abbandonato, Linda, "Rewriting the Heroine's Story in *The Color Purple*." In *Alice Walker: Critical Perspectives Past and Present*. Eds. Henry Louis Gates and K. A. Appiah. New York: Amistad, 1993. 296–308.

Abelove, Henry et al., eds., *The Lesbian and Gay Studies Reader*. London and New York: Routledge, 1993.

Adams, Stephen, "*Giovanni's Room:* The Homosexual as Hero" (1980). In *James Baldwin: Modern Critical Views*. Ed. Harold Bloom. New York: Chelsea. 1986. 131–40.

Allen, Graham, *Intertextuality*. London and New York: Routledge, 2000.

Altman, Dennis, *Global Sex*. Chicago, IL, and London: University of Chicago Press, 2001.

——, *Homosexual: Oppression and Liberation*. New York: Outerbridge & Dienstfrey, 1971.

Angelides, Steven, *A History of Bisexuality*. Chicago, IL, and London: University of Chicago Press, 2001.

Anzaldúa, Gloria, *Borderlands/La Frontera: The New Mestiza*. San Francisco, CA: Aunt Lute Books, 1987.

Awkward, Michael, "Appropriative Gestures: Theory and Afro-American Literary Criticism." In *Gender & Theory: Dialogues on Feminist Criticism*. Ed. Linda Kauffman. Oxford and New York: Basil Blackwell, 1989. 238–46.

Baldwin, James, *Giovanni's Room*. 1956. New York: Dell, 2000.

Barthes, Roland, "The Death of the Author." 1968. In *The Norton Anthology of Theory and Criticism*. Eds. Vincent Leitch et al. New York and London: Norton, 2001. 1466–70.

Bauman, Zygmunt, *Life in Fragments: Essays in Postmodern Morality*. Cambridge: Blackwell, 1995.

Beemyn, Brett, "'To Say Yes to Life': Sexual and Gender Fluidity in James Baldwin's *Giovanni's Room* and *Another Country*." In *Bisexual Men in Culture and Society*. Eds. Brett Beemyn and Erich Steinman. New York: Harrington Park Press, 2002. 55–72.

Benhabib, Seyla, *Situating the Self: Gender, Community, and Postmodernism in Contemporary Ethics*. Cambridge: Blackwell, 1992.

Berlant, Lauren, "Race, Gender, and Nation in *The Color Purple*." In *Alice*

Walker: Critical Perspectives Past and Present. Eds. Henry Louis Gates and K. A. Appiah. New York: Amistad, 1993. 211–38.

Berlant, Lauren and Elizabeth Freeman, "Queer Nationality." In *The Queen of America Goes to Washington City.* By Lauren Berlant. Durham, NC: Duke University Press, 1997. 145–74.

Berlant, Lauren and Michael Warner, "What Does Queer Theory Teach Us about *X*?" *PMLA* 110.3 (1995): 343–49.

Bersani, Leo, *Homos.* Cambridge, MA and London: Harvard University Press, 1995.

Boswell, John, *Christianity, Social Tolerance, and Homosexuality: Gay People in Western Europe from the Beginning of the Christian Era to the Fourteenth Century.* Chicago and London: University of Chicago Press, 1980.

Brannigan, John, *New Historicism and Cultural Materialism.* Basingstoke: Macmillan – now Palgrave Macmillan – 1998.

Bray, Alan, *Homosexuality in Renaissance England.* London: Gay Men's Press, 1982.

Bristow, Joseph, *Sexuality.* London and New York: Routledge, 1997.

Brown, Judith C., "Lesbian Sexuality in Medieval and Early Modern Europe." In *Hidden from History: Reclaiming the Gay and Lesbian Past.* Eds. Martin Duberman, et al. New York: NAL Books, 1989. 67–75.

Burns, Christy, "Re-Dressing Feminist Identities: Tensions Between Essential and Constructed Selves in Virginia Woolf's *Orlando.*" *Twentieth-Century Literature* 40.3 (1994): 342–64.

Butler, Judith, *Bodies That Matter: On the Discursive Limits of "Sex."* London and New York: Routledge, 1993.

——, *Gender Trouble: Feminism and the Subversion of Identity.* 1990. London and New York: Routledge, 1999.

——, "Imitation and Gender Insubordination." In *Inside/Out: Lesbian Theories, Gay Theories.* Ed. Diana Fuss. London and New York: Routledge, 1993. 307–20.

——, *The Psychic Life of Power: Theories in Subjection.* Stanford, CA: Stanford University Press, 1997.

Califia, Pat, *Public Sex: The Culture of Radical Sex.* Pittsburgh, PA: Cleis Press, 1994.

Carpenter, Edward, *The Intermediate Sex: A Study of Some Transitional Types of Men.* London: Mitchell Kennedy, 1908.

Case, Sue-Ellen, "Tracking the Vampire." *Differences* 3.2 (1991): 1–20.

Chasin, Alexandra, *Selling Out: The Gay and Lesbian Movement Goes to Market.* New York: Palgrave, 2000.

Chauncy, George, *Gay New York: Gender, Urban Culture, and the Making of the Gay Male World, 1890–1940.* New York: Basic Books, 1994.

Christian, Barbara, "The Race for Theory." In *Gender & Theory: Dialogues on Feminist Criticism*. Ed. Linda Kauffman. Oxford and New York: Basil Blackwell, 1989. 225–37.

Cixous, Hélène, "Sorties." In *The Newly Born Woman*. 1975. By Hélène Cixous and Catherine Clement. Trans. Betsy Wing. Minneapolis: University of Minnesota Press, 1988. 63–132.

Cohen, William, *Sex Scandal: The Private Parts of Victorian Fiction*. Durham, NC, and London: Duke University Press, 1996.

Conerly, Gregory, "Are You Black First or Are You Queer?" In *The Greatest Taboo: Homosexuality in Black Communities*. Ed. Delroy Constantine-Simms. Boston: Alyson Books, 2000. 7–23.

Constantine-Simms, Delroy, ed., *The Greatest Taboo: Homosexuality in Black Communities*. Boston: Alyson, 2000.

Cruikshank, Margaret, *The Gay and Lesbian Liberation Movement*. London and New York: Routledge, 1992.

Danahay, Martin, *A Community of One: Masculine Autobiography and Autonomy in Nineteenth-Century Britain*. Albany, NY: State University of New York Press, 1993.

de Certeau, Michel, *The Practice of Everyday Life*. Trans. Steven Rendall. Berkeley, CA: University of California Press, 1984.

"A Declaration of Sexual Rights." Adopted at the National SexPanic Summit, San Diego, California, November 13, 1997. Available at www.sexpanic.org.

de Lauretis, Teresa, "Habit Changes." *differences* 6.2/3 (1994): 296–313.

——, "Queer Theory: Lesbian and Gay Sexualities." *differences* 3.2 (1991): iii–xviii.

Deleuze, Guy and Félix Guattari, *Anti-Oedipus: Capitalism and Schizophrenia*. Trans. Robert Hurley et al. Minneapolis: University of Minnesota Press, 1983.

——, *A Thousand Plateaus: Capitalism and Schizophrenia*. Trans. Brian Massumi. Minneapolis: University of Minnesota Press, 1987.

D'Emilio, John, "Capitalism and Gay Identity." 1979. In *The Lesbian and Gay Studies Reader*. Eds. Henry Abelove et al. London and New York: Routledge, 1993. 467–76.

——, *Sexual Politics, Sexual Communities: The Making of a Homosexual Minority in the United States, 1940–1970*. Chicago, IL: University of Chicago Press, 1983.

Dinshaw, Carolyn, *Getting Medieval: Sexualities and Communities, Pre- and Postmodern*. Durham, NC: Duke University Press, 1999.

Dollimore, Jonathan, *Sex, Literature, and Censorship*. Cambridge: Polity Press, 2001.

——, *Sexual Dissidence: Augustine to Wilde, Freud to Foucault*. Oxford and New York: Oxford University Press, 1991.

Drucker, Peter, ed., *Different Rainbows*. London: Gay Men's Press, 2000.

Edelman, Lee, *Homographesis: Essays in Gay Literary and Cultural Theory*. London and New York: Routledge, 1994.

Ellis, Havelock and John Addington Symonds, *Sexual Inversion*. London: Wilson and Macmillan, 1897.

Faderman, Lillian, *Surpassing the Love of Men: Romantic Friendship and Love Between Women from the Renaissance to the Present*. New York: William Morrow, 1981.

——, *To Believe in Women: What Lesbians Have Done for America – A History*. Boston and New York: Houghton Mifflin, 1999.

Foucault, Michel, *The History of Sexuality*, Vol. 1: *An Introduction*. Trans. Robert Hurley. New York: Vintage Books, 1978.

——, "So Is It Important to Think?" (1981) In *Essential Works of Foucault 1954–1984*. Vol. 3. Ed. James D. Faubion. New York: The New Press, 2000. 454–58.

——, "The Subject and Power." 1982. In *Essential Works of Foucault 1954–1984*. Vol. 3. Ed. James D. Faubion. New York: The New Press, 2000. 326–48.

Frantzen, Alan, *Before the Closet: Same-Sex Love from "Beowulf" to "Angels in America"*. Chicago, IL: University of Chicago Press, 1998.

Freud, Sigmund, *Three Essays on the Theory of Sexuality*. 1905. New York: Basic Books, 2000.

Friedman, Lawrence M., *The Horizontal Society*. New Haven, CT: Yale University Press, 1999.

Fuss, Diana, *Essentially Speaking: Feminism, Nature, and Difference*. London and New York: Routledge, 1989.

——, *Identification Papers*. London and New York: Routledge, 1995.

——, ed., *Inside/Out: Lesbian Theories, Gay Theories*. London and New York: Routledge, 1991.

Garber, Linda, *Identity Poetics: Race, Class, and the Lesbian-Feminist Roots of Queer Theory*. New York: Columbia University Press, 2001.

Garber, Marjorie, *Vice Versa: Bisexuality and the Eroticism of Everyday Life*. New York: Simon and Schuster, 1995.

Gay, Peter, *The Tender Passion: The Bourgeois Experience: Victoria to Freud*, vol. 2. New York and Oxford: Oxford University Press, 1986.

Giddens, Anthony, *The Consequences of Modernity*. Stanford, CA: Stanford University Press, 1990.

——, *Modernity and Self-Identity: Self and Society in the Late Modern Age*. Stanford, CA: Stanford University Press, 1991.

——, *The Transformation of Intimacy: Sexuality, Love & Eroticism in Modern Societies*. Stanford, CA: Stanford University Press, 1992.

Gide, André, *Corydon*. 1924. Trans. Richard Howard. New York: Farrar, Straus, Giroux, 1983.

——, *The Immoralist*. 1902. Trans. Richard Howard. New York: Vintage, 1970.

Gilbert, Sandra, "New Uses for Old Boys: An Interview with Sandra Gilbert." In *Professions: Conversations on the Future of Literary and Cultural Studies*. Ed. Donald E. Hall. Urbana, IL: University of Illinois Press, 2001. 244–54.

Gilbert, Sandra and Susan Gubar, "From *The Madwoman in the Attic*." In *"The Yellow Wallpaper."* Eds. Thomas Erskine and Connie Richards. New Brunswick, NJ: Rutgers University Press, 1993. 115–24.

Gilman, Charlotte Perkins, "The Yellow Wall-Paper" (1892). In *The Yellow Wall-Paper and Other Stories*. Oxford and New York: Oxford University Press, 1995. 3–19.

Glover, David and Cora Kaplan, *Genders*. London and New York: Routledge, 2000.

Gordon, Colin, "Introduction." In *Essential Works of Foucault 1954–1984*. Volume 3. Ed. James D. Faubion. New York: The New Press, 2000. xi–xli.

Grahn, Judy, *Another Mother Tongue: Gay Words, Gay Worlds*. Boston, MA: Beacon, 1984.

Grosz, Elizabeth, *Volatile Bodies: Toward a Corporeal Feminism*. Bloomington, IN: University of Indiana Press, 1994.

Haggerty, George E., *Men in Love: Masculinity and Sexuality in the Eighteenth Century*. New York: Columbia University Press, 1999.

Halberstam, Judith, *Female Masculinity*. Durham, NC, and London: Duke University Press, 1998.

Hall, Donald E., *Fixing Patriarchy: Feminism and Mid-Victorian Male Novelists*. New York: New York University Press, 1996.

——, "Graphic Sexuality and the Erasure of a Polymorphous Perversity." In *RePresenting Bisexualities: Subjects and Cultures of Fluid Desire*. Eds. Donald E. Hall and Maria Pramaggiore. New York: New York University Press, 1996. 99–123.

——, "The Private Pleasures of Silas Marner." In *Mapping Male Sexuality: Nineteenth-Century England*. Eds. Jay Losey and William Brewer. London: Associated University Presses, 2000. 178–97.

——, ed., *Professions: Conversations on the Future of Literary and Cultural Studies*. Urbana, IL: University of Illinois Press, 2001.

Hall, Donald E. and Dennis W. Allen, "An Introductory Dialogue." *Victorian Poetry* 38.4 (2000): 467–90.

Hall, Donald E. and Maria Pramaggiore, eds., *RePresenting Bisexualities: Subjects and Cultures of Fluid Desire*. New York: New York University Press, 1996.

Hall, Radclyffe, *The Well of Loneliness*. 1928; New York: Anchor Books, 1990.

Halperin, David, *One Hundred Years of Homosexuality: The New Ancient World*. London and New York: Routledge, 1990.

——, *Saint Foucault: Towards a Gay Hagiography*. New York and Oxford: Oxford University Press, 1995.

Haraway, Donna J., *Simians, Cyborgs, and Women: The Reinvention of Nature*. London and New York: Routledge, 1991.

Harper, Philip Brian, *Are We Not Men? Masculine Anxiety and the Problem of African-American Identity*. New York and Oxford: Oxford University Press, 1996.

Haslett, Moyra, *Marxist Literary and Cultural Theories*. Basingstoke: Macmillan – now Palgrave Macmillan – 2000.

Hawley, John C., ed., *Postcolonial Queer: Theoretical Intersections*. Albany, NY: State University of New York Press, 2001.

Heilmann, Ann, "Overwriting Decadence: Charlotte Perkins Gilman, Oscar Wilde, and the Feminization of Art in "The Yellow Wall-Paper." In *The Mixed Legacy of Charlotte Perkins Gilman*. Eds. Catherine Golden and Joanna Zangrando. London: Associated University Presses, 2000. 175–88.

Hemphill, Essex, ed., *Brother to Brother: New Writings by Black Gay Men*. Boston, MA: Alyson, 1991.

Henderson, Mae G., "*The Color Purple*: Revisions and Redefinitions." (1985) In *Alice Walker: Modern Critical Views*. Ed. Harold Bloom. New York: Chelsea House, 1989. 67–80.

Herdt, Gilbert, *Guardians of the Flute: Idioms of Masculinity*. New York: McGraw-Hill, 1981.

——, *Sambia Sexual Culture: Essays from the Field*. Chicago, IL, and London: University of Chicago Press, 1999.

Hocquenghem, Guy, *Homosexual Desire*. 1972. Trans. Daniella Dangoor. Durham, NC, and London: Duke University Press, 1993.

Hovey, Jaime, "'Kissing a Negress in the Dark': Englishness as a Masquerade in Woolf's *Orlando*." *PMLA* 112.3 (1997): 393–404.

Irigaray, Luce, *Speculum of the Other Woman*. Trans. Gillian C. Gill. Ithaca, NY: Cornell University Press, 1985.

——, *This Sex Which Is Not One*. Trans. Catherine Porter. Ithaca, NY: Cornell University Press, 1985.

Jagose, Annamarie, *Queer Theory: An Introduction*. New York: New York University Press, 1996.

Katz, Jonathan Ned, *The Invention of Heterosexuality*. New York: Plume, 1996.

Kirsch, Max, *Queer Theory and Social Change*. London and New York: Routledge, 2000.

Krafft-Ebing, Richard von, *Psychopathia Sexualis*. 1886. New York: Putnam's, 1965.

Lanser, Susan S., "Feminist Criticism, 'The Yellow Wallpaper,' and the Politics of Color in America." In *"The Yellow Wallpaper."* Eds. Thomas

Erskine and Connie Richards. New Brunswick, NJ: Rutgers University Press, 1993. 225–56.

Levinas, Emmanuel, "Ethics of the Infinite." In *States of Mind: Dialogues with Contemporary Thinkers*. Ed. Richard Kearney. New York: New York University Press, 1995. 177–99.

Martin, Robert K., *The Homosexual Tradition in American Poetry*. Austin, TX: University of Texas Press, 1979.

McClaren, Angus, *The Trials of Masculinity: Policing Sexual Boundaries 1870–1930*. Chicago, IL: University of Chicago Press, 1997.

Meese, Elizabeth, "When Virginia Looked at Vita, What Did She See; Or, Lesbian: Feminist: Woman – What's the Differ(e/a)nce?" *Feminist Studies* 18.1 (1992): 99–117.

Mill, John Stuart, "Nature." 1874. *Prose of the Victorian Period*. Ed. William E. Buckler. Boston, MA: Riverside, 1958. 312–42.

——, "On Liberty". 1859. *Three Essays*. Oxford: Oxford University Press, 1975. 5–141.

Miller, D. A., *Bringing Out Roland Barthes*. Berkeley, CA: University of California Press, 1992.

Moraga, Cherrie, and Gloria Anzaldúa, eds., *This Bridge Called My Back: Writings by Radical Women of Color*. Watertown, MA: Persephone Press, 1981.

Muñoz, José, *Disidentifications: Queers of Color and the Performance of Politics*. Minneapolis, MN: University of Minnesota Press, 1999.

Murray, Stephen O., *Homosexualities*. Chicago, IL: University of Chicago Press, 2000.

Murray, Stephen O. and Will Roscoe, eds., *Boy-Wives and Female Husbands: Studies in African Homosexualities*. New York: Palgrave, 1998.

Namaste, Viviane K., *Invisible Lives: The Erasure of Transsexual and Transgendered People*. Chicago, IL and London: University of Chicago Press, 2000.

Nietzsche, Friedrich, *The Gay Science*. 1882. Trans. Walter Kaufmann. New York: Vintage, 1974.

Parkes, Adam, "Lesbianism, History, and Censorship: *The Well of Loneliness* and the Suppressed Randiness of Virginia Woolf's *Orlando*." *Twentieth-Century Literature* 40.4 (1994): 434–60.

Reid-Pharr, Robert F., *Black Gay Man: Essays*. New York: New York University Press, 2001.

Rich, Adrienne, "Compulsory Heterosexuality and Lesbian Existence." 1980. In *The Lesbian and Gay Studies Reader*. Eds. Henry Abelove et al. London and New York: Routledge, 1993. 227–54.

Robbins, Ruth, *Literary Feminisms*. Basingstoke: Macmillan – now Palgrave Macmillan – 2000.

Robinson, Dave, *Nietzsche and Postmodernism*. New York: Totem Books, 1999.

Rose, Phyllis, *Parallel Lives: Five Victorian Marriages*. New York: Knopf, 1984.

Rothblatt, Martine, *The Apartheid of Sex: A Manifesto on the Freedom of Gender*. New York: Crown, 1995.

Rubin, Gayle, "Thinking Sex: Notes for a Radical Theory of the Politics of Sexuality." 1984. In *The Lesbian and Gay Studies Reader*. Eds. Henry Abelove, et al. London and New York: Routledge, 1993. 3–44.

Rule, Jane, *Lesbian Images*. Garden City, New York: Doubleday, 1975.

Rupp, Leila, *A Desired Past: A Short History of Same-Sex Love in America*. Chicago, IL, and London: University of Chicago Press, 1999.

Sartre, Jean Paul, *Saint Genet: Actor and Martyr*. 1952. Trans. anon. New York: Signet, 1971.

Seabrook, Jeremy, *Love in a Different Climate: Men Who Have Sex with Men in India*. London and New York: Verso, 1999.

Sedgwick, Eve Kosofsky, *Between Men: English Literature and Male Homosocial Desire*. New York: Columbia University Press, 1985.

——, *Epistemology of the Closet*. Berkeley, CA: University of California Press, 1990.

——, *Tendencies*. Durham, NC and London: Duke University Press, 1993.

Showalter, Elaine, *Sexual Anarchy: Gender and Culture at the Fin de Siécle*. London and New York: Penguin, 1990.

Sinfield, Alan, *Faultlines: Materialism and the Politics of Dissident Reading*. Berkeley: University of California Press, 1992.

——, *Gay and After*. London: Serpent's Tail, 1998.

Solomon, Robert and Kathleen Higgins, *What Nietzsche Really Said*. New York: Schocken Books, 2000.

Somerville, Siobhan B., *Queering the Color Line: Race and the Invention of Homosexuality in American Culture*. Durham, NC, and London: Duke University Press, 2000.

Stengers, Jean, and Anne Van Neck, *Masturbation: The History of a Great Terror*. Trans. Kathryn Hoffman. Basingstoke: Palgrave Macmillan, 2001.

Stevenson, Robert Louis. *Dr. Jekyll and Mr. Hyde and Other Stories*. (1866) London and New York: Penguin, 1979.

Storr, Merl, ed., *Bisexuality: A Critical Reader*. London and New York: Routledge, 1999.

Stryker, Susan, "The Transgender Issue: An Introduction." *GLQ: A Journal of Lesbian and Gay Studies* 4.2 (1998): 145–58.

Trumbach, Randolph, "Sodomitical Subcultures, Sodomitical Roles, and the Gender Revolution of the Eighteenth Century: The Recent Historiography." *Eighteenth-Century Life* 9: 109–21.

Turner, William B., *A Genealogy of Queer Theory*. Philadelphia, PA: Temple University Press, 2000.

Vance, Carol, "Social Construction Theory: Problems in the History of Sexuality." In *Homosexuality, Which Homosexuality?* Eds. Dennis Altman et al. Amsterdam: Dekker Schorer, 1989. 13–34.

Vanita, Ruth and Saleem Kidwai, eds., *Same-Sex Love in India: Readings from Literature and History*. New York: Palgrave, 2000.

Walker, Alice, *The Color Purple*. New York: Pocket Books, 1982.

Warner, Michael, "Introduction." In *Fear of a Queer Planet: Queer Politics and Social Theory*. Ed. Michael Warner. Minneapolis, MN: University of Minnesota Press, 1993. vii–xxxi.

——, *The Trouble with Normal: Sex, Politics and the Ethics of Queer Life*. New York: Free Press, 1999.

Weeks, Jeffrey, *Coming Out: Homosexual Politics in Britain from the Nineteenth Century to the Present*. 1977. London: Quartet, 1990.

Williams, M. Kellen, "'Down with the Door, Poole': Designating Deviance in Stevenson's *Strange Case of Dr. Jekyll and Mr. Hyde*." *English Literature in Transition (1880–1920)* 39.4 (1996): 412–29.

Wittig, Monique, "One Is Not Born a Woman." 1981. In *The Lesbian and Gay Studies Reader*. London and New York: Routledge, 1993. 103–09.

Wolfreys, Julian, *Deconstruction•Derrida*. Basingstoke: Macmillan – now Palgrave Macmillan – 1998.

Woolf, Virgnia, *Orlando: A Biography*. 1928. San Diego and New York: Harcourt, 1956.

Zimmerman, Bonnie, "What Has Never Been: An Overview of Lesbian Feminist Criticism." 1981. In *The New Feminist Criticism: Essays on Women, Literature and Theory*. Ed. Elaine Showalter. New York: Pantheon Books, 1985. 200–24.

Index